THE JOY OF HORTON

Andrea Comer

Book Layout ©2013 BookDesignTemplates.com

The Joy of Horton/ Andrea Comer. -- 1st ed.
ISBN 978-0-9953904-0-9

This book is dedicated to the loving memory of Vivienne Anne Mort, my Mother and my friend. Mum your love knew no boundaries and for that I thank you over and over again.

CONTENTS

CHAPTER ONE

A Little Ray of Sunshine has come into the World

I can clearly remember the first email I received about Horton. It was August 2008 and a friend of mine in rescue contacted me to see if I would be interested in taking in a puppy that had very little use of his back legs. Years ago, when first talking to this lady, she had told me about her special needs pug. I remember commenting at the time about how lucky she was to have a pug like that in her life and mentioned that one day I myself would love to have a pug like hers to take care of. I enjoyed listening to her talk about this little pug of hers and asked a good many questions. Her life with this little soul sounded ideal to me – she had saved her from death and the two of them had developed an incredible closeness – and I told her how special I thought her life was. I guess when Horton came along she must have recalled our conversation and I'm glad that she did. His name was Sparky back then, named by the rescue lady. Before Sparky it was Monkey; his breeder had called him Monkey because she thought he was ugly. I don't know whether she meant his face or his body but she was wrong on both counts. He was far from ugly, but of course the breeder couldn't see that; she was only looking at the money to be made out of her puppies. All she saw when looking at this little black pug was a deformed body, and deformed bodies don't bring in the cash. She couldn't see Horton for what he truly was; her heart would never allow her to look at him and see the diamond, the little gem she was about to give up on.

My rescue friend described Horton as a dear little chap who was absolutely adorable. She said he dragged his back legs around behind him and didn't know if it was a birth defect or if he'd been sat on by his mother. Coming from a breeder, his mother was probably kept in a small, enclosed area and wouldn't have been able to move around much. At that point it wasn't known whether he would improve and end up being able to walk upright or whether he would remain a paraplegic for life. However, his condition didn't seem to impede him in the slightest, she said. In fact, nothing seemed to bother him at all. The way she talked about him left me in awe; he seemed like the most gutsy, determined little guy, a true little hero in my eyes and I was captivated already.

She'd only had him in her care a few days but he was happily discovering his new surroundings; he was curious about her cat and scooted along after it trying to figure out what this strange creature was. He had bad skin and his pads were cracked, but that wasn't anything to worry about; we both knew an improved diet and some tender loving care would fix those things pretty quickly. She wrote that she knew I only took in older pugs but asked me to please consider Sparky as he was just the most delightful little boy. She ended by saying she thought our home would be one where he could have a chance at having a good life and I had to agree with her – our pugs were the most important things in our lives.

I'd had a busy day so turned the computer off to go feed the livestock and take the seven pugs I already had for their afternoon walk. I thought about the little black puppy as I broke a bale of hay and scattered it around for the sheep and horses; I had so many questions racing around in my head. I tried to picture what his back legs looked like, but this was new territory for me. In all the years I'd been rescuing pugs I'd never had a case like this before and I couldn't imagine what he would look like. I pictured a human being walking along the floor on their hands, dragging their legs behind them. Was that close? I didn't know. For all I knew this little pug's legs could have been curled up or sticking out to the sides. I wished that she had attached a photo to her email or, better still, a video. Yes, seeing the little pug moving around would have answered a lot of the questions I had.

I finished with the livestock, began walking towards the gate and glanced up at the row of pugs sitting patiently waiting for me. My seven pugs went everywhere with me and followed me around the farm watching everything I did. Wherever I went a cloud of pugs scurried after me. They made me happy and I loved having them by my side. For their own safety they weren't allowed in the sheep or horse paddocks; all of them were elderly and too slow-moving to get out of the way of an irritable ewe. Although the horses were placid I never took any chances with my pugs. A windy day or a game of push and shove over food and the mood in the livestock paddock changed. Today, the late afternoon sun was still warm so my little pug family sat panting beneath a tree. It was shady there and they seemed quite content to be out and about. Shaking flies off their faces was definitely more enjoyable and entertaining than being inside the house. Ruby sat to one side on her own, Sarah, Harper, Steffy, Tommy and Grace lay quietly beside one another and Emily, my youngest, bounced about all over the place as she does. I wondered what they would think about having a puppy in the house. Would the little guy be too much for my dear old babies, too boisterous, too nippy and playful, that sort of thing? Not that it would have been the little guy's fault; he was a puppy and deserved to behave the way all puppies do. That's what being a puppy is all about. But my elderly lot were well set in their ways. They were used to a quiet household, a peaceful existence. I had to think of them. Although the little black puppy sounded wonderful, the pugs I already had needed to be my first priority. I couldn't let anything disturb their world; it wouldn't have been fair on them. Some had ailments, illnesses and special needs. They ranged in age from eight to fourteen. In fact, our farm was like a pug retirement village – well, that's what my friends called the place anyway. It would be like throwing a toddler into an old folk's home and expecting the residents to cope with it.

I needed to find out more about this puppy: his personality, what was that like? All puppies are playful, they are babies, they chew on things, they wrestle, they bark, they squeak, they just enjoy life, but some are less boisterous than others, so I emailed again, asking a couple of questions, with the first and second being, "Was he in pain?" and "Would he ever be in pain?"

A phone call would have been easier and quicker, but my friend did shift work as well as the countless hours she devoted to rescuing pugs. I always felt guilty when I called, like I'd just woken her up. Emails were best because she could answer those at her own leisure.

The answers came back quickly. "No" and "No". That was a relief, so more questions followed. The return email said he was a very quiet type of puppy. A friend of mine once said that there was no such thing, but perhaps there was; perhaps this little pug was a deep thinker; perhaps he just sat quietly taking in the sights of the world he had just been born into. Also, maybe his legs slowed him down a little bit; that would be a good thing in our elderly pug household. He'd fit in well. It'd mean he wouldn't be rushing around sending my unsteady little old darling Ruby to the ground. These days it didn't take much to set her off-balance and she was the pug I worried about most when I was asked to take in this special needs pup. I also thought about Thomas, my massive old boy Tommy was a huge pug by anybody's standards. He towered over his six elderly sisters. He was taller, longer and much more solidly built than they were. Would he be too much for this little paraplegic pug to cope with? That thought didn't last long because I figured they'd be okay together. Yes, Tom was huge, but he was such a quiet, gentle soul; he moved gracefully around the house and never once knocked any of the others over or pushed them about in any way. He assisted them if anything; when Ruby was running in amongst the pack she'd often teeter over, bounce off Tom and be able to remain upright. I do think I worry about my pugs too much because time and time again I have seen them all helping each other out without any interference from me. They seem to be able to sense what each other needs and then get on with it. I guess after all these years I should learn to trust them more than I do.

Although Grace was a tiny pug and the oldest of the pack, I didn't have any concerns regarding her. She was such a lively little thing, always running about everywhere, not a full-out racehorse kind of a run, more an elegant little trot that made her ears rise and fall in the most hilarious way: a bouncy jig done at a steady speed until she got tired then she'd just stop and stand still until I went and got her. I never tested the theory on the walks around the farm; I always went and picked her up and carried her back to the house, but I do think she would have stood in the middle of the paddock all day long if I hadn't gone and rescued her. Grace was so slender and sprightly that people used to think she was the youngest in the pack because she looked and acted that way. I knew she could look after herself if the puppy became too much. She wouldn't have any trouble telling him to back off if he got in her face. She was good at sticking up for herself; not nasty, just good at letting the others know when she'd had enough.

Sarah had that black pug thing going on and I wondered how she'd feel about having another black pug in the house. Emily and Steffy I didn't need to worry about and Harper was such a loving, nurturing soul that I knew she would probably love having a special little baby to look after.

I mulled things over for a long time; yes, worrying again but also trying to think of every scenario, trying to work out if everything was going to be okay. I always gave a lot of thought to the consequences of bringing another pug into the fold and with this little one having special needs there was a lot more to consider. I wanted to think of everything, wanted things right in my mind before saying yes. My thoughts again turned to the puppy, to little Sparky, and I worried about how he would cope living amongst all of us. Would living in a multiple-dog household be too much for him? Were there perhaps too many pugs here for him to be able to live comfortably? He was only a tiny puppy; would he get trampled underfoot by the sheer number of them as my cloud of pugs followed me about? Even elderly dogs can move fast, especially at dinner time; would he get squashed in the stampede?

It had been over ten years since I'd had a pug puppy in the house. I tried to think back to how small pug puppies were, but it did no good; my mind had forgotten. I searched through a box of old photographs, trying to find photos of Sarah when she was a pup. She was the only one of my pugs that I'd had since she was a baby; the others, because they were all rescues, came into my life as adult dogs. Impatiently, I tipped the box on the kitchen table and spread them out. We'd taken hundreds of photos of Sarah as a puppy but there didn't seem to be any in there. Perhaps they were in another box. I came from a photo-taking family; every gathering and social occasion was well documented in our house. I alone owned two cameras, my sister was the same, Mum only had one camera at a time but she'd replace it every six months or so. She had to; either they'd die from overuse, become lost or accidently get dropped and trod on in the frenzy of flashing bulbs. We'd try and get Mum to take to a more expensive camera, one that was sturdier, shatterproof perhaps, but she had always preferred the cheap ones. She was stuck in her ways. Even today she still has a camera that requires film. 'Digital' is a swear word to my mother.

Picturing the row of brightly coloured boxes, I got up and headed for the top shelf in the wardrobe, but as I passed the wall unit in the hall a photo of Sarah caught my eye. I held the gold frame in my hands. She looked beautiful and young, very young, black mask, glossy black fur. She was wearing a little red and white jumper. I remember how she hated that thing, the neck especially. She'd had a fit when I put it on her and ran around rubbing up against furniture trying to get it off. Some pugs just don't like wearing jumpers and Sarah was one of them. She only wore it the one time. I never put it on her again. That's probably why I took the photo in the first place, as a keepsake I guess, because she did look pretty cute in it. I looked down at the few pugs that had followed me out of the room. Four little old faces glanced up at me. Their old eyes held my gaze for a while then went back to looking at the frame in my hands. They were probably hoping it was food because it was past their dinner time. Thinking about the little paraplegic pug had slowed me down with the afternoon chores and my elderly brood were well aware of the delay even if I wasn't.

Apart from looking younger in the face, Sarah didn't look much different to how she looked now. Her body seemed the same as it did now. Of course she'd grown, but the photo was of her just sitting on the ground, not beside any furniture, so there was nothing to compare her size to. I lingered in the doorway looking up at the boxes. There were so many of them. Too time consuming, I thought. Besides, I really needed to feed the pugs. I couldn't keep them waiting any longer. Ruby had just come over to join the others and now stood swaying and giving little sharp, quick barks the way she always did when dinner time approached.

You can set your clock by Ruby's stomach and she was good at letting me know when her routine was out of whack. I headed for the kitchen and the hurried pitter-patter of small paws followed me in. If pugs were human beings I'd say a great deal of them would be chefs because they seem to enjoy the preparation and the smell of food almost as much as they enjoy eating it.

With this little black pug I certainly had a lot to think about. I needed to do some research, find out all I could about this pug's condition before I could make a final decision. My friend told me to take all the time I needed. I knew she loved this puppy; she would never want anybody merely feeling sorry for him, saying they wanted him on impulse. He needed and deserved better than that. He needed a home where he could be both loved unconditionally for who and what he was and one where every one of his needs would be fully taken care of, not only for a week or a month until the novelty wore off but every single hour of every single day for the rest of his life. I've never envied people in rescue, the job they have. Imagine how worrying it would be to find the right home for the dogs that come into their care. And when you have a special needs pug, well, that concern multiplies tenfold. I know I couldn't do the job they do. I'd be up all night worrying about whether I'd made the right decision. It'd be a huge responsibility. I'd be constantly wondering if I'd done the right thing by the dog. I'd be a nervous wreck by the end of the first month and that's why I have such high regard for those amazing souls who devote their lives to rescuing and rehoming unwanted dogs.

I did a bit of research on paraplegic dogs, emails went back and forth as I learnt more and had different questions to ask. I bet I was a bit of a pain with the amount of questions I had but I just wanted to get it right and make sure I knew everything I could about the little one's needs before saying yes. His needs were important and I wanted to make sure our home was the right one for him. What if he came to the farm and was miserable or found life here with all these other pugs too hard to cope with due to the limitations of his body. It would have broken my heart to see him struggling and it wouldn't have been fair on him to keep moving him from home to home just when he was getting settled.

There wasn't as much information out there about hemivertebra as I would have liked, but I did learn that there are degrees of it and that each case is different. Some with the condition only have a slight curve of the spine and are able to walk upright. Little Sparky was a full paraplegic and needed to wear a nappy. Every night when my husband came home from work I would talk to him about what I had learned. The more I found out about Sparky the more admiration I had for him. Not only did I desperately want to share my life with this amazing little pug but deep in my heart I knew he was meant to be with us. And although I wanted to go ahead with the adoption, I was still a little bit concerned – not about the workload, that didn't worry me at all; I was looking forward to looking after him – I mainly worried because having never had a pug with hemivertebra I didn't fully understand what would be required for his care. It was a fear of the unknown, I guess, but apart from that I couldn't wait to meet the little guy, bring him to his forever home and start living our life together.

David wasn't so sure. At first he didn't want me to take on this little black pug. It wasn't that he didn't want Sparky, more that he was concerned that I had enough on my plate taking care of all the elderly pugs we already had. I understood where he was coming from; elderly pugs are easy to look after but they do have needs and seven elderly pugs in the one household does take up a lot of time. I didn't push David. I couldn't; it wouldn't have been fair. My husband was always so good with our pugs, loving them, paying our hefty vet bills time and time again without complaining and I loved him for that. But it wasn't just David; I also had to think about little Sparky. He deserved to be brought into a home where everybody living under that roof wanted him. This little soul already had a lot to deal with in life; I didn't want him to come here and feel any negative vibes coming from his new daddy. We both had to be on board with it before saying yes. I wanted Sparky to be able to come to our farm and feel total acceptance from the first moment he shuffled through the door. He deserved to have a family who wanted him and loved him completely. If I loved him and David merely tolerated him then I had no right bringing him here. I cared about Sparky too much for that and so prayed to God that my husband would come around to my way of thinking or I would have had to email the rescue group and tell them no. So we talked everything over then I just dropped it, not just for a few days but a few weeks. I thought about the paraplegic puppy every second of every day but I no longer spoke to David about him. I had to let David think about things without pressuring. He needed to be all right with it and to come to that decision on his own. I suppose I must have been confident of him saying yes because while David thought, I set about finding a name for the little one. I didn't have anything against the name Sparky. In fact, I quite liked it and thought it was kind of cute, but I don't like people belittling dogs and I figured that if this little pug needed to use a cart to get around the thought kept going round in my head that people would make jokes at his expense like, "Oh look, Sparky's running so fast his wheels are sparking." I mean it may never have happened but still I couldn't get this thought out of my head and knew I had to give him another name. I went through my name list; I always have a name list and it's very long. With lambs being born and all sorts of different rescue animals arriving here it helps to be prepared. I think names are important and I've found that you can never think of the perfect name when thinking on the spot, so I have a list of names that I'm constantly adding to when I hear something I like. That way I don't have to end up calling something Blacky or Goldy or some other name I would later regret. While David was off thinking things through, I'd narrowed my huge selection down to just three names and by the time my husband finally got back to me I'd already decided our new son's name was going to be Horton. I remember the night David said Horton could come, he walked through the door and after greeting the pugs and me with the usual amount of hugs and kisses he turned and said "I think he'll do alright here". I instantly knew who he was talking about and ran over and hugged his neck. My husband doesn't dramatize things the way I do, if I was the one who'd gone away and thought things through for the length of time he did when I'd finally come to a decision I would have burst through the door and made a big song and dance out of it. But he just quietly and calmly let me know what was in his heart. And really I wouldn't have it any other way.

Him being quiet and softly spoken has served me well over all the years we have been together, I can be pinging off the walls, anxious, a nervous wreck and he has the ability to bring me back down to earth with a simple word spoken in a quiet calm voice. When we first got together I thought he needed livening up and bit and I do believe he got a little bit of that with me, but what he brought to my life was something that I desperately needed. A stillness, a wisdom, a voice of reason when once there wasn't very much of one and I have been grateful to have such a presence in my life for many years now. David saying "Yes" to Horton though is one of the things I will be most grateful to my husband for. He could have easily said no and would have been quite justified in doing so, and I would never have held it against him if he had come back with that answer. How could I really, he had already given up so much for me and the pugs, we were living in a beautiful home on the side of a lake before coming to our farm, David loved that home I know he did and yet said yes right away when I could no longer hold off on the desires of my heart for one second longer. We were always going to go and live in the country, we were always going to rescue needy animals, it was something we were aiming for but never given any real deadline. When I said "Life is short, what are we waiting for, let's do it right now" David supported me in it and our home by the lake sold within ten days of being put on the market. I think the universe was looking after us with that. It was as if the stars aligned and we sold and we bought and we moved so fast it was like it was all meant to be. And in all the years we've been living here David has never once complained about the extra traveling to and from work he's had to do.

I couldn't type fast enough when emailing the rescue group. I pounded the keyboard so hard I'm amazed the letters didn't go flying through the air. I said I would really love to bring this little pug into the family fold. I said I couldn't stop thinking about him and that although I knew it would be hard until I got used to caring for him, I really felt I could make a difference in his life and I knew he would definitely enrich mine. At the time I had no idea how true those words were when I wrote them. I had absolutely no idea how much my life was going to change once Horton was in it, no idea about the wonderful journey I was about to be taken on when this little pug entered my life, no idea of the amount of pure joy, of laughter and happiness he was going to bring to my life. And definitely no idea about the huge amount of love I was about to feel for and receive from this beautiful little champion.

The night before Horton arrived I didn't sleep much. I was both nervous and excited at the same time. As we did the nightly routine of putting the pugs to bed, I worried if this was going to be their last night of peace and quiet for a very long time. I wondered if they would have to wait until the puppy matured a bit before their serine world returned. The old pugs got into their beds and I kissed their heads as I covered them up. It was the middle of September and the nights were still pretty cold; the days were lovely and sunny but once it got dark the temperature plummeted, so I covered my little old darlings up every night to ward off the cold. We have a large wood heater that we pack to the hilt before going to bed, sometimes we are lucky and it's still glowing red in the morning but more often than not it dies somewhere between the hours of three and four so I wrap the pugs up snuggly for extra protection. Although on the really cold nights I have been known to tiptoe across ice cold floorboards to toss a few more logs on if I find myself awake. I try and make it into the lounge and back again without anybody following me otherwise I've got to re-tuck them in again and sometimes they'll want a tummy rub and once that starts they all line up for a turn and then you've got buckley's of ever going back to bed again.

David met Horton before I did. He was coming a great distance to be with me so two rescue ladies drove in relay, half the journey each, with the last one delivering him to David at work. David worked just over an hour's drive from the farm. The rescue lady changed Horton's nappy before she left so David got to see how it was done and could then show me once he got home. Horton spent the afternoon crawling around the office floor and peeping at David as he worked at his desk. He'd been placed on a blanket spread out on the floor with his toys on it but Horton wasn't in a playing mood and didn't stay put for very long. The office must have been interesting to him because he set off to discover it more or less as soon as he'd been put down. He went over to the pot plants and had a little sniff then over to the filing cabinet and sniffed there too. Then he either smelt or spotted the rubbish bin and scooted over for a closer inspection. There was a banana skin in the bin so he circled round trying to see if he could find a way in. The office bin amused Horton for quite a while then he went back over to David's desk and sat looking up at him. He'd come a long way and was tired, so he took a short nap on the carpet while David tried to finish off the project he was working on. But Horton was too cute, too much of a distraction, and David spent most of the afternoon playing with his new son.

I talked to Horton on speaker phone and said hello. I wanted him to hear my voice. I would have sang him a song but David's secretary was in the office, sitting on the floor, playing with Horton, so I just told him that I was his new mummy and that I couldn't wait to meet him later on that night. Like I said, with Horton, I wasn't sure what I was getting, so I asked David to describe Horton's legs to me over the phone. I was anxious to know what he was like but I was protective of him as well. I told David not to let the whole company come into his office to see Horton. I didn't want him on show for everyone to view, with people gathering round just to satisfy their curiosity. This was Horton's life and he deserved to be respected. David did as I asked; he closed his office door, which kept Horton in and the noise out. Only a few people in the entire company knew Horton was even in the building and that's only because they'd seen him being carried into David's office by the rescue lady. Hearing David's happiness as he talked about his new son made any anxieties I had disappear. David loved him already; I could hear it in his voice. He didn't get much work done that afternoon and spent most of the time on the phone to me. Everything Horton did David thought was so adorable that he had to keep ringing me back and telling me about it. At 5.00 p.m. David popped Horton in the car and drove back to the farm. Before they left, David gave Horton a drink and changed his nappy then the two of them headed off to pick my sister up from work and Horton rode all the way home in her arms.

It was dark by the time they got home. I couldn't wait for the car lights to appear at the gate. I left the blinds open and sat in the dark, watching the road like a hawk. If the pugs thought it unusual to be sitting in the dark they obviously weren't overly concerned about it because they fell asleep in no time. At that time there weren't any street lights on our road so everything outside was in total darkness. Not too many cars go past our place at night but the few that did had me bolting upright in the hope that they were going to turn into our drive. When the headlights were ours I raced around closing the blinds and turning on the houselights because I didn't want Horton being brought into a dark home. I watched David coming up the back ramp, carrying Horton in his arms and strained to see his little face in the dim glow of the porch light. Five pugs danced at my feet; they had no idea their new brother was here. They were more interested in Dad and each one scampered about wanting to be the first in line for a hug. David stepped inside the door and I could clearly see Horton's face now. He was magnificent, so beautiful, a totally gorgeous little baby and, yes, small, very, very small. I thought he was wonderful and it took me about half a second to fall for him. His enormous baby pug eyes darted about all over the place. There was no fear in them, just wonder, curiosity and excitement, and this made me happy.

Horton sat there in his daddy's arms, taking in his new surroundings and heard the other pugs pitter-pattering on the wooden floorboards. He glanced down and there wasn't even a hint of being scared. His expression changed, his ears altered, but he seemed to be fascinated by them if anything. I cupped his little face and kissed his forehead. Honestly I have never fallen in love with anything so quickly and so deeply in my entire life.

"Hello, Baby Horton," I said. The name suited him perfectly. David had chosen a few other names, sci-fi type names from memory, but in my heart he was always going to be Horton and looking at him now, I was glad I had stuck to my guns.

David put Horton on the floor in an area where he could see things but not get trampled in the stampede, then set about greeting the other pugs. I looked at this gorgeous little bandy-legged thing sitting on the floor looking up at me and the lump in my throat was so big I knew there was no way I could push it down. I smiled at Horton regardless. Pugs are extremely good at reading facial expressions and I wanted him to know from the very first moment that he was home, that I loved him and that everything was going to be all right in his world from now on. "Don't cry! Don't cry!" I told myself over and over again. "You'll be no use to him if you do. He needs you to be strong, so stop it, stop it, stop it!" He had a battle ahead of him and I had to be brave for his sake; he needed me to be an asset to him not a blubbering mess. And besides, he wasn't crying, so why on earth was I? Horton shifted his body round and sat looking at his new siblings gathering around their dad. While he was distracted, I took my leave. I grabbed a tissue from the kitchen and wiped the tears away before he could see them. I wasn't gone long. I didn't want to leave him. When I came back he was still sitting in the same spot, but was now happily giving kisses to the pugs that had gathered round to meet him. Looking down from the safety of his dad's arms was one thing, but I thought he may have been frightened to meet so many pugs at the same time, but he was handling it well, taking it all in his stride, just sitting on the floor, spinning round, kissing every snuffling, flat face that came his way. I thought this just showed what a wonderful nature he had dwelling within him; he'd had a big day, come a long way and yet there he was sitting in the middle of the pack giving everybody kisses. I suppose he was doing the submissive puppy thing, letting everybody know he had no interest in being top dog. He didn't want to take anybody's job away from them; that's not what he was here for. He didn't care if he sat at the bottom of the pack. All he wanted to do was make a few friends and all I wanted him to do was concentrate on becoming healthier and stronger. He looked better than when I first saw him; he'd spun around and his legs had straightened out. He looked happy, almost as if he was smiling, and his mouth kept opening and closing – his way of saying I am a baby I mean you no harm.

Sarah stomped over, puffing herself up as she always did with a newcomer. She isn't a big pug, so had to make herself look as threatening as possible and the puffing up thing was her way of looking mean. Horton was bright and quickly realized that Sarah was top dog, so had a big submissive kiss for her. Grace did her jumping little bark thing then once she settled down she came close and sniffed Horton and he licked her tiny old face. She was only a fraction bigger than he was. Harper stood in front of Horton, sniffing and snoting. I think she was delighted to have a puppy in the house. She came from a backyard breeder so was used to having many puppies around. Emily and Steffy were more interested in Dad and got quick submissive kisses as they dashed from David to Horton and back again. Ruby and Tommy, who had been asleep when Horton first came in, now rose from their beds and staggered over to sniff the new arrival. Both were hard of hearing, both could sleep through anything and I always envied them this. I wasn't sure what Horton was thinking, whether it was, "Oh hell, there's even more of them," or "Oh wow, two more pugs to love." Tommy stood looking down at the little newcomer; he looked massive beside him. His head was almost the size of Horton's entire body and he must have looked like a giant to him. But Horton wasn't fazed. If I were in Horton's shoes I would have been scared stiff, but the look on his face didn't alter. He just conjured up more kisses and planted them on the two old faces that had appeared in the crowd. Horton let everyone have a sniff at him. He didn't particularly like them sniffing his back legs but I guess he knew it had to be done. They had to familiarize themselves with him as much as he had to familiarize himself with them. It was all part of the settling-in period and he was patient as a few came back for a second and third sniff. Then he just sat in the middle of the lounge looking around at everything in his new home. Now that he had met everyone and I had composed myself I went over and picked him up. I couldn't hold off any longer; I just wanted to feel him close. He was so beautiful. He nestled his face into my neck and gave kisses. He had puppy breath and it was the most wonderful thing in the world. Gosh, how I'd missed puppy breath. It'd been so long since I'd smelt it I'd almost forgotten it existed. My mind went flooding back to all those years ago when Sarah first came into my life. That was the last time I'd experienced it. I held Horton close, closed my eyes and concentrated on the moment. He was so lovely and this was our very first snuggle. I just wanted to stay there like that forever. I began swaying. I don't know why but whenever I'm snuggling one of my pugs I always sway. I suppose it's like when mothers holding their human babies rock. I held him a little while longer and he didn't struggle to get away; he just stayed in my arms and was peaceful. It was like we belonged together, we were meant to be. After I tore myself away from that embrace, I put Horton on the floor and showed him around the house, making sure he knew where the water bowl was, that sort of thing. He scooted along the floor behind me, pausing every now and then to have a sniff, still no fear just total curiosity. I thought he was such a champ.

After the house tour, David showed me how to change Horton's nappy. I couldn't believe how easy it was to do and how well Horton handled the procedure. The nappy was something I had been worrying about, how it stayed on him and whether it was a hindrance to him, to his back legs, that sort of thing, but the Tinkle Trousers were fantastic little devices and made everything so easy. I had peace of mind now. Caring for Horton was going to be a breeze.

CHAPTER TWO

A Gift of Pure Joy

The previous worries about looking after Horton vanished in those first few days; he was so easy to look after and everything I did for him was an absolute pleasure to do. With all dogs – not just Horton, but especially ones like Horton – it's like you're taking an oath when bringing them into your life, an oath to do whatever it takes, whatever the cost, whatever the time in order to give them the very best life they can possibly have. And you get up every morning and you do it and you do it and you keep on doing it. But you don't have to worry because it's not a chore, more of a pleasure, an honour, a privilege and in my case, an absolute, one hundred and fifty percent pure pure joy. Horton was a delight to be around, he was just lovely and David and I would often squabble over who got to do things for him because any time spent in his presence was fantastic. There was something very special about him, which was evident the first moment he came through the door. I just loved being around him, loved watching him discover his new home, loved feeding him, loved changing him, loved talking to him. He would look at me with those huge puppy eyes of his like he understood everything I was saying. He seemed to enjoy being spoken to and he scooted along after me everywhere I went, so I thought it'd be good to explain to him what I was doing as I did it. I basically just chatted away, giving details of what I was doing around the house or farm and why I was doing it. I figured Horton was new to the world and just as toddlers are curious, puppies are the same.; everything is wonderful to them when they are seeing it for the very first time. I talked to him about everything really, getting him used to the sound of my voice and the goings-on in our home. I didn't just do this with Horton; it's what I do whenever I have a new pug in the house. I feel that rehoming is traumatic enough for them and you've no idea how much they understand. I feel a calming voice helps them settle. The rest of the pugs followed on behind Horton. Well, Tommy didn't. He was asleep on his special chair, but the others stood around watching as if to say, "It's okay, little brother. We were new once as well and you're going to have a wonderful life here."

I always feel for all our pugs during that initial settling-in period. You always worry about what's going through their minds in this time of uncertainty and want to rush this period along as fast as you can, but basically there is nothing you can do but talk them through it and let them know how much you love them and want them in your home. Ninety-five percent of my pugs come to me unwanted, unloved and rejected. That must be an awful thing for a little dog to be feeling, especially when they've done nothing wrong but grow old or become sick and this is when they really need their original family the most. It's sad to watch sometimes because these beautiful souls mourn their families a lot longer than their families mourn them. Some in my care have mourned so deeply for the family who gave them away, and you grieve for them as you watch them go through the process because they have lost their entire family and are mourning each member. They don't fully understand that the family no longer wanted them to be a part of it and that is the thing that really breaks your heart.

Those first few weeks in my care are a time of comforting and reassuring. It's a time of getting them used to my touch and the quiet little routine that is our life on the farm. It's also a time when they are figuring out where they stand in the pack. It's a lot for them to go through really, especially when most have spent time in a pound before coming to the farm. So, by the time they are fully settled and feel totally at ease here they will have gone through many weeks of upheavals and uncertainties and your heart goes out to them for that. I just try and make up for what they have lost and help their little hearts heal. I cloak them in love and sometimes they'll let me in; other times they'll reject me because at that point I am not the one they love. They are still being loyal to those they have lived with for most of their lives. It can take a long time for some of them to give you their heart, but when it happens it's a beautiful thing and there is no greater gift in the world. It's wonderful when they finally love you, when you become their darling. For me, it's like a true honour has been bestowed. Everything about them changes; you can see it in their eyes and how they react when you hold them. It's as if you can physically feel their hearts opening up to you and I thank them for it over and over again for it. Then I go off and think to myself, "Oh, I truly am your mummy now."

Horton's story, however, was slightly different to what his elderly brother and sisters had gone through. But I do believe he felt the same rejection, the same lack of love and the same level of uncertainty, all that plus dealing with and working out the little body he had been born into. But Horton was incredibly happy during it all, ecstatically so. It was as if he was so young and new to this world that he didn't fully realize this wasn't how it was meant to be. He loved life. It was like, "Hey, I've gone from my breeder to the vet to rescue to this farm." He was loving the journey and couldn't wait to see what came next. It was a great attitude for little Horton to have and I believe it helped him in a good many ways. I was glad he didn't have to go through that initial mourning period, to have to heal from a broken heart plus his dear little body would have been a difficult thing for me to watch, probably a lot harder on me than it would have been on him. But he took things in his stride whereas I was worrying constantly. I just wanted everything to be all right for him and I believe his incredible attitude to life made it so. I learnt a lot from him during that time and enjoyed the first of many lessons that this incredible little pug would teach me.

In the early days of his arrival I think I must have driven Horton mad with the amount of times a day I would change him, so worried was I of leaving him sitting in a wet nappy that I over-changed it. When he'd first gone into care he'd had little welts on his tummy, urine burns, and it was because of this that I over compensated. I even got up two or three times a night in those first couple of weeks, woke the poor little soul up and changed him because I didn't want him suffering neglect on my watch. But he was good with me, always gave me little kisses on the nose when I changed him and settled back into sleep a lot faster than I did. The night time did worry me the most; I kept worrying that he would have a wee half an hour after we turned the lights out and then have to sit like that until morning. What a terrible thing it would be for him to have to go through, once the urine cooled it would be freezing, like an icepack on his tummy. I couldn't possibly leave him in that state while I slept soundly, oblivious to what he was enduring.

After a while I got used to the routine of his bladder and bowels. I kept an eye on his daily nappy changes so knew what nights he did and didn't need to be woken and checked. And if I did misjudge it, my incredibly intelligent baby boy alerted me to the fact that he needed changing and as all new mothers sleep with one ear open, I woke up instantly on his first little woof. I liked that he'd figured out how to let me know when he needed my help. I liked that he knew I was always there for him. Even during the day, if I was busy with one of the other pugs and my routine with Horton got disrupted, he was good at letting me know when he needed something. Also, as he grew, he didn't need changing as much. Once his little puppy bladder became more like an adult's he was able to go through the whole night most times. Then David, who is up early for work, always changed him before jumping into the shower and I would check and change him again as soon as I got up.

I remember waking up early one morning in the second week Horton came, neither David nor Horton were in the bedroom so I went to see what was going on. The rest of the pugs were sleeping so I tiptoed out of the room, trying not to wake them. As I got to the entrance of the lounge I could see two figures in the wood fires glow. David was changing Horton's nappy and he was doing it in the warmest place in the house so our son wouldn't get cold.

David was crouched down talking to Horton who was sitting directly in front of him. I wasn't close enough to hear what was being said and I really wish I had have been, but I could see that Horton was totally engrossed. I couldn't make out his expression because there wasn't enough light, but I could see Horton's little face tilted up, listening to everything his dad was saying to him. It was a beautiful moment and I didn't want to disturb the two of them, so I turned and crept back to bed. Later in the day I asked David what he was saying to Horton, but he couldn't remember. Both of us were constantly telling Horton how wonderful he was, what a good boy he was and how much we loved him, so it was probably along those lines. I have that image captured in my mind and I can see it now as I'm writing this. I just wish I had been able to capture that special moment on camera as well, but the flash going off would have ruined everything and probably made Horton jump and I would never have scared him like that.

I think Horton was very happy when my new mum nerves settled down into a nice easy routine. I wasn't fussing about as much and he seemed to appreciate that. I was no longer getting on his nerves by checking the state of his nappy when there was simply no need to do so. But certainly Horton's favourite times were when he was nappy-free. On warm days I used to put him on the veranda with a few scatter cushions, half in the sun, half in the shade, and he would run along looking at anything and everything that took his fancy then sprawl out on one of the cushions when he wanted to have a rest. The others were all out there with him and I just used to check the cushions for wee before bringing them in at the end of the day. I loved that Horton could get the sun on his tummy and if I had to be washing cushions every single day then that's what I was going to do. It wasn't a big deal really. I'd just throw them in the washing machine then hang them up to dry. A friend commented on the extra work and I asked her what she meant. Everything is so convenient these days; it's not like I had to go down to the river and beat them against a rock. She laughed at that.

I'd always put a big water bowl out there for them and freshen it regularly. Horton wasn't a big drinker; he'd sometimes go for hours without fluid and that used to worry me. I mentioned this to my friend in rescue but she thought he just didn't know where the water bowl was and that once he figured it out he'd be all right, but he knew where the bowls were and every time I freshened them I always put the bowl down in front of him and lifted it up near his face so he could easily have a drink. He just wasn't ever that interested in it. Unless it was a very hot day he never went near the water bowls much at all. I'd go in and out numerous times, checking on the pugs and freshening the water bowls, sometimes with a book or a cup of tea, then go back inside again finishing the housework. The other pugs would walk down the ramp to have a wee and sometimes Horton would follow them and I'd always shoot outside when he went off the veranda because he was so little, I was scared of losing him. With the size of him and the size of the property he could have very easily become lost. He generally only ever went down the ramp and started sniffing around there, but he was curious about everything and I never knew if he was going to go further on that particular day, so I'd run out to be with him whenever I saw him scooting past the windows. He'd probably have never gone too far, staying near the house or under the ramp or off near the row of tree's sniffing away happily, but I knew if I didn't watch where he went I'd be running all over the place looking for him. I could imagine me not seeing him in my panicked state, racing right past and ending up searching the entire property with my heart in my mouth.

Actually, I did lose Horton once. It was about a year or so after he came so he was used to the place and I was used to his favourite areas, so I always knew where to look for him. On this day, though, he wasn't in any of his favourite spots. I knew he couldn't have gone far because I'd only gone inside to put my empty cup in the sink, but he'd used that time to get off the veranda and disappear. He must have seen something he thought needed further investigation and taken himself off to study it up close. He often did this type of thing and I used to like him doing it. I always loved that he was interested in everything going on around the house and the farm. He was such an intelligent boy and his interest in life and all it had to offer made me as happy as it obviously made him. Once I noticed that he was missing I came off the veranda in a hurry, glanced up to see where the others pugs were and saw that Horton wasn't amongst them. I did a quick sweep of his favourite spots then took off, circling the house looking for him and calling his name as I went. I didn't go near the shed because I knew he couldn't have gotten over there in the short amount of time he had. He could move fast but not that fast. I did an entire lap of the outside of the house twice with no sign of him. I was panicked beyond measure. A few of the other pugs had come and joined me but Horton hadn't come out of his hiding spot. I asked the other pugs where their baby brother was, but none of them set off to show me, so I figured they were in the dark just like I was. I wasn't sure where else to look for him so turned and went back the way I had come. I turned the corner of the house on the south side and there was Horton shuffling towards me. He was panting and a little hot and bothered, but other than that he was okay and he had the most amazing smile on his little face, as if he had just participated in the most fun game ever. I was hot and bothered too, but for very different reasons. Our house is up on blocks, which makes the summer months more bearable because when the cool winds come they blow straight underneath, which changes the temperature of the house in no time. What had happened was that Horton was peeping through the slats, watching my legs and he must have seen me come off the veranda and so set about shuffling after me, but we were both going in the same direction and unbeknown to both of us, had been circling the house chasing one another. I was faster than he was, but I also kept stopping, my eyes, searching across the open paddocks looking for him and he had used that time to cover quite a bit of ground. Thank goodness I turned and doubled back, otherwise it could have gone on a lot longer than it did and poor Horton would have been totally exhausted by the end of it. Although I didn't find it particularly funny on the day it happened, I have since looked back on this and been able to laugh about it. Others have laughed too when I told them what happened. Those who know his speed and curiosity find it very amusing.

Right from the start, Horton gave me a lot of enjoyment. I was so besotted with him that I used to stay awake at night watching him sleep. He was so beautiful, lying there, huffing and puffing in deep peaceful sleep, his eyes disappearing into the folds of his face. I didn't use a torch – too cruel; I didn't want to startle him – I used to wait for the full moon nights then sleep with the curtains open so I could see his face more clearly. I just took pleasure in every single aspect of him. I loved watching his facial expressions and hearing the noises he made when something delighted him or when he saw something for the very first time. I'd forgotten how much fun a puppy could be. People said that I was wonderful for taking this special needs boy in, but what they didn't realize was that Horton gave me far more than I was giving him. I woke up in the morning happy because of Horton and I'd go to bed at night content because I'd really enjoyed my day. You just couldn't have a bad day with Horton around; it simply wasn't possible. He made everything we did so much more fun because I could watch his reaction to things and there was a whole world of happiness gotten by doing that.

Having a puppy in the house was a novelty to all of us and a new air filled our home. The oldies were as besotted with Horton as I was and he relished all the attention. Ruby's old arthritic tail would go ten to the dozen when she was around her baby brother, moving like I've never seen it move before. Tommy liked Horton but, Tommy being Tommy, he never got involved with the goings-on down on the floor. He was content to watch everything from the comfort of his special chair. Most of the time he slept and Horton would shuffle over and sit looking up, watching him sleep. Sometimes he'd give a little yap, you know, just so Tommy remembered he was there. It hardly ever woke Tommy up, but on the rare occasion that it did, Horton thought it was the best thing ever. His face changed and he looked so proud of himself.

When Tom is in a deep sleep he sucks in air then blows it out fast, making his jowls flap about. One day, Horton was sitting looking up with his head on the side, listening to Tommy snore.

He didn't try and wake his elderly brother this time, just seemed content listening to the unusual noises. I stopped what I was doing and watched on as Tom slipped deeper and deeper into sleep, his breathing becoming heavier and heavier. I knew the bellowing jowls show was about to start and wanted to see Horton's reaction to it. When it came it was priceless. Horton's eyes practically doubled in size and he pushed his little body backwards as fast as he could. He wasn't sure what to make of it, yet was fascinated all the same. He kept coming closer then backpedaling and his facial expressions were wonderful to see.

Although Tommy and Horton never played together I always felt they had a very special relationship. They seemed to have an unspoken closeness, a natural bond, as if they understood one another and accepted each other for who they were. Tommy was a huge pug and yet he was incredibly graceful when he was on the floor. He'd slowly side-step Horton, never once making contact with his little brother's body. Seeing the two of them together was comical, the size difference incredible. Tommy is by far the biggest pug I have ever seen and Horton the smallest. Horton was so tiny he could scoot right underneath Tommy without his head making contact with his tummy. He made a game out of it and moved so quickly that I think Tom figured the best thing to do was stand still and let the little guy exhaust himself. Also, when Horton first came, you could uncurl Tommy's tail and it fit all the way round Horton's tiny head like a headband. I tried it once when they were both on the bed with me sleeping. I uncurled Tommy's tail gently and slowly so as not to wake him up, then moved Horton's head a little bit closer. I just wanted to know if it would go all the way round. I'd been thinking about it while watching them sleep and wanted to satisfy my curiosity. I managed to do all this while they were both sound asleep then went and ruined everything, waking them both up by laughing when it actually went all the way round.

All the pug nanas loved having a youngster about. They were in awe of him, much like a human grandmother is when a new baby arrives. And Horton loved being around all of them. He'd follow his elderly sisters everywhere they went and scoot about at the back of the pack, always interested in what they were doing. I think he thought they were going to lead him to something magical and for a newborn pup discovering the world, everything is magical if you haven't set eyes on it before, so he was rarely disappointed. When they stopped and sniffed, he stopped and sniffed. When the pack moved on, Horton would scurry along after them, his little head turning from side to side as he went. If he saw something that held his interest, he would pause for a few moments, never long enough for the pack to get too far ahead, though. I guess he figured that the pack knew where they were heading and he could always come back to everything he saw along the way later in the day while the rest of his pug family slept.

Harper mothered Horton the most. She is a natural-born mother and he let himself be nurtured by her. She looked after him but and didn't guard him in a nasty way, like she did with her toys. It was more that she was aware of him, kept a close eye on where he was and what he was doing, making sure he was okay. He liked being around her. In fact, in those early days when he first came, Harper was the one that Horton chose to be close to. She is one of my most gentle pugs, so beautiful and loving in nature and Horton seemed to like that. I think Harper was a comfort to him. He would sleep side by side with her; there were plenty of spare beds and also beds with other sleeping pugs in them but he scooted past the lot and shuffled himself in next to her. After a while he decided to give the other pugs a go. Then, as he got stronger in his body and more outgoing in his personality, he would find himself a bed of his own, but there were times when he was particularly tired from exploring the farm, chasing insects and watching butterflies and dragonflies and anything else that moved, that he'd once again go looking for the comfort of Harper and snuggle in next to her.

Most of the time, Horton wouldn't make a sound. The rescue lady was right when she had told us that he was a very quiet puppy, but when there was a game on he was very vocal and his excited little yaps floated throughout the house. Emily soon became Horton's playmate. Being a lot younger than the others, she was always up for a game. She was never selfish with him, shared all her toys and enjoyed having a tug of war with him and her floppy-legged teddy bear. Emily did have a tendency to play a little roughly at times, which in the early days once or twice caught Horton off-balance. It wasn't that she meant to do it, because I know she was aware that Horton wasn't like her. Actually, all the pugs quickly became aware of Horton not being like they were; they knew his back legs were very different to theirs. They could tell that he didn't like anybody sniffing his back legs in the early days of his arrival, which was hard because when he first came his back legs were of the most interest to them. He didn't like the others getting behind him where he couldn't properly see them either and the first few weeks he was here it bothered him because I think he was unsure of what they were going to do. But he soon came to realize that they were not going to hurt him, so he tolerated the excessive sniffing and circling until his legs were no longer a novelty to them.

After Horton had toppled over a few times and became no longer interested in the game, Emily must have gotten the message because after that she used to give him an advantage. She would lay on her side and let him pounce on her tummy, even enduring the occasional overzealous bite and his puppy teeth were really sharp. For his part, Horton was having the time of his life. He would fly round her body, squeal then pounce on her tummy, head or back, then be off, circling her again as fast as lightning. She never knew where he was going to pounce next. I think that was all part of the game; well, for Horton it was because deep down I have the feeling that Emily knew exactly where he was all the time. That's the thing when your little body is always making contact with the ground it makes it kind of hard to creep up on somebody. But Horton thought he was being super sneaky. You could see it; his facial expressions would change just before he pounced and God bless Emily, because she always gave him a wonderful reaction. She never let on, never ruined his fun. She'd either lift her head slightly and bark or jerk her entire body about like he'd just scared the living daylights out of her. This thrilled Horton no end and made him shoot off, circling again, ready to scare her one more time. He loved playing with Emily; he always sought her out for a friendly afternoon play fight and she never once refused to engage him in a bit of fun, no matter how many times he asked her to come play. Horton knew exactly where he could find her, too. Actually, he soon got to know where on the couch each of his siblings liked to sleep. He'd scoot past Tommy's chair, bypass Sarah, ignore Steffy and kept scooting right to the end of the couch where he knew Emily liked to lay.

As Horton grew and became stronger their games became different. She no longer gave him an advantage; she didn't have to because such was his strength that he proved to be quite a match for her, to the point where he wore her completely out and she had to jump back up on the couch just to get away from him. Horton eventually got to know when she needed time out and would sit staring up at her for a few moments, you know, just to be sure she was really serious about having a rest this time. Then he'd scoot off and find himself a bed and have a little rest himself. And I'd be creeping round the house so as not to wake him up. I swear Horton always slept with one eye open in case he missed out on something.

I needn't have worried about him being too boisterous for my elderly household. Horton was inquisitive and lively, but he was never annoying. He never once tormented his elderly sisters while they slept. Emily was the only one he played with; the others were too old and he got to know they liked to sleep more than he did. Horton learnt that lesson early on. At one time he would go from bed to bed, pause then tap the blankets with his paw, trying to initiate play, but that didn't work at all so he only did it for a little while. If Emily had had enough for the day Horton just more or less set about amusing himself while everyone else rested. He'd scoot past the rows of beds to the stack of toys near the window and play with them. He had a few that were his favourite, so I'd bury those underneath the ones he had no interest in and watch him search the stack. It gave him something more to do, it occupied him longer and he seemed so excited when he found his special toys. Even if Ruby, Grace or Harper happened to have flopped in the middle of the floor and were having a snooze Horton simply scooted around them. I was worried at first that he may plough through them and once or twice he stopped and sniffed, but mainly he veered off, such was his hurry to get to the toys. Occasionally, he would fall asleep amongst the stack, with his little head using a soft toy as a pillow. This was a beautiful sight to see because it rarely happened. Mainly he'd just quietly lay and chew for hours. Once somebody woke up, though, the toy was quickly spat out, he'd scoot over, fall in line behind and follow where they went. Sometimes it only led to the water bowl for a drink then back to bed for more sleep, but he always followed them, waiting for the times when it led outside for a sniff.

When friends dropped by, Horton thought they'd come especially to see him because basically they had. Once people knew we had a special boy joining the family they all wanted to pop over and meet him. Horton used to scoot to the door and greet each one like a proper little socialite. Sometimes I'd pick him up so he wouldn't get knocked off-balance in the mad rush to say hello to whoever had knocked at the door. But he didn't like waiting in my arms while the other pugs got greeted. He wanted to be down on the floor where the action was. He never liked people who spoke loudly, though. That seemed to unnerve him quite a bit. Actually, loud noises of any kind seemed to upset him terribly. That's the good thing about living on a farm; it's always quiet here. I believe he wouldn't have done well living in a heavily built-up area, not just because of the noise level but the pollution level as well. Heavy fumes in the city wouldn't have been good for him, health wise. His little lungs wouldn't have done well living amongst pollution. The fresh air here on the farm did wonders for him and he relished in the purity of the air, the food and the lifestyle. Also, a home with rowdy children wouldn't have suited him either. He was deeply bothered by noisy children to the point where, after witnessing his reaction, I no longer allowed certain children back into the house. It wouldn't have been fair on Horton. This was his home, the one area he needed to feel safe, happy and secure, and I needed to keep our home a haven for him. But it wasn't just for Horton; I've always done this with my elderly lot, always kept their home a place where they felt comfortable, a sanctuary really, one where they could thrive. I believe that's how to get the long years out of them. No frail elderly person wants to be bothered by unruly youngsters, especially if they're not feeling well or are just settling in. Not everyone agrees with me of course, so this has caused a few ruffled feathers in the past when people have been told to be quieter or leave, but this is my home and one can like it or lump it. It's basically a case of my castle my rules. I also no longer allow negative people into my house because I don't want their presence around my pugs. This did start with Horton. In those first few weeks that he was here, life was hard for him. He was adjusting to his new life and his body was adapting to our wooden floorboards. He was not doing terribly well with them but he was a trooper, he was so determined and had such strength of mind. Yet it was very hard on me watching his weak little legs sliding about all over the place. There was actually a point where I thought of giving him back to the rescue group so they could find him a home where he could better handle the floors. It felt like I was being cruel to him, making him struggle with the slipperiness. I rang my rescue friend in tears after a particularly hard day, telling her about my concerns for Horton. I said I didn't want him to go but I loved him too much to keep him here if a home with different floor coverings would be of more benefit to his needs. What if a more suitable floor could have been the difference between Horton being able to one day walk upright? I loved him too much to keep him here if I knew doing so would be holding him back. My heart was so heavy with grief for over a week and that day I just broke down. We couldn't afford to carpet the entire house and with elderly pug bladder accidents, carpets are no good for us anyway.

My friend listened to my blubbering, anxiety-filled ramblings before butting in. She had to cut in really, such was my distress I was going round and round in circles and not pausing for breath. She reassured me that puppies where very resilient, even those with special needs. She said that a carpeted floor was no good for Horton because it would give him carpet burns. Yes, our floor was proving a challenge for him now but that would all change. She told me to take a deep breath and allow Horton to work it out for himself; he would be able to adjust and figure out how best to maneuver himself across the floor. I didn't really believe her when I hung up the phone and decided that I would do what I'd been told not to do, and carry my baby around all the time. When I had doubts about being able to look after Horton in those early days before he came I had been told that the only way I could fail at this was if I over-mothered him, if I carried him around and did everything for him. But in that moment I decided I would go against the advice given to me and do my own thing. I just didn't want to see him struggling any longer. It was agony watching his little, weak body slipping and sliding about all the time. It hurt my heart too much. But the next day I woke up and realized she was right; carrying Horton around was no good for him and no good for me. I had to resist the urge welling up inside me to go over and help him every time he slipped. I had to let him do this on his own. I realized that as much as I may have wanted to I couldn't protect Horton from everything nor could I do everything for him. That wouldn't have been right or fair, it would have even been robbing him of what he could do and the life he could live. So, as he struggled on I occupied myself with housework, I didn't stand watching him as much as I had been doing because I found it too hard so and I set about keeping my hands and mind busy. If I was idle and forever watching him I knew I would be tempted to run over and pick him up. Besides, Horton wasn't asking for my help and he didn't seem half as upset when he slid as I was. I wouldn't go as far as to say he was totally enjoying himself, but he wasn't too bothered about it either, so I just had to learn to leave him to it. After a while he figured it out, he knew how best to project himself across the room and he ended up being able to do it with incredible speed as well. As Horton's body developed, became stronger, I was rewarded by seeing how much he could actually do on his own. His strength was amazing – such a little body but so incredibly strong. Horton was truly an amazing and inspirational little guy and that's why I couldn't have anybody entering my home that wasn't totally supportive of him. There are many times in your life when you find out who your real friends are and this was one of them. I mean, here little Horton was having so many obstacles to overcome, everyday battling so hard to make his body stronger and he was doing brilliantly with it. To have somebody standing in his home projecting negativity or making a joke at his expense, well, I was never going to allow that to happen. Words are powerful and I believe dogs understand far more than most people give them credit for. Some folks said things without thinking and I'd pull them up on it and they'd do better next time, so I allowed them to come back and be around Horton. But they had to be careful because whether they meant it or not, there was Horton sitting nearby, his little ears would hear it and he was taking everything in. He'd be able to pick up on the negativity and I couldn't allow anybody or anything to hinder his progress. I gave people a few chances, but if they couldn't be supportive and encouraging of Horton then they had to go. Sometimes you just have to remove poisonous people from your world, even if it's uncomfortable to do so. You owe it to yourself and those you love most in life to make their environment as happy and healthy as possible. Create a haven where everything thrives and nothing withers. How could I have this beautiful little soul on the floor fighting hard for every achievement only to have negative, degrading comments floating above his head? Horton deserved better than that and it was my job to make sure he got it.

CHAPTER THREE

120kg of Vodka

Because having a pug with hemivertebra was new to me, I more often than not allowed myself to be guided by Horton. He knew his body better than I did, he knew how things felt on the inside and so I spent a lot of time watching him closely and learning from how he handled himself. He was very good at letting me know what he wanted and needed from me. He was incredibly independent and never asked for help unless he definitely needed it. It was a time of Horton figuring out what he could do with his body and me learning how to read his signals properly. After my initial meltdown about him sliding around on the floor, I settled down a lot and stopped stressing about every little thing because it wasn't doing either of us any good. I felt my job was to observe Horton, to try and be as in tune with him as I could and to figure out what he was telling me. Things worked out pretty well for the two of us in this area, but I often worried about dogs in other homes whose owners maybe weren't as in tune with them as I was with Horton. I'd lie in bed at night and feel sorry for the dogs out there trying to let their owners know what they needed only to be ignored. I had a lump in my throat for those dogs left to live their entire lives in backyards. How could they possibly get messages across to their owners if all they did was dart outside with a bowl of food and back in the house again without a backward glance? Dogs can't talk; the only way they have of communicating with us is through their actions. That's why it's so vital that we watch and learn, block out the noise and distractions of the day and really be in tune to what is going on with our four-legged companions. That, to me, is what being a good guardian is all about and it's a must if you want to give your furry family members the best life possible. This is important for all dogs, especially elderly dogs, because certain issues start arriving once a dog reaches a certain age. It's the same with humans, although we can verbally communicate. Our dogs can't, so they need us to be ever watchful for the signals they are sending us. I lucked out with Horton because he was a fantastic little communicator, never loud, never whiny, just a little noise to alert me and then he'd talk with his actions or his eyes.

I remember when Horton let me know I was picking him up wrong. It was the right way to pick a normal pug up but it must have been uncomfortable for him due to his condition. He would be out on the veranda then call to let me know he wanted to come back inside the house. In the early days before his front legs got stronger he couldn't get himself over the long small metal strip that the glass door slid along and so always asked to be lifted over. I heard him call and walked across the room to get him but every time I bent down and reached out my hands he turned and shuffled off. At first I thought he hadn't called me, that I must have mistaken his unique little dolphin noise with something else, so I went back inside and carried on with what I was doing. Horton shuffled over to the strip, peeped his head inside the door and called for me again. No, it was definitely my little prince calling me this time. I was certain of that. I went back out to get him and the same thing happened again. I thought he must have wanted to play. He did like being chased; that game delighted him no end, so I played with him for a while, which pleased him. After he grew tired of the game I went back inside. A few moments later he called to me again. He didn't need his nappy changed because he was on the veranda and it was a lovely warm day, so he was nappy-free. I took more notice of Horton this time. We made eye contact, so he knew I was coming to get him but before I had even reached out my hands he turned round. This time he didn't move away; he stayed put and glanced slightly over his shoulder. He didn't want to be chased; we'd already played that game. He just sat there waiting. I side-stepped his little body and went round the front of him to pick him up in the way I always did. He turned again and I moved round the front once more only to have him turn his back on me again. So, I thought, "What the heck!" I'll just pick him up backwards. Horton gave me the biggest kisses when he reached my face, like he was saying, "At last, Mummy, you got it, you figured out what I was telling you and thank you for that." After that, every time Horton wanted me to pick him up he'd come scooting over then turn just as he reached me and up he'd come. I figured it must have been easier on his spine to lift him this way and like I said, I had no idea it was uncomfortable for him being picked up the other way because he never complained. Perhaps he'd just gone through another growing phase and his body had once again changed. I was glad we'd worked it out, though, because the thought of causing him any discomfort or pain saddened me. I was also glad that I was so in tune with him. What if I had merely thought he was being silly when he turned round? What if I just thought, "Well, if you're playing games you can just stay out there."? If I hadn't taken the time to work out what Horton was trying to tell me he would have eventually given up and I would have just gone on picking him up in a way that wasn't right for his body. What a terrible thing that would have been for him. Our animals speak volumes with their actions or sometimes it's only with a slight look in their eyes. But it's easy to figure out the messages they are trying to get across. That's why it's important to be in tune with the animals we share our lives with. It's our job to look out for the signs they are trying to send us. We at least owe them that after all they give us throughout their lifetimes.

It was very important to both David and me that Horton be allowed to live a very full life. We wanted him to be able to experience everything. We didn't want to hold him back just because of the body he had been born into and it was a good thing we decided this early on because the spirit that dwelt within Horton wasn't going to allow him to live any other way. He was so full of life, effervescent, just wanting to discover new things and have a go at everything. As soon as his body grew strong enough for him to try something new he would try it. Once he tested it and knew his body was up to the task, there was no holding him back. He was just the most curious little boy and fearless, incredibly fearless, he needed to be constantly watched because he could quite easily have hurt himself. Naturally, we never pushed Horton to do anything, not only would it have been unfair and cruel but we just couldn't see the point in it really, so we just loved him and waited until he felt ready to take new things on. New achievements weren't for us, they were only for Horton because basically we never really cared if he didn't achieve anything. We loved him regardless, but we wanted him to feel that he could try new things if he wanted to and our job was to make sure he was healthy and happy and had the confidence to do so. Of course we would always be there beside him in everything he chose to do, one of us would always be around to make sure he wouldn't hurt himself physically, we weren't ever going to send him out into the world unaccompanied, he needed us to be with him because the bottom line was that he was different to other dogs. He was like a newborn baby really and needed that level of care every single day, but we were never going to let him miss out on anything because of this.

I remember the first time I saw his little body and the reaction I had. I remember walking out of the room to get my head together and I also remember walking back in with a different mindset. I thought, "Right, let's get on with it. Let's give this little darling the best life any pug has ever lived. Let's do everything in our power to make him the happiest, healthiest pug baby in the world." And that's what we did. After a few months Horton glowed with health, his coat was black and glossy, his body became stronger and his eyes were bright and beautiful and took in everything that was going on in the world around him. He grew a lot in confidence in those first few months and he was so happy; well, not just happy but ecstatic. He greeted each new day with enthusiasm; he was full of life, full of energy and full of personality. And this seemed to confuse a lot of people. It even confused our country vet. I think people projected their thoughts onto Horton. They saw his little body and thought he should have been sadder, shyer, uncomfortable maybe. What I believe they were doing was putting their own feelings on him, which was a mistake, because he didn't think the same way they did. Perhaps if they had been born similar to Horton they may have sat in the corner and been miserable. But that just wasn't Horton. He wouldn't participate in self-pity; he didn't know what that was. All he knew was that this was his body, the only one he had. He didn't know that this wasn't how he was supposed to be or how he was supposed to look. How could he, really? So he just got on with living.

To be honest, I don't think he gave his body a real lot of thought. Human beings tend to over think things, which can make them worse, but dogs don't do that. It didn't seem to bother Horton that some of the other pugs could do more than he could. I don't even know if he knew he was different to them. He was too busy enjoying every moment. He just slotted himself in amongst the pack, scooted along happily with his siblings and basically became one of them very quickly after he arrived. And besides, being placed in this home with all these oldies, where no two pugs were completely the same, was probably a blessing for him. The right decision had been made.

Some of my pugs move better than others, some have arthritis and some don't. Ruby walks with an unusual gait; she shuffles along like a little penguin and yet she does okay. It doesn't hold her back. She can even outrun some of the others. She used to be my special needs pug or at least I used to think she was until Horton got here and blew her disabilities out of the water. She looked like a normal pug next to him. Some of my elderly pugs move differently because they are blind and some tend to act that little bit differently because they can no longer hear. But the beautiful thing that I have seen over and over again is their ability to help one another. I believe that this was the best home for Horton to be placed in because he was around so many pugs with so many different needs. Basically, he was just one of eight special needs pugs. Only human beings saw him differently, but to Horton he was just a normal member of our beautiful little pack.

One warm day in spring, we called a vet out to the farm to de-sex Vodka, our Ram. Voddy was about two years old at the time. We waited until winter was over and done with because we didn't want him to have stitches and soreness during the cold, damp months. The vet they sent out was the same one who'd seen Horton on one other occasion when he accompanied Ruby to her appointment. The other pugs stayed home but we never left Horton on his own, so he came with us when Ruby had an ear infection. There were no other dogs in the surgery, so I put Horton down and let him go where he pleased. He scooted around the waiting room, checking the place out thoroughly, then dashed behind the desk and said hello to the nurses. He then went near the window and sat looking out onto the street, watching people walk by. When the vet came out to call us into the consultation room he forgot all about Ruby, his patient, and went straight to Horton, even Horton knew he had gotten the wrong pug because the look on his face told me everything he was thinking. Horton wasn't scared of the six-foot vet rushing towards him; his Daddy is tall, so tall people didn't worry him. He just sat there looking up at him as if to say, "Dude, we're here for my sister."

David carried Ruby in and I scooped up Horton. There was a rather high step into the surgery area and I knew Horton wouldn't be able to manage it by himself. He was content sitting by the window, looking at new things, but he had to come with us, so in we all went. While Ruby was being examined Horton scooted under the table but looked up every time he heard his name, which was a lot because the vet was still fixated on the little fella and began asking all sorts of questions. He thought Horton was gorgeous and said he had no trouble getting around. He seemed amazed at his speed and spent more time smiling down at Horton than he did looking at Ruby. Ruby didn't mind. She sat slumped on the table, waiting for the treat she knew followed every examination. The vet also asked if we had sought the advice of a specialist. We said that Horton had seen the best there was but sadly nothing could be done for him. I think because there was a lot of carrying around of Horton on that visit the vet may have presumed that's how Horton's life generally was, but Horton in his natural habitat and Horton on an outing are two very different things, so I was glad when this same vet hopped out of the ute the day I called a vet out to the farm. It gave him a chance to see the real Horton and I knew his mind would be forever changed about how this little boy truly lived.

Vodka's a pretty big ram and weighs about 120kg. Even though his parents had rams, I don't think this vet had seen one like him before and didn't seem to believe me when I told him how much he weighed. He thought he was around 80-90kg, that's what his parents' rams weighed, so he only gave Vodka enough serum to sedate him for that weight. But after an eternity of watching and waiting and Vodka only swaying, never dropping, the vet finally realized I was right. Seeing as we didn't want to over sedate Vodka and possibly kill him, our big ram was released from the holding pen and staggered out into the open paddock like a drunkard on his way home from a big night at the pub. Vodka eventually got de-sexed, but the vet had to come back a week later to do the job. It wasn't a wasted trip, though, because while we waited for Vodka to fall asleep, the vet came into the house and had a chance to spend a bit of time with Horton, which he loved. This was a vet who truly loved dogs, you could see it in the way he looked at Horton and as usual, when all eyes were on him, Horton was a bit of a show off, scooting round the lounge, sneaking up on the vet then as he turned, scooting off again at lightning speed. He was playing with our visitor the same way he played with Emily and the vet seemed amused by it. Horton even brought his yellow duck over and started shaking it like crazy until the vet actually acknowledged that he had a little ducky in his mouth. I think Horton wanted the vet to follow him over to the window so he could show him his special stash of toys, but the vet didn't realize this so eventually Horton gave up trying.

The vet crouched down on the floor, checking out all the other pugs. I never asked him to but a good vet will always check on the health of any animal he comes into contact with when called out to a farm, especially when out on a large property where sometimes the dogs don't receive the care they need. And with me having so many pugs I suppose he wanted to double check I was looking after them properly. He did it on the sly but I knew what he was doing and didn't mind because I look after my pugs better than I look after myself. Besides, I would rather have a vet double checking healthy dogs than not checking out the dogs that really do need his help.

My pugs gave him kisses and bobbed about as he studied each one. We talked about their overall health and I was quite happy to pick his brains on a few things. But he couldn't wait to get back to Horton, which was fine because Horton couldn't wait to have the vet's attention solely on him. You could see it in his eyes when he finally got some quality time with my special little boy; he was in awe of him. While he quickly looked at the others Horton had been busy scooting about all over the place. He was at the window woofing at the birds then he scooted across the room to see what the vet was doing then he was off again to play with a toy then back again peeping through the bunch to look at the vet's face. He then rushed over to me because I'd spoken and he thought I was talking to him. He was giddy with excitement at having somebody new in the house; well, not just somebody new, but somebody new who thought he was wonderful. Dogs are very good at sensing when somebody adores them and Horton was in his element having a new member of his fan club. I was a little bit embarrassed at the amount of showing off he was doing but the vet thought Horton was the best thing he'd ever seen, so I didn't rein him in. I just cringed, let it go and looked the other way. One word and a point of my finger would have been all it took for Horton to calm down a bit. He was well behaved and very good at understanding what I said. He could easily be called over from across our big lounge with one or two words. He was always listening to what was going on. He may have been involved in a game with Emily or studying a fly crawling up the window but one word was all it took and in a flash he'd be right in front of me, looking up, smiling, wondering what was coming next. Did I have a treat for him? Were we all going outside for a bit? Did I want to hug or kiss him – a thing I did as often as I possibly could – or was it simply time for his nappy to be checked?

The vet was mesmerized by Horton and said that seeing him at home and how well he moved, how happy he was, how much he loved the rest of the pugs and how beautifully he interacted with them, was well worth all the hanging about waiting for the ram to drop. When Horton did his silly face the vet said he looked like he was actually smiling. I'd always thought Horton's two-teeth smile was pretty special and it was nice that the vet thought so too. If I spoke Horton came over to me and when the vet spoke he dashed back over to him in case he was about to dish out more praise. When Horton sat in front of me I would clap and say, "Good, good boy." Whenever I said this he would begin bouncing up and down on his nappy. The vet had a huge smile on his face every time Horton did this. He commented on our closeness, said we shared a special bond and he was right. We did. We simply loved each other and it always showed because time and time again I'd hear this same thing said.

I believe that the vet left our home happy that day and I think those images of Horton would stay with him for a long time. At least I hoped they would. This vet was a man with a heart for dogs, but I've found that not all country vets are because they prefer dealing with the larger animals. Their sole interest is livestock, which is why they come out to work in country practices. Some of them just don't have an interest in small domestic animals. I liked this vet; he was different and I was glad he was able to have a glimpse into my little boy's life. Even if it was only a small glimpse, I think it was enough for him to realize the kind of wonderful life Horton lived and it was important for him as a professional to see that: to witness what could be done with a special needs dog if they were placed in the right situation, the right home with the right people. Perhaps he would now think twice before putting a dog to sleep that doesn't really need it. Hopefully the next time he came across a special case he would remember his time with Horton and know that there are other options besides that final needle. This vet came into contact with a lot of people on a daily basis; he could spread the word about what could be done for a dog that wasn't in any pain but merely needed lots of loving care and special looking after. This vet already had an open heart when it came to dogs; I hoped his time with Horton opened his mind up as well. And I believe it did. You couldn't meet Horton and not be forever changed by the experience. I truly believe that meeting Horton would have impacted on this young vet's future and the future of every dog in his care. That which was witnessed in our home on that sunny day in spring would be carried with him for the rest of his life. After all, it was a precious vet with an open mind and a heart full of pure gold who saw something in Horton that his breeder had failed to see. If Horton had seen a different vet, been taken to a different surgery by his breeder on that fateful day, everything would have been different. His breeder would have gotten her wish and Horton's life would have ended as quickly as it had begun. There would be no wonderful little soul scooting across the floor, enjoying life and leaving a tiny paw print on the hearts of everyone he came into contact with. And what an enormous tragedy that would have been.

CHAPTER FOUR

Stronger and Stronger

Horton was so tiny and weak in his body when he first came to the farm. He wasn't used to moving much; he had been kept confined so his front legs were like thin sticks with no definition. He was moving around but quite slowly, covering small distances at a time then stopping to rest. I guess from the time he was born to the time he came to us nobody really knew what he could and couldn't do. It was a period of him being born and nursed by his mother and the breeder noticing that he was different. He was then taken to the vets to be put down, but ended up in rescue, being looked after by the experts, and finally arrived in our home.

In those early days I remember him scooting over to say hello and without thinking, I would lean down and stroke him on the head like I did with all the other pugs. But because he didn't have a lot of strength or muscle tone he was very unsteady and even a gentle pat would send him toppling over. The first time it happened I was on the computer typing away when Horton came over looking for a bit of love. I leant down and patted him and over he went. I jumped up from the chair thinking, "Oh Bloody hell, I've injured him," and bent down quickly to help him up and check he wasn't hurt. He was fine. The incident didn't faze him at all. In fact, the only one panicking was me. It was a bit of a shock to see how easily Horton could topple over. He lay on his side, flopping about, doing all he could to flip himself over but he couldn't manage it. Due to the condition of his spine, if he was lying on his side he simply could not get himself upright again without my help. I only set him off-balance once or twice but it let me know what his limitations were and once I knew where his weaknesses lay, it made life easier for both of us. It let me know to make extra sure he wouldn't fall over again when I was otherwise occupied. If I was about to have a shower I'd bring his bed into the bathroom with me and build the blankets up on all sides of his body so that he would be okay while I washed my hair. And I took extra special care when patting him from then on. I used to cup his little face in the palm of my hand and gently massage the top of his head, the side of his face and his ears with my thumb as a way of saying hello. That's how I kept hold of him and for a couple of months that was how Horton got his greeting and remained upright at the same time. He had the tiniest head and used to lay his chin on my palm and close his eyes as I stroked. I used to massage and tell him over and over again how much I loved him. I think I must have told him how in love with him I was a million times a day and he used to love hearing it, because wherever I was in the house I would hear his little Tinkle Trousers tapping along the floorboards and knew he was coming for another massage and another vocal outpouring of love. I also used to tell him how very special he was and how glad I was that he had come into my life. I'd tell him how happy he made me and that his daddy and I were so lucky to have him. Horton's huge eyes used to look up at me when I spoke, soaking in every utterance, but sometimes he was so into the massage that he'd close his little eyes and almost fall asleep. He never actually started snoring but I knew I had to make sure he was fully awake before taking my hand away, otherwise he would have fallen over again and I didn't want that. In every single area Horton was just the most beautiful little boy. The massages soothed him and when he got sleepy I'd carry him over to a bed so he could have a nap.

I remember the first walk we ever took Horton on. It was his first morning on the farm and we were told to keep him on the ground, to more or less let him do what our other pugs were doing, but I believe my friend in rescue had no idea about the distance my old pugs used to walk in a day. Poor Horton was getting exhausted so we quickly ignored what had been suggested and picked him up. Horton arrived on the farm in spring time and there was lots of dew on the ground and he was getting wet so David rushed him back to the house while I gave the rest of the pugs their normal walk. When I came inside Horton was sitting on his dad's knee, wrapped in a big blue towel. I couldn't see him at first then this little black face emerged from the center of the fluffy cocoon. He must have heard his new siblings pitter-pattering in and wanted to see what was going on. Horton was happy to have been out for a walk but it really was too much for him to cope with. He wanted to jump right in and do what all the others were doing but he needed to build up his little body first. After that, I would let him on the ground for five minutes then up in my arms for ten to catch his breath then down on the ground again for five and I'd take a towel with me to dry him off while he was resting. Of course if he stopped for a sniff I'd leave him down a bit longer because he rested as he sniffed, but I had to let him build his body up very slowly. Horton's mind was a lot stronger than his body, so it became a battle of wills sometimes, especially if he happened to be in my arms when the others found something interesting to sniff. He'd wriggle like crazy so I'd lower him. Even in his less than robust state he wasn't about to miss out on anything. He was ecstatic if he found a leaf or a stick to chew. He'd lay on the ground with his find, all the while keeping an eye on the others in case they found something better and more interesting than he had. When he saw them gathering in a bunch he'd quickly spit out his newly found chew toy and shuffle off to see what they'd come across.

If the weather was cold I'd carry him most of the way with only little intervals on the ground at the start and end of the walk. He seemed fine with that. As long as he knew he was going to get some time on the ground he was happy. From the first moment he arrived on the farm he just loved being outside. If a door was left open, out he would shuffle and sit watching the goings-on in the livestock paddock. I wanted him to enjoy himself and build up his body at the same time, so that's what he did as far as his strength training went. We just took each day as it came and altered things according to the weather and how Horton was feeling on the day. If he'd done too much one day I made sure he rested more the next. This went on for months and all the while the weather was getting warmer and warmer as he was growing stronger and healthier.

Horton loved his food and was diving into four small, yet highly nutritious, mini meals every day. Over time, he grew incredibly strong. The power in his front legs and shoulders was amazing and such upper body strength developed at a nice steady pace. I remember lying on the floor with Horton playing Throw the Ducky one day while the others were asleep. That's when it hit me how much his body had changed. At first I was looking at his bright eyes and how shiny his coat had become, then he turned slightly and I was able to see that those once-little, stick front legs were more like solid tree trunks now. His side profile was very different to how it once had been. Huge bulging muscles protruded from the tops of his legs and his entire upper body was massive in comparison to when he first came. We used to call him Horton-Schwarz-a-pug, as in Arnold.

You could pat him like a regular pug now and he wouldn't fall over. He still came over for massages, so I gave them to him whenever he asked. He could drag himself on any dog bed in the house and those slightly higher beds that he was never able to get in proved no challenge for him now. He would simply scoot over, lean up and swing his body in. A few quick turnarounds and he was settled. Sometimes his back legs would get in his way so he'd move round until he was comfortable. But it was never a strain, always done with ease. Because his back legs didn't do much, he just dragged them around behind him like little logs really, but I remember the horror when a vet mentioned amputation. I had never even considered such a thing. I suppose he was looking at him with the eyes of a professional and I was looking at Horton as his mother.

"Why have them there if he's never going to use them?" was what he said to me. To the vet a simple amputation would mean the little fella would have been able to move around that bit easier, but to me it was like somebody wanted to cut my baby's back legs off. Inside I was raging. I wanted to scream at this guy, tell him exactly what I thought of both him and his suggestion, but Horton doesn't like loud noises and besides, my little boy was still in the vet's arms. So I calmly grabbed my handbag, ignored the vet, made eye contact with Horton and spoke directly to him. I said, "Come to Mummy. Come to Mummy," in the softest, sweetest voice I could summon up. Horton immediately started wriggling because he always wants to come to Mummy. He wriggled hard until he was finally handed over to me. Once I had hold of my son I put his head against my shoulder, faced him away from the vet and began massaging his head and ears to sooth him. I told the vet I thought his sensitivity button had been switched off at birth and walked out of the room. It was the one and only time we ever used that particular vet. I couldn't believe he'd actually said such a thing. Perhaps he was merely thinking out loud, mulling things over in his head then voiced his thoughts. People did that a lot with Horton the first time they saw him. They'd meet him then you could see their minds ticking over. Sometimes people would ask questions so you'd know where their mind had gone, others must have felt it impolite to do so, so would just stand and stare without saying a word. I loved Horton's back legs and his back paws looked like little seashells to me. I loved those little seashell feet of his. Those little seashell feet were part of him and they were beautiful. He wouldn't have been Horton without them.

As Horton's strength improved so did his confidence. He was growing up fast, becoming more independent and he sure did love the outdoors. Such was his strength, he used to prop himself up on one leg and try to open the sliding doors with the other. He'd be at it all day, but that door was so big and heavy and he was so little, I never thought he'd be able to manage it. I thought he was just amusing himself until the day he actually made it move, which turned him into quite the little escape artist and I needed eyes in the back of my head after that. I used to have to lock the door that faced the shed because he had to go over a gravel driveway before reaching it and I didn't want him hurting himself. If he managed to open the doors that lead onto the front veranda it wasn't too much of a problem because something out there always distracted him from his mission and he forgot all about trying to make it round to the shed.

Most of the time Horton was an independent little bugger and told me off if I intervened when he was happy doing something by himself. He had such a strong mind and such powerful determination to do things on his own. If he came up against an obstacle his little face would change and you'd be able to see his mind ticking over then he'd go at it from a different angle or push his body harder. If that didn't work he'd pause, have another think and try something new. He was brilliant in that way and lovely to watch and I was always watching him in the early days, always ready to help when help was needed. I was told not to over-mother him and so in a split second I had to decide whether to help or just let him be. There were also times when I felt he may have appreciated a hand but knew it would be better for his development not to intervene. I had to stand back and just watch what his body could do. He was so young when he came to us and his body went through a good many changes in the first eighteen months of his life. He'd have a growth spurt and his capabilities would change. It was a series of grow and change, grow and change. Every growth spurt brought new things and of course in those early days, always in the back of my mind was the hope that the new growth stage would see him walking, but I knew in my heart that it was not possible; Horton was never going to be able to walk upright due to the curving of his spine. But if love could have made Horton walk he would have been doing it the first week he arrived in our home.

In the end, I learned to just enjoy the growth spurts, concentrate on them and watch what new changes they would bring. In fact, no six-week period was exactly the same, but it was interesting to see the changes. Both David and I were always there, always noting what was going on. When he conquered something new we would both stand around clapping for him, saying, "Good, good boy! Good, good boy!" over and over again. Horton loved to be clapped for and told how wonderful he was. He'd do a silly face and smile showing his two bottom teeth only, as if he knew why we were clapping. Sometimes, when he was really excited by his shower of praise, he would do a lap of honour around the lounge before finally settling down. I think all the praise and attention made him giddy with excitement and he needed to release that energy, so off he would fly. When he got overly excited his run changed; there was more bounce in it. A quick scoot around the lounge normally sufficed and he'd come back and sit in front of us until he was lifted up for a hug.

When visitors came they'd always ask what Horton could do now so I'd tell them and they'd watch him for the entire visit so as not to miss seeing it. I never made him show anybody his new accomplishments, never coerced him in any shape or form, I didn't want to have him as a performing seal, I loved him too much for that. It was just a case of if they happened to be here when Horton did something they hadn't seen before then good for them. If not, they'd just have to wait and see it on the next visit. Most of the time their eyes were on Horton and they'd barely be able to keep up their side of the conversation with me. They'd take quick sips of tea, shove a biscuit in their mouths, politely glance at me when I spoke but mostly they'd be watching my boy. Funny thing was, after the initial circling dancing fit of excitement of having a visitor in the house wore off, all the elderly pugs would climb in one of the beds and quickly fall asleep. And once Horton saw them getting in bed he would scoot off to the toy corner and amuse himself until they woke up or if he was a bit tired, he'd shuffle in next to somebody and have a rest. There were a lot of disappointed faces when he did that. Definitely, more people watched Horton sleeping than any other pug I've ever had here on the farm. You'd have thought he wouldn't have been able to sleep with so many eyes on him, but he just shuffled onto a bed, got himself comfortable and shut his little eyes, blocked them all out and was snoring away in no time. But there was the odd occasion when somebody got to see him doing something he hadn't been able to do the last time they were here and knowing what David and I did with his new accomplishments, they too would stand, clapping and saying what a "Good, good boy!" he was. And when a different person to his parents was praising him he'd do his silly smile even bigger and sometimes the lap of honour became two.

Horton soon became a real ham and was a shameless show off when he had an audience, to the point of becoming embarrassing, but he didn't care. He was the center of attention and that was a very addictive drug for a little pug. He always scooted along the floor faster, doing his best run when somebody new was in the house. And he'd be looking around, making sure he was being watched and of course he was never disappointed because everybody always had their eyes on him. There were times when I worried he may bang into the wall or furniture because he wasn't watching where he was going, but he never did. He always turned round just in time to right himself and veer off.

It got to a point where he'd expect a round of applause every time he came scooting into the room. He hadn't done anything new, just entered the room a few seconds after everybody else had, but he still wanted us to clap. At times I think he deliberately held back a bit so he could be the last one in the room, but his little face did seem awfully disappointed if we didn't make a fuss. And of course, us being the twits that we are, we clapped for him and said, "Good, good boy!" over and over again. I mean, how could we not? He had been through so much and had accomplished so much; if clapping was what brought the little guy joy then clap we would. After a while, however, he got a bit tired of it. The novelty had worn off, the applause didn't thrill him as much as it once had and when he was fully grown and settled into himself a bit, he wasn't as interested in the applause anymore. He still loved being praised and adored being the center of attention but the clapping wasn't nearly as important to him as it had once been.

The early days, when Horton was learning how to best handle himself, when his body was growing stronger, were hard in many ways, but they were also really lovely and David and I have a lot of fond memories that I hope never fade. David and I have always been incredibly compatible, we rarely fight about anything, but we used to fight like school children over who got to change Horton's nappy. That's how in love with him we were. It only lasted about twelve or eighteen months, however, and looking back there was really no reason to fight. There were always enough nappy changes to go around. Even though we finally got that well out of our systems, there has never been a time when Horton has had to sit in a wet nappy and I am incredibly proud of that. Neither of us ever wanted him to be uncomfortable and changing Horton became second nature to us very quickly. It's one of those things we were both always aware of. It was always in the backs of our minds like a timer going off, even when we had people over and were preoccupied, Horton never missed a change. We have a routine and we stick to it. It's as easy as that. I think you can handle any amount of dogs with any amount of special needs if you work out a routine then stick to it. If you lose the routine then everything crumbles, although I do think that working out a routine in the first place is the hardest part. Once you've watched your dogs and realized what they need and when they need it the rest is easy. Then again, an oldie will develop something new and you'll have to adjust your routine slightly to accommodate, but that's our life and we're used to it.

I think the hardest part with Horton was in that first fortnight when he came. My friend in rescue thought Horton may have been able to be housetrained and in those first few weeks I thought it may be possible too, so I gave it a try. I really wanted him to be housetrained because I knew he didn't like his nappies and I knew how wonderful his life could be if he didn't need to use them. He would have more or less been free to live his life like any other dog and I wanted that for him, I truly did, but sadly it was not to be. Those first few weeks were very hard on me because I could see it wasn't going to happen, but I kept persisting, trying to give Horton the best shot possible of controlling his bladder. But by the end of the second week I was totally exhausted. I hadn't been sleeping because I was always worried about my new baby during the night. What if he needed me and I got into a sound sleep and didn't hear him call? He would be sitting in a wet nappy until morning and I didn't want that.

His bladder functions were all over the place when he first came. He was just like any other puppy in that way. When he got excited he'd wee, you'd just finish changing him and he'd wee, just little droplets but I still changed him again because even one drop sitting on his delicate puppy belly would have caused a rash and like any other mother, I wanted my baby to remain rash free.

Day in, day out, I was caring for all my elderly pugs and trying as hard as I could to get Horton housetrained. There were accidents happening all over the house and the blind pugs were walking through it, spreading it everywhere. The dog beds needed to be washed and dried daily and poor little Ruby was slipping and sliding about in the urine, so I was constantly washing and drying her off and she was full of arthritis, so the constant falling over was painful for her already sore little body. I was mopping the floor several times a day but you could still smell it and the smell of Horton's urine made a few of the others start weeing in the house again, re-marking their territory. It was all a bit of a disaster really. I'd clean up one puddle and another one would appear and if I hadn't gotten to it fast enough, it became bigger and bigger when some of the others started adding to it. I've always found it amusing that pugs want to wee in the exact same spot somebody else has been. Even in the open paddocks where there is such a huge area of grass to go on, they always huddle together for a group wee. I know why they do it but it's still comical to see. In the house, though, it's a different matter. David would walk through the door of an evening and the house would really smell. I didn't think it was fair on him to work hard all day then come home this.

The Friday night of Horton's second week here found me sitting at the kitchen table with my head in my hands. I was an over-tired, emotional mess and I felt like a failure. I felt as if it was my fault that Horton was going to have to wear nappies for the rest of his life and that pained me no end. I would have given anything for him to be without nappies and felt bad he'd have to continue wearing them. I felt like I'd let him down because I couldn't make it happen. David said I was being silly, blaming myself for something I had no control over and certainly Horton didn't hold it against me. He just got on with his nappy-wearing life and would come and tap me on the foot or I'd feel him pawing the back of my leg if he needed changing and I hadn't realized right away. I'd feel this little tap tap tap and knew he needed something and his nappy was always the first thing I checked. Most times his nappy was fine and he just wanted to be picked up and hugged or he'd want a massage.

We did try again over the next couple of months with Horton's housetraining, when the weather became warmer and David was on holidays, so that he was there to help out. It was always our hope that by the time David returned to work Horton would be nappy-free, but it didn't happen. His little bladder just released itself whenever it needed to and there was nothing any of us could do about it. Actually, I thought it was kind of cute the way he used to run along and urinate, leaving a little snail trail of wee wherever he went. On the veranda, you could always see where he had been. There would be a long, zigzagged stream then a concentrated little puddle where he'd stopped to look at something.

David used to take over Horton's full care when he was on holidays or at the weekends and I figured I may as well let them be together and stay out of the way. Horton loved David being home and sometimes forgot he had a mum when his dad was in the house. I used to miss caring for him terribly, but figured it was the least I could do because any time spent with Horton was a gift and David deserved to share the enjoyment. He went out and worked hard all day, providing for our family, the least I could do was drop back and let him have his special time with Horton whenever he was home. Besides, I knew I was the lucky one because I got to be with Horton the most. David used to tell me all the time that I was so blessed because I got to spend my days with Horton while he was away at work. He hated leaving Horton in the mornings and raced home to see him at night. I knew how privileged I was to be Horton's main care-giver, so even though it killed me and I missed my time with him, I dropped back and allowed David to take over when he was on leave. But, boy, was I happy to have my son all to myself again once David returned to work.

I have to confess that when David was in charge I used to sneak around and check that he hadn't become absorbed in something and forgotten to change Horton, but he never let him down. He always had him changed and sitting next to him in a clean Tinkle Trouser. Even when he was busy or brought work home, he never once forgot to change Horton.

Whatever David did on the weekends or holidays Horton was always in on it and that's the way they both liked it. If David was at his desk, Horton sat on an office chair right beside his dad. And when David was doing something in the shed, Horton would sit watching him. I'd leave the back door open and the others would come and go, but Horton stayed put. He was fixated on his dad. But if David was doing something that may have been dangerous I'd put Horton in his pram so he could still watch everything his daddy did but wouldn't come to any harm. There were occasions, though, when Horton had to come inside, when a power tool was being used and he needed protecting. I suppose I could have got him a pair of Doggles, but I don't think he would have been happy out there with the noise that high-powered tools make, so inside he came. Horton was never very happy with me for bringing him inside because he wanted to be out there with David. He wouldn't come near me at those times. Normally, he would follow me around the house, but not when I'd taken him away from his dad. I think it was his little way of letting me know that he was displeased. Instead, he would sit at the back door watching and waiting until it was safe for him to join David again. I had to make sure all the sliding glass doors were locked in case he opened them himself and shuffled out. If he'd gotten loose and dragged himself across the gravel driveway he would have scuffed his back legs up. I remember we always used to carry him over the driveway. We did think about resurfacing for Horton's sake but with the driveway running half the length of our property the cost would have been enormous. It was easier to carry him across then pop him down on the other side and he'd scoot off, happily exploring the shed. We once put a little sand pathway on top of the gravel. It reached from the shed to the bottom of the ramp that led up to the house, but it proved useless because Horton refused to use it. He didn't like it for some reason, perhaps the texture of the sand, but he didn't have to worry about it for long because the first time the winter rains hit, the path got washed away.

Because it was impossible for me to have my eyes on Horton every single second of every single day, it was inevitable that he was at some point going to scuff his back legs up. He was such a fast mover and so interested in checking everything out, I just couldn't watch him all the time, so he did end up following his siblings onto the driveway before I could grab him up. He'd be sleeping in the sun when I left him and I'd go out to check on him a little while later only to find he'd gone over the driveway and was happily playing near the trees on the other side. I cried when he first scuffed himself up. He was so beautiful, so black and shiny and to have this happen really upset me. It'd taken some time to get his coat that lovely and it made me sad that he had gotten scuffed. But I couldn't predict every move he made. Sometimes he would be on the veranda cushions for hours on end without moving then all of a sudden spot something, go after it and be off the veranda at lightning speed. I monitored Horton a lot, but couldn't have my eyes on him all the time because the other pugs needed me as well. I protected him as much as I could but I couldn't pre-empt his moves and there were always going to be times when I was off doing something else and he'd go investigating and get a little graze. It was mainly one leg, though. Because he was lopsided only one leg constantly made contact with the ground. We did think of making him a sort of little sleeping bag type of thing so he could go wherever he wanted around the farm and not mark himself. But it gets pretty hot here so that wouldn't have worked. We couldn't allow him to overheat and with the speed he went that would definitely have happened. Plus, at some point he would have had a wee in the sleeping bag and ended up with urine burns and welts, so it definitely wasn't a good idea. It was really a case of dammed if you do, dammed if you don't. Besides, when he was outside on the veranda it was his nappy-free time, a time for him to be free of the constraints in his life, a time of getting fresh air and sunshine on his tummy, a time that he truly did love. If he was constantly out there wrapped up in a sleeping bag because of the slight chance he may go off the veranda and get a little scrape it wouldn't have been fair on him. I felt that the fresh air and sunshine on his skin was a lot more beneficial to his overall health.

Horton used to get a bit fed up with his nappy being on all the time. He lived for the days when the weather was good and he could be nappy-free. He especially loved it when he was outside at last after a long cold winter. He couldn't wait for me to pop him down once his nappy was removed. He would squeal and scoot off before I caught him and put a new one on. He thought he was being sneaky and escaping, he didn't realize I had no intention of putting his nappy back on. After a few days out there he'd get to know that I was giving him some nappy-free time and would stay outside as long as he could.

In the heat of summer I tried to keep his nappy off as much as possible. When he came inside I'd lay him across hand towels to soak up the wee. This is basically how we did things in the warmest months. We couldn't have him wrapped in a nappy on forty-degree days. All dogs cool down by exposing their tummies and Horton had to be able to do the same thing. Summers were survived by me running around after him with a towel in one hand to put under him when he finally settled and wiping the trail he'd left behind him with the other. Sometimes he'd settled down fast, other times he thought it was a game we were playing and he'd run around all over the place. He loved games and the more excited he got the more he'd wee. There were little snail trails all over the house and once he'd tired himself out, I'd go back and mop the floor while he lay on his island of towels watching me. Summer with Horton was a juggling act, just doing all we could to get him through it. Extreme heat is kind of unfair on a little nappy-wearing pug.

Horton had a cart to use on the longer walks and even though he never had his nappy on when using the cart he still didn't much like it. I actually think it was uncomfortable for him due to the way his body was. For some dogs, carts are fantastic. For Horton, not so much. In the end we opted not to persevere with it. As I said before, we were guided by Horton and how he reacted to things. He knew how his body felt better than we did so we had to put our trust in him. We had him in it a few times just in case he merely needed time to adjust to the strange device attached to his body. Both David and I watched Horton's reaction and decided never to put him in it again. I do believe these carts are brilliant and make life so much easier for some paraplegic dogs, but you must always be there beside them when they're using it. You can't have them in the cart after the walk is over; they're not designed for day-long use and again I must stress: never ever leave dogs unsupervised while in a cart because all manner of accidents could happen.

With Horton, I guess it mustn't have hurt him too much to be on the gravel, otherwise I doubt he would have gone across. It wasn't like he didn't know what was over the other side of the driveway and was going across hot coal to an undiscovered land, because I'd taken him over many times so he could go have a sniff with the other pugs. I showed him all round the farm, every inch of it actually. I carried him across the hard surfaces then put him down and stood around watching while he sniffed and scampered about on the soft grass. Sometimes he'd be there for the longest time, checking everything out and I'd get a bit antsy because I had loads of things to do, but I figured, "To hell with it! It can wait." So I'd just lean against a fencepost and wait until he'd finished enjoying himself. I think the reason he ventured across on his own was because he wanted to be over there looking at things when he wanted to be and couldn't be bothered waiting around for me to take him over. He probably wanted a bit of independence, to be a big boy or the boy who didn't need help.

Once the fur got rubbed off, we used to massage cream into the top of his legs every night, keeping the skin supple. My dad suggested I leave it, let the skin toughen up so he could go on rough surfaces and not be affected as much. But I felt I had to keep the skin in that area soft otherwise it'd be uncomfortable for him when curling his legs up and going to sleep. Horton was out on that gravel only about one percent of the time, half a percent even, the rest of the time he was on soft grass or polished wooden floorboards or curled up asleep in one of the dog beds. I think this is one of the many things you don't think about until you have a special needs pug in your life and with everything about a special needs dog you just have to think things through and do what you feel is the best thing for each dog in your care. But every case is different so you stop, give it some thought and do what you think is going to work. If it doesn't then you try something else and something else again, all the while making sure to allow yourself to be guided by the dog in your care because this is so very important.

I was sad when Horton lost his newness, when his beautiful little seashell feet became a bit worn. But, as David would tell me, you just have to let some things happen. You can't possibly protect Horton from everything as much as you may want to. That wouldn't be allowing him to fully live his life. No living creature goes through life untarnished. To truly live is to become marked, blemished and stained. You can't go through life and remain in perfect condition. It's impossible to do. We both felt a little bit of scruffiness wasn't the worst thing in the world for Horton and our vet agreed with us. I suppose I could have kept him inside, let him watch the world go by from the safety of the house, just sitting by a window and watching everybody else having a good time, but what kind of life would that have been for him? Yes, his little body would have been kept in pristine condition but what state would his soul have been in if he was made to live being constantly restricted like that? He wanted to be in the thick of everything that happened on the farm and he enjoyed being involved. It would have been unfair and cruel to not let him join in. Also, I think Horton would have realized that there was something wrong with him if he'd been singled out like that, left in the house while the others explored. I think that would have destroyed his spirit. I believe we did the right thing in allowing him outside to play amongst it all and to participate in life. And if he got scuffed up a bit, had a little graze, chewed on a leaf or a stick, ate a bit of dirt, played in the mud or pawed a puddle, at least he was out there experiencing it himself instead of watching while everybody else did.

I remember the day Horton fell into a puddle. Well, not so much fell in, more dived in. I didn't see him enter it but knowing how much he liked water I know he would have jumped right in as soon as he discovered it. Horton just loved being in and around water and in summer the hose and sprinkler were two of his favourite things. I'd turn the rain water tank on (we couldn't use town water; that was far too expensive, but towards the end of summer if the tank was still looking good I would go out in the afternoon sun and prop the hose up so Horton could watch the trickle and play in the little bubbling brook I'd created for him). As we have gone through years of drought here in Australia I am always water conscious, so I'd set the hose up in amongst the fruit trees so they would benefit from the soaking as much as Horton did. Horton was beautiful to watch, just a gorgeous little boy having the time of his life in amongst the flow. Water gave him so much joy. He would sit doing little woofs as he watched it. He even liked the sound and sat with his head on the side, listening. Horton could hear water from quite a distance and would go after it. He more than once over the years alerted me to the fact that I'd gone inside and left the rain water tank on after filling up the livestock trough.

All of us enjoyed those late-summer afternoon wind downs. I would sit on the ground leaning up against the tank feeling its coolness, the other pugs would lay with me and we'd all watch as

Horton patted at the stream of water with his paw. He'd then scoot over the top and get a little wet, but he didn't care. His nappy was off and he was having the time of his life.

He never liked going over the top of the hosepipe for some reason and would go to great lengths to avoid it. Perhaps he didn't like the feel of it underneath his body. Or maybe it was uncomfortable for him to go over. He was never bothered about most other surfaces but the hosepipe was a thing he never got used to. He was the same way with the vacuum cleaner lead. He never once went across an electrical lead either and would scoot around the house trying to get away from it. He didn't mind being with me while I vacuumed. The movement and the noise didn't bother him at all, just the lead. He'd be behind or beside me, looking on, watching the dust balls being sucked up, but as soon as the lead started moving towards him he shot off.

Horton sure did love water though and knew that the two went hand in hand, so he allowed the hosepipe near him but never touched it with any part of his body. When he got to the other side of the stream he would spin around as fast as he could. I never knew if it was due to excitement or if he perhaps thought the water was going to try and chase him the way me and David would do when playing with him in the house. He loved the water game and never grew tired of it. It was always me being water conscious that ended things before Horton ever ran out of steam. Then he'd be totally soaked to the skin so I'd bring him inside, wrap him in a towel and sit holding him for a few moments until most of the water had been absorbed. He'd look up and lick the side of my face as if to say, "Thank you, Mummy. Thank you for letting me play."

The day he dived into the puddle could have worked out very differently to how it did. Horton had opened the door himself and gotten outside while I was on the phone. It was my sister; she was having a crisis and I wasn't concentrating on Horton as well as I normally did. The first I knew that something was amiss was when Grace came racing into the house. Out in the distance, I had been aware of a dog barking but as I was trying to help my sister, I hadn't paid all that much attention to it and didn't realize it was one of my own who was barking. To be honest, it didn't even sound like one of my dogs. I know all the different dog barks around here and the bark Grace was doing that day didn't sound anything like her usual one. I believe she thought Horton was in great danger so her bark was frantic because she knew she had to get me out there as quickly as possible. Grace circled me a few times then dashed back down the ramp. I figured she wanted me to follow her and thought she'd found a turtle or a baby bird had fallen out of its nest or something, so I hung up the phone and went out to see, just on the off-chance that she'd found a baby snake. We keep our farm pretty clean and clear of rubbish so have never had a snake on our property, but knowing there's a first time for everything, I raced outside. I was halfway down the ramp when I saw that Horton had made it all the way across the driveway and was sitting in a puddle near the shed. He was up to the top of his back legs in water and Grace was doing her bouncy bark on dry land right next to him. Every now and then she'd look back to see if I was coming. Horton was playing but Grace was deadly serious. She had the most terrified look on her little old face, one I've never seen her have before. I don't think I've ever crossed the driveway so fast in my life. Horton had his nappy on and it was soaking wet. He was caked in mud and his nappy was caked in mud, with no visible white anywhere. It would have been heavy being waterlogged and he may have found it hard to drag himself out of the puddle. Without the nappy he could have gotten himself out in no time but with that nappy strapped tightly in place, it would have been quite the challenge to drag himself onto dry land. Not that Horton wanted to; he was splashing about and really enjoying himself. He was pawing and licking at the water in the happiest of states, he had no intention of going anywhere, but I knew it would have been hard for him to maneuver his body with the extra weight. Well, that and the sides of the puddle would have been slippery too. Basically, he was stuck and didn't know it. Grace must have realized this, though, because she was going absolutely nuts.

As I crossed the driveway, so many thoughts were going through my mind. What if he had fallen on his side? The water wasn't overly deep but if he'd toppled over, due to the condition of his spine, he wouldn't have been able get himself upright. He wouldn't have been able to hold his head up out of the water. If he fell forward he would have simply pushed himself back up with his strong front legs, but a sideways fall was different. A sideways fall and everything would have changed for Horton. It became a dangerous situation and I believe Grace realized this. If she hadn't alerted me, if I'd been on the phone any longer, then things could have ended badly and I would never have forgiven myself. Thanks to Grace, everything turned out okay. She was a true hero in our house that day I can tell you. Horton complained a bit when I lifted him out of the puddle but Gracie was so relieved.

Once I'd gotten Horton washed, dried and sitting in a clean nappy I rang David at work and told him we were having roast chicken that night for tea. That's Grace's favourite meal and heroes in our house get exactly what they want to have for dinner. The funny thing was that Grace had never before shown any signs of being in tune to danger like that. I suppose before Horton came here she had no reason to really; this house was like an elderly pug retirement centre before Horton entered our lives. But she proved to be a real hero to all of us that day and I couldn't thank her enough for what she had done. She had saved her baby brother. While Horton opened the back door and scooted over to the shed all the other pugs had been asleep in the house, even Harper and Emily had slept through it. And if anybody was going to become Horton's saviour I would have thought it'd be one of them. They were the two in the pack who always seemed to be more aware of where Horton was and what he was doing than any of the others.

I suppose, because Horton was making his happy noises, they must have assumed he was okay. Although, I don't know why none of the others went out to see what Grace was going crazy about. Harper wasn't feeling well that day, she had been to the vets, but here was our oldest pug outside taking care of her little brother like it was the most natural thing in the world for her to be doing. God bless Grace for being so observant, that's all I can say.

When David came through the door that night he picked little Gracie up and gave her the longest snuggle. I think Horton's nose was put out of joint a bit because he always wanted David's attention first. He sat looking up at his daddy and bouncing up and down on his nappy so he could be seen. It was like he was saying,

"Hey, I'm the one that was in danger here. What the hell are you hugging her for?"

There normally isn't a puddle near the shed, but with the flooding rain we had experienced the day before everything was wetter than it had previously been and Horton, having a keen nose for water, must have smelt it once he'd gotten outside and shuffled over to take a closer look. We have a walk-around phone and if I'm talking I don't usually sit in one place unless all the pugs are asleep at my feet. If they are scattered about I walk around checking on them as I'm talking. I even walk around outside, giving the pugs a wee while talking on the phone. But this day with my sister's drama I had been distracted. The thought of what could have happened to Horton, or any of the others for that matter, stayed with me for a long time. It haunted me actually, enough to never let such a thing ever happen again.

Grace sat on David's knee that night while eating her dinner. She had pride of place and knew it. Then after tea we put a fence around the puddle. It was only temporary but soon got replaced with a permanent fixture so that whenever the heavy rains came I no longer had to worry about Horton being in danger. He seemed disappointed not to be able to gain access to the area and would sit with his face pressed up to the new fence before scooting along the edge, trying to find a way in, but David had Horton-proofed it so there was no chance of him being able to gain entrance.

CHAPTER FIVE

To Thine Own Self be True

When Horton had only been here a few days, I sent an email asking if there was anything more we could do to help him. I'd had time to have a good look at his body and saw how he moved, what he could and couldn't do. I was getting used to his differences and I loved him just as he was with all of my heart. But I wanted to do more than just love and care for him, change his nappy and keep him clean. I wanted to know if there was any way of us helping him to become all he could be. A long email came back describing a set of exercises that may have been beneficial to our son. We were told to do these exercises with Horton for six months, otherwise, due to lack of muscle movement, he may have forgotten that his back legs existed and once forgotten, the specialist said he would never remember them again. His mind would close off to that part of his body. The physiotherapist said that if there was no improvement after six months we may as well stop doing them because we'd just be wasting our time.

When Horton first came here his back legs just lay there. There was no movement, nothing, perhaps a flicker of a nerve making his little seashell feet jump when he was dreaming, but that was about it. We were thrilled with the email. To have something to do that may have been of assistance to Horton was fantastic news for us as parents. The hope that we may be able to help him got both of us very excited.

Every night when David got home he would take Horton into the bathroom on his own and do the exercises with him. Horton hated doing the exercises and although his body was weak, he fought them as hard as he possibly could. One of his back legs has always been stronger than the other and that was the one he used to make his true feelings known. David did the set of exercises every single day and every single day Horton resisted, but we were persistent, we had to be, it was for his own good. The exercises didn't hurt him, that was in the back of our minds, so we doubled checked that we were doing them right. We were. The strong-minded little bugger just didn't want to be doing them, that was all. Perhaps Horton felt it was time wasted, time he could have been spending doing something he enjoyed more. We tried to make it special for him, giving him a little treat afterwards and talking to him in an excited voice when he was going off to have the exercises done. I'd watch him being carried from the room and he'd peep at me from over David's shoulder.

"It's your remembering-leg time, Horton. Go remember your legs, baby. Go remember your legs," I'd say in the happiest, most excited voice I could muster, but it didn't make any difference. Horton never changed his mind about his exercise routine. Oh, he was thrilled when they were over and ecstatic when chewing on the treat but apart from that he didn't like going through the ordeal.

With David away at work all day it was a lovely bonding time for the two of them and Horton liked his time alone with dad but loathed his leg routines. It took him about four or five weeks to give in and finally stop fighting David on them. David would put his hand under Horton's body to hold him up then start with the sets. Horton would sometimes look up and kiss his dad's face once or twice but that was about it for affection until the exercises were over. Then he'd go ballistic, plastering David's face with little kisses. After six months, however, there was still no improvement and we sort of expected that, as it was what we'd been told. But we decided to keep doing them because, really, what did it hurt? It wasn't costing anything, it kept Horton's back legs limber and David got to have some one-on-one time with Horton. I was lucky I got to have Horton to myself all day long; those ten minutes of leg exercises were special to David, and Horton persevered because at the end of it he was getting a treat. Horton would do anything for a treat. David said Horton knew when the exercises were coming to an end, almost as if he was counting them in his head, and would start looking for his reward as soon as they began the last set.

One day, I was sitting at the computer when I heard a funny scratching noise followed by a slight thump. It was an unusual noise, one I couldn't ever remember hearing before. It wasn't loud but I could hear it whenever there was a lull in the chorus of snoring. I knew all the pugs were asleep but I couldn't see some of them from where I was sitting, so got up and checked to make sure everyone was okay. I checked Horton first. I always check on

Horton first, just to be sure he was all right, then I went down the row of pugs in beds, checked the two couch potatoes, Steffy and Emily, as well but they were all still asleep, all still breathing. Everybody was okay. Horton was about fifteen months old at the time and he was doing brilliantly, really sturdy in his body, healthy, muscular, beautiful; Horton Schwarz-a-pug was as strong as an ox. He could pull himself up onto any dog bed he liked, which was a far cry from the early days when I had to fold a blanket and put that on the floor in between the other dog beds so he could sleep in amongst his siblings without feeling left out. Harper liked the lower beds too, so he was never without a friend, but these days he was doing marvellously. He could get around the farm with ease and even attempted chasing the sheep. He never caught any of course but it didn't stop him trying. He was fearless and so confident within himself and his surroundings, he was maturing and a beautiful little personality had come through. It was a joy to see.

Horton's days were full; he'd go from lying in one of the dog beds to jumping up and scooting out the door. I'd always go after him to make sure he was okay but he'd be fine. He'd go puppy barking all along the veranda, chasing a dragonfly or something else that had caught his eye. He always managed to get himself out the door fast, yet never came back inside on his own. He always called for me to lift him over the metal strip. I think he didn't really like crossing over that strip but when something caught his eye or he heard the sheep and horses in the paddocks, in the mad rush to be out amongst it all, he forgot about what he had to cross over and just flew out the door. But today Horton slept soundly. He'd had a big morning and was content to rest for a while. He had fallen asleep quite quickly and was doing big puffy breaths when I stood over him. I always liked to pause for a while when checking Horton, just in case something was amiss. But he was definitely fast asleep, so I went back to my computer and started typing. Again the noise, again a pug check and again nothing wrong. When you hear something like this in a houseful of oldies you always worry in case one of them is having a seizure and I think because I hadn't heard that exact noise before that was what I was looking for. This went on a couple of times and in the end I didn't get up. I just looked across at Horton who was in the nearest bed to me then carried on typing. About the fourth or fifth time I looked across at Horton my heart skipped a beat: his back legs were moving. I couldn't believe what I was seeing. I looked away then back again and they were still moving, scraping along the floor, left then right, left then right, kicking out like a little frog swimming. As his feet came into contact with the cupboard his bed was backed up against, Horton flexed his little seashell feet and kicked, kicked, kicked. He kicked out at the old worn cupboard door that was always a little bit open since the latch broke. That was the thumping sound: his little feet kicking the old cupboard door.

I had a lump in my throat. Horton was still sound asleep. Perhaps the poor little soul was dreaming he could run. Why not? If I can be thin in my dreams why the hell can't he be running in his? But I felt a bit sorry for him. Was the poor little thing so desperate to run in real life that he was dreaming about it every time he slept? That thought made me a bit sad because I knew he would never be able to walk. All the experts had said so. I knew I could never make my baby's dreams come true. If there was an operation that could fix Horton, regardless of the cost, David and I would have paid it. We'd spoken about it often when he first came. If money could have fixed Horton's spine we would have made it so. We would have carried him into our bank manager's office and begged for a loan, but sadly there wasn't anything anybody could do to make Horton walk upright. And if love was all it took for Horton to walk he would have been walking long before now. Because Horton was loved – boy, was he loved – loved by that vet who gave him the chance to live, dearly loved by the rescue lady who gave him to me, truly madly and deeply loved by David and myself, loved by members of our family, loved by our friends. Horton had more aunties and uncles than any pug I've ever known and they all just adored the little fella. He was even loved by people who'd only ever seen a photo of him. He was loved by people all over the world. Heck, he was even loved by strangers who met him in the street. I could tell by the way they flocked to him, how they spoke to him. I could see it in their eyes. They loved Horton even before they got talking to me and realized he couldn't walk and then of course they loved him all the more when they found out his story and how courageous he was. Horton was loved a hundredfold and there were many good thoughts and prayers sent his way on a daily basis.

I watched his legs move for about five minutes longer, half afraid to look away in case I was never to see it again. Those spindly little legs that had never done anything more than drag along behind him were full of movement now. It was the most beautiful thing to see and I think I could have sat there watching this scene for the rest of the day and never gotten bored. But I moved because I had to go get the video camera. If this was a one-off thing then I had to record it for David to see. He was the one who, night after night without fail for over a year, regardless of how tired he was when he got home, had done the leg exercises with Horton. He was the one who'd persisted even when Horton said no. If anybody should have been here witnessing this wonderful moment it should have been David not me. I had to get that camera and fast. David had to see this. Just telling him about it wouldn't be enough, not after all the work he had put in. I got up and wanted to run across the room so as not to miss a second of getting it recorded, but I had to tiptoe otherwise I would have woken Horton up. As I went into the other room to get the video camera I heard a few paws pitter-pattering behind me. Harper, my shadow, always followed me whenever I left the room. The others would come find me if I'd been gone a while but my little shadow always followed me wherever I went, no matter how long I was going for. I prayed it was just Harper. If the others came, especially if Emily and Steffy jumped off the couch, they would wake Horton up. If he woke his feet may have stopped moving and I'd have lost the chance to show David. I grabbed the video camera, spun around, patted Harper's old head, told her I thought a miracle had happened and raced back into the lounge. As soon as I rounded the corner the couch potatoes bailed, hit the floor at the same time, as they so often did. With the thunderous thud on the floor, Horton's head shot up. His back legs stopped moving, he yawned, he stretched and although I could have cried, I smiled at him instead. I started telling him what a "Good, good boy" he was as I reached down to pick him up for snuggle. Of course he had no idea what he'd done to be such a good boy but he loved the attention. When you pick Horton up you always have to support his back end, otherwise he will just hang there and it'll be uncomfortable for his spine. As I cupped both his back paws in my hand and brought his bottom up to rest on my arm one of the little seashells slightly curled around my finger. It didn't exactly grip it like a canary does its perch, but there was a definite difference there. Horton had just done something I'd never felt him do before and I was overwhelmed with joy. I felt how the mother of a human baby would feel when her newborn holds her finger for the very first time. That tender touch, that connection was the best thing I'd ever felt in my life. I stood there laughing and crying at the same time, I couldn't believe what I was experiencing. I was so excited. I knew the moment I felt that first soft touch was going to be with me forever. It would be embedded in my mind for the rest of my life. I kissed Horton's ears, told him what a good boy he was again and raced to ring David at work. I carried Horton with me and kissed his ears over and over again as I went. Although David was in a meeting with a room full of people when he answered the phone, I heard his voice soften. It went from being all business-like to that of a proud, proud daddy in about two seconds flat. It took about a week before David got to see Horton's back legs kicking and probably a month or so before any visitors did. But once news got out, we had a lot more visitors than we usually did and a lot more tears than we usually had, but they were the good kind of tears. They fell due to pride and a whole lot of joy.

After a while, Horton began kicking his back legs all the time. They didn't just get dragged around behind him anymore; they moved now, curled and pushed. Once he realized he could actually move them they were rarely still. The top part of his body stood like a still solid unit while his bottom part was going nuts. He reminded me of a duck, with his top part still while his legs pedalled away like crazy, and when he paused he'd lean on one side with the free leg moving about like he was pedalling a bike.

Horton now kicked while he slept and when he was awake. It was as if he was making up for lost time. He'd go scooting across the veranda and be kicking his little legs as he went. He used to run round the house then pause, looking at something and then kick, kick, pedal, pedal. He'd scoot over to watch Tommy sleeping and kick, pedal, kick as he sat looking up at the chair. And both of his legs kicked about the same; he wasn't just using his strongest one, both took equal turns. He'd play with Emily and be kicking away excitedly as they played. He used to put a bit of pressure on his back legs to leverage himself up so he could slam dunk on Emily's tummy harder than he could previously do. It was his strongest leg he used most for doing this because that's the one that got him where he wanted to be. If she noticed the difference in her little brother she wasn't reacting. She just lay there enjoying the game. When she'd had enough and go hide on the couch, Horton would follow her and sit, trying to get her to come back down and play again, all the while kicking and pedalling away happily.

I'm not sure if Horton would have naturally started moving his back legs of his own accord if we had decided to stop those leg exercises after six months. I'm just glad David kept on doing them because he kept those vital muscles flexible and gave them a little bit of strength. That way they were ready when Horton's mind told him to start moving them. I know the extra effort paid off. What if Horton had gotten to fifteen months of age and wanted to move his back legs only to find they were useless to him? What if they just seized up, failed him due to lack of movement? Honestly, that would be the true meaning of being imprisoned in your own body and we would never have wanted him to experience that. Due to his dad's perseverance Horton's little legs were there waiting for him, supple and well used to movement by his daddy's loving hand. I believe David's persistence paid off. To be honest, there were some nights when we were busy and could have missed a leg session but David never did, and there were also nights when Horton was fighting real hard against them and we wondered whether we were doing the right thing in persisting. It was hard on both of us, making the little fella do something he clearly didn't like doing. I wanted every single moment of Horton's life here on the farm to be happy and wonderful and joyous. After all he'd been through in his first twelve weeks of life it was very important to me that he was happy here all the time and knowing he wasn't really tore at my heart. That's why we made sure we were doing the exercises properly. We had to double check we weren't hurting him. How horrible would it have been to be making him do something that was causing him pain? Horton wasn't usually a complainer so when he started complaining about the exercises we had to make sure we were doing them the right way, handling his dear little body properly. And deep in our hearts, we both felt we should keep doing the sets with him. Both of us had a strong feeling it was what we had to do. Even when the six months came and went we talked about it and both still felt it was the right thing to do. We stayed true to the promise we had made to Horton when he first arrived, to do all we could in order to make his life better, and we went with our gut instinct, we stayed true to ourselves.

And the leg movement, what did that mean for Horton? Well, to be honest, we didn't know what changes it would bring. We knew Horton wouldn't be able to fully walk upright but perhaps in time when those muscles were built up a bit it would mean that he'd be able to put more pressure on his legs, lift his little body higher off the ground, balance differently and possibly be able to develop his own kind of special amble. When he was out in the paddocks, from a distance, he looked like a crow with a broken wing flitting across the ground. Now, perhaps that motion would become smoother, more controlled maybe. There was a lot we had no idea about, but what we did know was that Horton's brain now acknowledged that he had two back legs. We knew they were being used daily by him and that would mean his circulation would improve. His back legs used to be like ice in winter. I used to wrap them in a snuggly blanket at night while he was sleeping. I'd also massage his feet to help with blood flow. Now he was doing all this for himself. That meant that persisting with those ten minutes of exercises each night, even when we were told to stop because they were a waste of time, even though Horton fought against them, had paid off and there was no greater feeling in the world than that. As his parents, we both felt as if we'd won the lotto.

Once Horton started using his legs we stopped the exercises. There was no longer any point to them because Horton was doing all that David had done each night by himself now. Those muscles that David kept moving were now being moved by our boy. And I no longer had to massage his sweet little feet, but I kept doing it because I wanted to. He loved it and I loved it. I thought his little seashell feet were the most beautiful things I'd ever seen. I massaged Horton's body every night, mainly his upper body, shoulders, top of his front legs and his neck area, and he loved the contact. I mean, who doesn't like being massaged? It's so relaxing. And Horton would just sit there with his eyes closed really getting into it. He's so relaxed that he's often fallen asleep while I've been massaging his shoulders, especially when he was very little. He'd be so tired from his daily activities on the farm that he'd be asleep a few minutes after I began massaging.

I try and do the things he can't do for himself, like scratch behind his ears. He just adores this, loves having his little ears rubbed and will wear out my hands if I let him. An able-bodied dog can do all these things for himself, but Horton can't and I don't want him being uncomfortable or irritated in any way. Imagine having an itch you couldn't scratch; it'd drive you mad. He's even come over to me during the day and once I've checked his nappy and everything else and his paw is still tapping on my foot, I start massaging, mainly because I've run out of things to do and still haven't figured out what he wants. As soon as I start massaging I can quickly tell that that's what he needed from me all along. He does the same thing when he wants the back of his ears scratched.

Horton also has trouble holding a bone. He should be able to as his front legs and shoulders are so strong and powerful, but he just can't seem to hold onto it. He tries real hard and it just keeps slipping, which must be due to his spine. In the end he gets frustrated so I'll lay on the ground holding and rotating the bone for him. He goes out with all the others and if his bone slipped and I wasn't there Emily would probably steal it from him and that wouldn't be fair. None of the others would bother; they'd be too busy with what's in front of them, but not Emily. She always has one eye on her bone and one eye on everyone else's as well.

We all go out into the front paddock and have the bones in the sun. It's such a big area out there so all the pugs can eat quite a distance away from each other. I go out with a pile of bones in my hand and start dropping them as I walk around the paddock. Even though I spread them out all over the place, you will get somebody who'll pick up their bone and move it, sometimes its sun to shade or vice versa, but if they go too close to another pug I shout them back. Bones tend to make pugs very protective and you don't want fights starting. Once everyone is chomping away happily I walk back to Horton who is up on the deck waiting for me. He's been watching the bones being dropped and his siblings running over to them and starts bouncing when he sees me heading his way. I give him his bone then lay across the deck holding it for him. I suppose I could just leave Horton inside to eat the bone in peace and try and manage it as best he can, but I like him to be out with the family where he belongs. And he really does need me to hold it in place for him, but I also need to be out with the pugs in case somebody finishes early and tries to steal a bone and I can't be in two places at once. I like watching Horton chewing on a bone. He just loves it and it's so good for his jaw strength and teeth. He lays there gripping on it with all his might, one eye closed depending on which side he's chewing hardest on. I'm sure Horton would like to be the first one receiving a bone but if I don't do it in the right order everything gets out of control fast. Emily's bone goes down first and she always has the biggest one. Things tend to be easier that way. Then Tom gets his and you have to take him off a good distance from the others because he eats so slowly due to lack of teeth. Steffy just grabs her bone and runs. Sarah gets hers at the same time as Harper, with both bones handed to them at precisely the same moment so nobody thinks they're missing out on being given one. I keep Ruby and Grace nearest to me just in case Ruby needs me to help her out. Grace is fine on her own. She's like a little piranha actually, but she likes to eat with Ruby so the two of them eat side by side close to where Horton and I are lying. Arthur, being blind, gets his bone given to him then just sinks to the ground and goes nowhere. If he wanders around and puts it down he knows someone could swoop in and take it and he wouldn't even see the thief coming. That happened only once and he learnt from it. I had to go back inside and get him another one. The poor little soul was wandering around searching everywhere for it and it was on the other side of the paddock being devoured by Emily. The other pugs come onto the deck looking for me when they've finished with their bones. As they walk up the ramp I'll jump up and put them inside the house and they sit watching us from the window then somebody else will finish and I'm up again, putting them inside before they go too close to somebody else's bone, which leaves poor little Horton on his own, trying to hold his bone in place. He's always happiest when the last of his siblings is inside and he knows I'm not going anywhere until he's finished eating.

CHAPTER SIX

There's a Big World Out There

As Horton's body became stronger, his confidence grew enormously and we decided it was time to show him the world that existed outside our farm. But it was important to me that we waited until Horton was physically strong in his body and confident in himself and his abilities before we took him out to discover the rest of the world.

Our veranda wraps around the entire front part of the house and overlooks the front paddock. Horton would scoot from one end to the other, watching everything that was going on. He'd watch the sheep and horses in the paddock, watch cars going by in the distance, the trees blowing in the wind and he'd do his puppy woof at everything he saw. He loved insects, flies, ants, ladybirds, and beetles would keep him amused for hours, his little face tilted as his eyes followed them flying through the air or crawling along the edge of the decking and up and down the veranda posts. The following day when he got to go outside he'd once again go looking for them at the place on the veranda's edge that he'd seen them last. He was such an intelligent little boy, really smart and very quick-thinking. He was fearless on the farm so we decided he was ready to see a bit more of this wonderful world he had been born into. David and I both felt he deserved to see everything; we wanted him to experience all life had to offer at his own pace of course and with one of us always there beside him in case he was frightened or hurt himself, but never holding him back. That wouldn't have been fair on him.

Horton liked to experience new things. Even if he was unsure at first he was always more than happy to be near what was going on and took everything in with those huge eyes of his. I used to love watching his face change and his eyes fill with excitement and wonder when he was seeing something for the very first time. Naturally, I did on occasion worry about him, but had to let him guide me. He was the only one who knew how far he wanted to go. As a mother (of a human child or a furry one), we have to learn to sit back sometimes and allow our babies to grow. And it can be both hard and rewarding all at the same time.

The first time we took Horton out in the car he was literally shaking with fear. His entire body trembled. Even closing the car door bothered him; he didn't like loud noises, and loud unexpected noises bothered him even more. I closed the car door as softly as I could, but it had to be closed properly so there had to be a bit of a slam. Horton was sitting on my knee with his head resting against my body. I put my hand over his exposed ear to soften the noise but he still jumped when the door shut. I held him in my arms and talked to him while David put the key in the ignition. He didn't seem to worry about the engine starting, though, but our car is very quiet; it hums. Lucky we didn't have Horton at the start of our married life because the old bomb we had back then was the loudest piece of crap there ever was and used to rattle along the road like it was about to break into a million pieces. Our neighbours always knew when we were coming home because they heard us long before we were actually in view. An elderly couple lived next door and once they started talking it was hard to get away. We used to try and sneak into our driveway, try and keep that old car as quiet as we could, but it was no use. It was loud and annoying and our neighbours' heads would pop over the fence as soon as we pulled up.

I held Horton to my chest, explained to him all that was going on, and we went only about ten minutes down the road to the local oval. We let him out to play on the grass and smell new smells then brought him back home again. Each outing we took him a little bit further until he got used to being in the car. If a truck went by he would try and crawl over my shoulder, just doing anything to get away from the noise. We did think of putting him on the backseat on his own but figured that may make him worse, so whenever something frightened him I would stoke him, put my hand under the buckle of his tinkle trousers, rub his little back and talk him through it. After a while he no longer buried his head in my shoulder; he started to look all around, watching David driving and responded when David spoke to him as we went along, but he still shot his head back and buried it in my shoulder whenever a car passed on the other side of the road. He'd have his eyes on his daddy then this fast blur would whiz past outside the window and he didn't like that one little bit. Horton didn't seem to recognize them as being the same things he saw at the bottom of the front paddock whenever he was out on the veranda. Now they were noisy, fast-moving things he didn't see coming and they startled him. We were only on country roads so it took him a while to get used to passing cars as we only ever saw a few on our country drives. But he conquered that fear and eventually began looked forward to going out. If he hadn't settled down as quickly as he did then we would simply not have taken him out again. If he was happier to stay home and just scoot around the farm then that's what we would have allowed him to do. It was all up to Horton really because it had to be. This was his life and we made sure we allowed him to do exactly what he wanted to do. It wouldn't have been right to push him out into the world if he wasn't comfortable doing it. Horton was completely in charge of everything concerning this and I felt it so very important that we took notice of what he was telling us at all times.

Horton's first big trip was to my friend's antique shop a few towns over from where we live. He was more used to going out now and we wanted to introduce him to somebody who loved dogs, somebody who had wanted to meet him for a very long time. I also knew that she would allow Horton to come inside her shop and she wouldn't bother if he needed his nappy changed or wanted a drink. She loved dogs as much as I did so these things wouldn't be a problem to her at all. I didn't know how many people would be in her shop and didn't want to overwhelm Horton. I figured doing too much too fast may be hard on him and he was doing so well with the outings that I didn't want him going backwards, so he sat in the park opposite and shared a pie with his dad. Horton didn't have the pastry, just a few mouthfuls of meat, but I reckon his first pie experience was the highlight of that trip. I watched him bouncing up and down on David's knee while waiting to be given another mouthful. David said Horton didn't take his eyes off that pie until it was all gone. My friend and I stood in her shop, talking and watching through the window. She couldn't wait to see him close up, so I kept an eye on the shop while she dashed over the road to meet him. I saw her kneel in front of the park bench and knew that she was definitely a thoughtful person; getting down to Horton's eye level would have been less threatening for him. She sat out there for a while talking to David and patting Horton, and when she came back in she was rubbing her face saying she'd just been given a pile of meat pie kisses. She thought Horton was gorgeous and if he kissed her I knew he felt the same way. The longer trip and the meeting of new people was a big success and from then on we were able to take Horton out with us whenever we went out in the car. Horton's meat pie experience sealed the deal for him because he was always happy going out after that. I only had to touch my handbag and he'd start getting excited. At first I thought he just wanted to go out because he thought every trip involved a meat pie but he didn't care if food was involved or not. He just loved going out.

I used to pack a nappy bag for him with whatever he may have needed on the trip. It was a lovely, deep peach-coloured bag with fawn pugs running all over it. It was a ladies' handbag really but the compartments were perfect for us and what we needed to carry. The mobile phone pouch fitted Horton's Pawpaw cream in snuggly and I had places to put the clean and used nappies separately. I always had Horton's nappy bag packed and placed next to my handbag so I could just grab the two of them and head out the door. It was easier that way and made things quicker because once Horton knew we were going out he didn't like to be kept waiting. He would make a beeline for the door and sit bouncing up and down until David scooped him up and carried him to the car. If I used something from the nappy bag on one trip I replaced it as soon as we got home so I didn't forget. It just made it faster to get out of the house because once Horton saw my hand touch either one of those bags that was it; he knew he was going for a drive. He scooted and then bounced and bounced up and down on his nappy until he was put in the car. Horton sat high on my knee, watching David open and close the farm gate. Then he sat higher still so he didn't miss out on seeing anything as we went along. The car door slamming and the cars passing by didn't bother him anymore. He knew the door needed to be closed before we could go anywhere and he desperately wanted to be going out so just sat back and took it all as it came.

On the way home Horton was always so exhausted, he always slept. But he never wanted to miss seeing anything on the ride there and would sit with his head moving about all over the place, trying to take everything in. But no matter how deep a sleep he was in on the way home, as soon as our car pulled into the driveway Horton woke up. He must have been able to sense that we were home or perhaps he could smell the pine trees that grow each side of our driveway. Either way, he knew we were back at the farm and would sit woofing at the sheep as we drove up to the house. Horton was like me; I always love coming back to the farm. If I've been gone half an hour or half a day it's always wonderful to be home again.

The one thing that Horton never got used to was the windscreen wipers. I don't think it was the noise, more the quick action being so close to where he sat. He never knew when they were coming and jumped every time they appeared. Even if they'd been on a while he still physically jumped every single time they moved. He never figured out that they couldn't get him, that they were on the outside of the window. I don't think he could quite work out what they did or why they were there so he would hide his face in my neck and tremble. He even tried to crawl over my shoulder just to get away. He didn't mind light rain on the windscreen. He was okay with that, which surprised me. He didn't love it but tolerated it, nevertheless. However, anything heavier than that just terrified the living daylights out of him so we decided not to take him out in the rain anymore. Many a trip was postponed because it suddenly started raining when we were about to go out. If I'd already picked up my handbag and the nappy bag and Horton was already bouncing by the back door then we'd take him on the shortest trip possible because neither one of us could bear seeing his little face disappointed. But really it just wasn't worth taking him on an outing if he wasn't going to enjoy it. In one particularly heavy storm the windscreen wipers were going flat out so we put Horton in the backseat to see if that would calm him down, but he just cried. He didn't like being on his own. It was a two-door car so it was nice and cosy and secure for him back there and I was reaching round stroking him, but he never took to it. He liked being upfront where we were. In the end we just avoided going out if it was raining hard. We'd get online to check the weather forecast and save our trips out for the days when the weather was good, no dark clouds in sight.

I was really proud of the way Horton handled himself in the outside world. The ease with which he approached new people was wonderful to see. He oozed confidence, which let me know he was all right in himself. He felt good and secure in his body, and there was no fear in him. I couldn't have asked for better for him than this. It meant that we had done our job as parents. We had given him the self-assurance he needed to grow and develop and feel at ease in the world. That was a very good feeling for both David and me. It meant the fears I had of being able to do the right thing by this amazing little soul completely vanished. They were unwarranted because Horton felt confident enough in himself to go out there being as tiny as he was and scoot right up to new people and say hello. He was so small and it's a big world out there but he was doing it. He was living it and he made my heart swell. Every now and then he'd look back over his shoulder making sure I was there and I'd smile at him and softly clap my hands and nod as if to say, "Good, good boy! Good, good boy," just like we did at home, only without words, just the action and a smile of reassurance. Then he'd turn back and allow the person he had approached to bend down and pat him. It was a beautiful thing to see. To be able to witness this little darling come into himself was one of the most amazing gifts I have ever been given. To see this take place and know I had a small part to play in it was truly magnificent. A lot of things went through my mind at this time; I would look at him and see what he had become but also remember what he was and then everything he had accomplished would dawn on me and in an instant, there would be a lump in the middle of my throat and a tiny tear of joy in the corner of my eye. And, yes, it could quickly become a waterfall and, yes, I could certainly let it flow, but I didn't because I didn't want to miss a single second of watching my boy with the new friend he had made. It's one of those moments in life when I felt incredibly blessed because I got to witness everything he has accomplished from a front row seat and not too many people are lucky enough to be able to do that. But as I watched him with that new friend and then saw him move onto another, my mind would go back to all that had taken place over the past year. I would think about that first day, the first night even. Horton was very afraid of the dark when he first came. He feared it so badly that I wondered if he had perhaps been left in the corner of a dark garage sitting in his own filth, maybe even left to die. I will never know the truth. I'm just guessing really but something happened to make him feel so terribly fearful of the lights being turned out. We found this out the first night he was here. We got the older pugs into their beds, tucked up the ones who liked having a blanket put over them, and then we said goodnight to Horton who was sitting up, looking around the room. We put Horton near David's side of the bed as we knew he would be warmest there. My side of the bed is further away from the heater and this new little baby of ours needed to be kept warm. We figured he would settle down to sleep the moment the light went off. But that didn't happen. As soon as we turned off the light Horton shot out of his bed and flew underneath ours. We heard him scurrying off and turned the lights back on fast. He was so small and we didn't want to lose him. We weren't sure if he was small enough to fit behind the bookcase and to be honest, hadn't thought about such a thing until he fled. We were so used to old pugs getting into their beds and not moving till morning that we just assumed Horton would do the same thing. David knelt on the floor and peeped underneath the bed and there was Horton sitting right in the middle, his entire little body trembling, fear in his eyes and all across his face as well. It took a while to get him out as we didn't want to reach under and drag him. That would have made the experience for him even worse, so David went under the bed with him and spent time softly talking to him, reassuring him that everything was going to be okay. When he finally came out he needed his nappy changed. I got out of bed and changed him and while I did I explained to him that we all needed to go to sleep in a dark room because it helped us get a better night's rest. I told him how old some of his sisters were and that they couldn't sleep so well with the light on. I said he would be okay and that his new dad and I were still in the room with him even though he couldn't see us. I gave him a little kiss on the head then David popped him back in his new bed and leant over the edge of our bed, stroking Horton until he finally lay down and went to sleep. Only then did we turn the lights out. For weeks, that's how we got Horton to sleep. David would lie in bed with one hand hanging over, stroking Horton until he was sound asleep and snoring, then he would slowly move his hand away and turn the light off. Then one night David was so exhausted that he forgot and turned out the lights with Horton sitting up in his bed. David's hand was still stroking the little guy's head as the room became dark. This time Horton stayed put. Although he was wide awake when the room changed from bright lights to total darkness he stayed in his bed. I think with his dad's reassuring hand stroking his head, Horton knew that he wasn't alone in the dark and after a few moments, he lay down and went to sleep. We did try a night light at one stage, but that didn't seem to do anything except make Emily bark, which set everyone else off barking. Even Horton sat up and began doing little woofs from the middle of his bed. So the nightlight was discarded and we went back to dad's reassuring hand.

One night, when Horton had been here about ten weeks or so, David was having trouble getting him to sleep. He'd think he was settled and go to pull his hand away and Horton would bolt upright and start crying. He wasn't unwell and he didn't need a new nappy put on. Everything was checked and yet he still wouldn't settle. I said that he'd just have to be left whimpering and that he'd stop as soon as he knew it wasn't going to get him anywhere. David waited a while then said, "I can't stand it. I'm going to bring Horton on the bed."

I said, "You do it once and he's going to expect it all the time."

David told me that he didn't care. I think it tore at his heart strings, hearing the little guy cry. He felt that Horton had been through enough. We already had Ruby and Grace sleeping on the bed with us and David couldn't see any reason why two couldn't become three. I think Horton had a way of wrapping himself around his daddy's heart because until he came it had always been a two-pug-only bed. Those were the rules and it was David who brought the other two pugs onto our bed in the first place. He had a soft spot for dear old Ruby. She did to him what Horton was doing now and they both got away with it. I had to laugh at that. They knew exactly what they were doing and David was caught under their spell. I don't think he could have stopped himself bringing them onto the bed if he tried. They'd worked their magic on him and he didn't stand a chance. As soon as Horton came on the bed he glanced over at me then settled down near David's arm and went to sleep. In fact, he settled faster than he'd ever settled and David slept with a protective arm around him so that he would stay put and not wander over to the edge. After that night we brought Horton's little dog bed up and put it in-between our two pillows so he was safe from harm. It was the perfect position for him, actually, as it kept him away from the edge of the bed and out of the way of one of us accidently rolling on him during the night. And that's how it was. That's how we all slept from then on. He'd have his night time mini meal, wait by the back door while the others went outside for the last wee then have his nappy changed and be brought up onto the bed with us and go to sleep. We had to do some readjusting, however. Ruby had to be moved further down so Horton could go where she used to be. Thankfully, she didn't seem to mind, though. As long as she was in bed with her special pink blanket wrapped around her she was happy. And I thought it was kind of nice that Horton was surrounded by the three of us. It was as if he was in a little protective pod: Mum and Dad at either side and his older sister in front. He was completely protected, totally enclosed in love. Was Horton spoilt because he got to sleep on the bed? Perhaps some would think so, but in our house living in close harmony with our pugs is not considered spoiling, to us; it's just living the kind of life we want to live. Maybe somebody else wouldn't have a nappy-wearing pug on the bed but that's up to them. Each of us has a right to do what we want to do in our own houses and everybody has different rules. It's a personal thing and personally I'm glad Horton got to sleep with us. I'm glad Ruby and Grace did too. I'm glad all our pugs sleep in our bedroom with us and that we live our lives as a pack. I believe that doing so gives you a special connection. From my experience, living side by side with your dogs makes for a closer bond. I've never understood why people put their pugs in cages at night. I guess it's a step up from being left outside, but to me it seems kind of wrong to do it. The poor pugs would think they were being punished and would be locked away all night wondering what they did wrong. It's the same with putting them in the laundry; everyone knows that's the coldest room in the house and in the middle of summer it'd be okay, but in winter it'd be freezing. Having Horton on the bed made things easier. I slept better because I knew he was close enough to me that I would hear him call and it made keeping an eye on the nappy situation a breeze. I'd just lean over, check if he was wet, change him if he needed it or, as was more often the case, just roll over and go back to sleep. He wasn't any trouble either. Once he knew which bed was his he'd race over, jump right on in and be snoring by the time I'd finished brushing my teeth. A few times he got in Ruby's bed. Grace slept at the bottom of the bed so there was never any confusion there, but Ruby's bed was right near Horton's and occasionally he'd get in there while she was standing swaying in the middle of our bed waiting for us to finally hop in. When the lights went out she'd shuffle over to her bed, sense there was somebody else in there and go lay down right next to him. He didn't care and she didn't care so they sometimes slept together for the rest of the night with her pink blanket over both of them. Other times, we moved Horton out so Ruby had more room to stretch her arthritic old body out. We didn't want her lying there uncomfortable all night long. She had a good ten years on Horton and seniority rules here. It's greatly respected in our house, so Horton would be gently lifted up and placed in his own bed. Their beds were side by side so they could still be near each other, just in their own comfortable space.

Speaking of rules, what I love about living in the country is that different rules seem to apply here. For example, in the city Horton wouldn't have been allowed in half the shops that he goes in, but out here life has different meaning and people are more relaxed. If Horton wasn't allowed in a shop then I didn't go in either. I wasn't about to leave him sitting in his pram out in the street on his own while I idly went from item to item as if I had all the time in the world to do so. One lady I asked came back with the most brilliant reply I have ever heard in my life. She said, "Sure, love. Bring him in. We had a sheep in here last week." Comments like this let us know that we'd made the right choice by moving to the country and they would stick with us for a long time.

I was always weary of the shops in which I allowed Horton to be on the floor. My friend's antique shop was the one where I felt most at ease putting him down. The rest of the time he stayed in his pram or in our arms. Horton had the most beautiful royal blue and white old style baby pram, it wasn't brand new yet it was beautiful all the same and that pram of his got almost as many comments as Horton himself did. But we didn't buy it just for its beauty, that pram had an important job to do, it kept our boy safe from other dogs, fast-moving children who may have stood on him and people who didn't like dogs as much as we do. It can be a pretty cruel world out there and I didn't want Horton experiencing any more of that side of it than he already had as a puppy.

He loved going to my friend's antique shop and her customers were a nice bunch of people. I think they all took their lead from her; she was almost in as much love with Horton as I was. He was her special little man and she made a big fuss over him whenever he entered her store. He'd practically bounce out of David's arms, trying to give her kisses. The rare times we went out and didn't drop by the antique store, Horton seemed really disappointed.

She had a small bar fridge in the backroom that held milk for a cup of tea as well as anything she wanted for lunch. She also generally kept a little bit of cold meat in there for sandwiches. The first time she took Horton in the backroom he seemed a little unsure of what she was going to do to him. He glanced over her shoulder at me as she carried him away. I smiled and clapped so he knew what was happening was a good thing. I also followed close behind. When he saw I was coming with him he settled down and turned around to watch where she was taking him. Horton wasn't exactly frightened but he wasn't super happy either and kept glancing back at David and me as we followed them in. She put him on the floor in front of the little fridge and he sat looking around the small room. I don't know if he was looking for an escape route or just curious to see what she had in there. It was a cluttered little room so there was a lot for Horton to look at and he liked looking at new things so calmed down a bit once his curiosity took over. My friend got down on the floor with Horton. He didn't recognize the fridge as being a fridge because it was so much smaller than the one at home. But when she opened the door he must have smelt food because he scooted up close and peeped inside. His eyes went from the two small shelves in the fridge to my friend's hands then back again. He watched closely as she took a little package out and began unwrapping. As soon as he saw she had cold meat he began bouncing up and down. She gave him a little bit and he scooted closer so she would give him some more. She seemed amazed at how fast he ate and asked if it was okay for him to have another bit. She seemed to enjoy feeding him, seeing the look of happiness spread across his face. Horton definitely wasn't unsure of her now. He had his two front paws up on her knees and began doing little woofs, telling her he wanted more. The two of them were friends for life after that.

If Horton entered the antique store and my friend was busy and hadn't offered to take him to the backroom fast enough, he would scoot over to the entrance of the little room and wait by the door until she finished with her customers. Sometimes he'd get impatient, leave the entrance and go see what was causing the delay. He'd scoot round the back of the counter and tap her on the foot to hurry her up. Sometimes he'd go from the room to the counter and back again a couple of times before she finally took him in. There was a big step up into the room and he'd sit peering in, trying to see what was in there for him to eat. If he could have he would have scooted right on in but the step was too high so he'd rest his little chin on the step and wait for her to come over and say hello. The rare occasions that she had nothing in the fridge for Horton to eat were a huge disappointment to him. It was as if he couldn't believe she'd not been expecting him to call by. Of course Horton had no idea she was trying to run a business and had more on her mind than stocking the little bar fridge with special treats for him. I think he thought all she did all day long was sit around waiting for him to drop by. But whether he was given a treat or not, Horton sure did love visiting her shop. He knew the layout like the back of his paw and would scoot off investigating the place as soon as he was put down. There was always something new to see and smell and always somebody new looking around the place. David and I basically just wandered around after him, making sure he was okay. He brought a display of aprons down once when his back legs got entangled in the ties, but other than that you would have never known he was there. He used to like stalking the customers, sneaking up on them or hiding underneath a table and watching what they were doing. Half the time they didn't know he was there, which was how he liked it, because that was all part of the game.

If Horton got caught on something and wanted us to step in he would gain our attention by doing his little dolphin noises until one of us came to see what was wrong. It was the same way at home. If he wanted help the dolphin noises started, if he was happy doing it on his own you wouldn't hear a peep out of him. Horton's nappy is held in place by Tinkle Trousers. The inside where the sanitary napkin goes is plastic and the outer is plastic covered by a nylon netting material. When he went in or out of our kitchen the metal strip that sits on the edge of our cork tiles became a bother to him at times. Occasionally, the outer-netted liner of his Tinkle Trousers became caught on the strip if a nail was sitting a little higher than the others. The first time he got caught he dolphin noised me until I walked over and helped him out. The next time it happened he didn't call for me, so I just stood by watching seeing what he would do. He'd go backwards and forwards, think about things, then wriggle from side to side trying to become untangled. But he had no way of freeing himself because the head of the nail was caught in the holes of the netting, so we'd have to rip the lining to set the little guy free. After this happened a few times he began scooting into the kitchen then as he approached the strip, his face would change. He'd speed up and as he went over the area he had been caught on, he would jump his front legs into the air, clearing the strip. I thought it was fantastic of him to be able to figure that out all by himself. Of course he couldn't do anything about his back legs but by the time he came down again his tummy had cleared the strip: no contact, no nails, no getting caught. David had gone along with a hammer and knocked all the nails in but Horton had no way of knowing that. He was just doing what he could to get the problem solved.

That's the way he was with all sorts of things on the farm. He would work out in his mind how best to help himself then go ahead and do it. There were probably a lot of things he'd worked out that we will never know about, but that one I witnessed and thought he was brilliant and clapped my heart out for the little guy. It amazed me how much he was able to lift his body off the ground. Of course it wasn't a 'cow jumps over the moon' type of thing; more like there was enough room to roll a pencil under him, but he was off the ground for a second and he cleared the nail head. He did what he needed to do in order to not get stuck and I thought he was brilliant for doing that. There was definitely something amazing about this little pug. He was special and I'm not talking about special needs (of course he has those; a blind man can see that), I'm talking about Horton as a whole, the entire package of who he is: his mind, his personality, everything about him.

Some people used to think because there was something wrong with Horton's body that there was something wrong with his brain as well. There isn't. They assume he's stupid and he most definitely is not. He's vastly intelligent actually. He's had to be. He's had to use his brain a lot more than some of my other pugs have because they weren't born with his body. They've had no need to try and figure out ways to do things the way Horton has. Things that come easily to able-bodied pugs are what Horton has had to put a great deal of thought into every single day of his life and he's done brilliantly. Horton has been a great thinker from very early on. He hasn't had the luxury of being lazy with his intellect or his body, but I believe his personality has been born into the right body. You may think it's strange of me to say this but it's the truth. A different personality (one, say, with less determination) may not have been able to achieve all that Horton has done. What he has accomplished is solely a credit to him and him alone. David and I have always been there to guide him but everything Horton has done he has done on his own. Without that inner drive and steely determination I greatly doubt he would have been able to achieve all that he has. However, I do believe that all pugs are individuals, just as we are individuals. They all have a right to be exactly who they are and you can't push them. Even if a pug is born with hemivertebra and simply wants to have its nappy changed then sit by a window all day long enjoying the view, that's okay. Each dog has a right to be who he or she is. Our requirement is only to love them, completely love them for who and what they are, and I think if you can truly do that with all your heart then you are a success as a guardian and as a parent.

CHAPTER SEVEN

To De-sex or not to De-sex? That is the Question

The decision to de-sex Horton was not one we came to lightly. We worried about putting him under anesthetic and what affect that would have on his little body. There is always a concern when putting a pug under and with Horton that concern was multiplied. He was our first hemivertebra pug and there was not a great deal of information out there. Not much research had been done because the simple fact is that most of the pugs born like Horton are put to sleep at a very young age. We took a long time assessing him before we decided to go ahead with the operation. My friend in rescue said she wanted Horton to be de-sexed, but asked that we wait until he was at least twelve months old before we did so. Even though we promised her that we would have him de-sexed (it was part of the agreement made when she first contacted us about taking him in), we did at one point consider leaving him as he was. I think she was concerned he may be able to breed and perhaps father a litter of similar-bodied puppies. When she gave Horton to us he was so young and she, like us, just didn't know what his body would and wouldn't be able to do on reaching maturity. We were all in the dark really, but as he grew we could see that Horton becoming a daddy was not something we were ever going to have to worry about because he would never be able to reproduce. The physical act couldn't possibly have been performed. I suppose Horton could have been left as he was if preventing him from breeding was the only issue at hand but it wasn't. There were other things to be considered.

A lot of people asked why we bothered. Why put Horton through an operation if he couldn't impregnate? But they didn't realize the other issues that go hand in hand with a paraplegic pug. Horton was around thirteen months old when the operation took place and I was a nervous and emotional wreck when we were dropping him off. The effect of the anaesthetic on his body was what worried me the most. Putting any of my old pugs under is always a worrying time for me and with little Horton the concern was tenfold and my heart knew it. I trusted our vet but still couldn't help worrying. I dreaded the procedure and was crying as I left him with the vet. Our vet and the nurses there were all really good with me, reassuring me they would take excellent care of him and that everything was going to be okay, and I don't think I could have let any other vet besides our vet near Horton. I don't think I would have trusted anybody else with him. But our vet was fantastic in understanding our little boy's special needs and was good enough to be flexible with the rules due to Horton's condition.

The procedure was going to take place just after lunch. Most dogs have to be in at 8.00 a.m. on the day of their operation, but our vet allowed us to bring Horton in a few minutes before he was going to be operated on. That way, he didn't have to be left for hours sitting on his own in strange surroundings. I know that would have distressed him a lot. He didn't like being on his own because he never had been. He always had one of us around him twenty-four hours a day. David and I never left him alone; we never wanted to have him falling over on his side and lying there unable to get up until we got home. Horton came everywhere with us and if one of us had to go to the doctor or some other place that didn't allow dogs then the other one stayed home with Horton. That's how we did things. I had many offers from friends to babysit Horton but I never left him with anybody, not even my sister. It just didn't feel right in my heart to leave him. I suppose I never trusted anybody else with my special boy. What if they picked him up wrong and hurt him? What if they accidently dropped him or injured him in some other way? What if they forgot how fast he could move, left a door open and he got out and onto the road or into the hands of a stranger who didn't understand how special he was? Or worse, what if he came across a large, aggressive dog? He'd have had no chance of defending himself. Those thoughts haunted me every time somebody asked if they could look after Horton for me. One of my friends was desperate for me to leave him with her, to the point of pushing me out the door so she could be with him on her own. She would suggest all sorts of places I may like to go, you know, so that I could have a break from all the pugs and be off on my own for a few hours of pampering. But what she didn't realize was that I didn't need a break. My pugs weren't a burden to me. They never have been. I love being with them and time apart is agony for me. My time bobbing around the farm with my cloud of pugs trailing after me is exactly where I want to be and exactly what I want to be doing. I wouldn't have all these pugs in my life if I didn't want to be with them all the time. When I go grocery shopping I'll ring David halfway through the shop to check how the pugs are going. Then we'll discuss what treat they would like me to bring home for them. The only good thing about leaving them is how excited they all get when I arrive home. My homecoming is always a time of joy. I bring treats and make sure to bring something different back each time. But time away from my babies purely for the sake of being away from them is not necessary for me. It never has been. I don't want it and I don't need it, ever. Maybe with her only having one dog my eight-pug home seemed a little hectic to her, but it's not chaotic to me; it's pure contentment and you take my pugs away from me and I no longer feel content. I did let this friend of mine change Horton whenever she was visiting, which was about once a week because she missed Horton if she went for more than seven days without seeing him. She was so besotted with him and so desperate to help I almost felt sorry for her, so would let her change him even if he didn't really need it. If she was about to leave and Horton was due to be checked in half an hour's time, I would let her check him early so she didn't miss out. But the first time she changed his nappy had us both legless with laughter. She was so intent on doing a good job and so very careful in her handling of Horton, the way she touched him was as if he were made of thin glass and I liked that she was being so tender with him, but when she finished and proudly brought him over for me to check, she had put the sanitary napkin part of his nappy on his back. It was like he was wearing a little backpack. I could hardly tell her what she'd done wrong with laughing so much and when I finally got my words out she collapsed in a fit of laughter. Horton sat on the floor looking up at us, but we just couldn't stop laughing and the more we looked at him the harder we laughed. At first he seemed amused and sat smiling up at us then he got bored and scooted off to play with his stack of toys. As he went, he resemble a little baby turtle. He looked adorable actually, but with the nappy strapped to his back and nothing to catch the wee he left a trail all over the lounge floor and I was too weak with laughter to clean it up. After we'd composed ourselves, I went over and fixed Horton's nappy up. She was horrified at getting it wrong and couldn't believe she had been so stupid, but I told her not to worry. Horton wasn't bothered; he just went off to have a play. He even tried to run away from me with a toy in his mouth because he'd just been changed and was happy to be off having some fun. He didn't want to be disturbed again so soon. As she left she laughed and said, "Now I know why you won't leave Horton with me".

When people offered to babysit Horton I knew they were only trying to help and I was grateful for that, but David and I have always worked out our lives so that we never have to leave Horton with anybody else. Sure, I would have liked David to come to the doctors with me as he had always done in the past, and he probably would have liked me to be with him at those times too, but neither of us wanted to leave Horton. We both felt strongly about that and for him to be left sitting in the backroom of our vet's for hours waiting to have an operation didn't sit right with us either. We both knew such a thing would scare him, but I also worried about the mental effect it would have. He would be sitting there looking out at all those dogs in cages, and they wouldn't have been wandering around freely like Horton and his brothers and sisters do on the farm. That would have been confusing to him. Smelling all those strange smells, no fresh country air, just the smell of antiseptic and disinfectant wouldn't have been normal for him either. He wouldn't have understood what was going on, what was about to happen to him. He wouldn't have known why he was there or even if we were coming back for him. I couldn't have him feeling broken-hearted like that. I didn't want him sitting by himself in a strange place thinking we had abandoned him. All that time on his own would have left his little mind ticking over. What if he thought he had been taken there to be put to sleep? It wouldn't have been the first time that had happened to him. What if being there brought all those memories flooding back? I didn't want him feeling unloved, unwanted, worthless and rejected. What if Horton felt after all this time that David and I had gotten tired of looking after him? What if he thought we had changed our minds about him and didn't want him anymore? What if in the confusion of his day being so different to how it normally was he forgot how much we loved him? What if he was sitting there on his own thinking that he was a burden to us? It wouldn't have been the first time he'd heard something like that said.

I've always thought of Horton as a gift, a gem, my jewel. Sometimes you get given something so magnificent in life that it causes you to stop and wonder what on earth you could possibly have done that was so right and so worthy of you being the recipient of something as incredible as this. You rack your brain and come up empty every time because nothing you have ever done in your life thus far has warranted the honour that has been bestowed. That's how it has always been with Horton. I've always looked at him with a huge overwhelming feeling of love and a deep, deep sense of gratitude. I look at him and wonder: why me? Why was I the one fortunate enough to get chosen? I guess I will never know the answer to that but I just feel so incredibly lucky that he came to be with me. Perhaps Horton is a gift I've been given early. Maybe I've yet to do something to deserve him. Whatever it is, I'm ready. I'll do it. I'll pay my dues because life with Horton is so worth it. I have never taken the gift of Horton for granted. My heart is constantly full of appreciation and thankfulness. When I look at Horton, even when he's scooted off the veranda and raced through the mud for the third or fourth time that day and I'm busy, it doesn't matter. He's just living his life, doing what he loves to do. Cleaning him up again and looking after him is an absolute pleasure. The needle that was going to be used to put him down at twelve weeks of age would have been wasted and it makes you wonder how many of them actually are.

A lady I was in contact with when Horton first came to live on the farm referred to him as a burden. That was when Horton first heard the word used and it was the first and last time this woman entered my house. You have to be careful who you let into your home and what you allow them to say when they get there. Previously, all our conversations had been over the phone. She was an animal lover so we got on well. When she learnt that I had Horton she asked if she could come and meet him. I thought it was a good idea. All the pugs enjoyed meeting new people and Horton especially loved it when somebody new came to the house. I have found over the years that pugs can't have enough friends. They just love being around people and this lady was traveling a fair distance so I thought if she wants to make the long drive then she must desperately want to meet him. I'm not sure what image she had of Horton in her mind, though. Perhaps it didn't match what he was actually like. We'd had many a good conversation about his progress since he arrived and she'd always been so positive. That's why it was such a shock to hear something so negative coming out of her mouth. Now I look back I'm thinking perhaps she merely came out of curiosity not love. As for Horton, he wouldn't go anywhere near her. Normally he's first in line for a pat and pushes his way through the pack, making sure he's right upfront when meeting new people. Horton is well used to being adored. We spent a lot of our time adoring him so this reaction was foreign. He scoots into a room and expects that everyone is going to love him because he doesn't know any other way. Horton has been surrounded by love since the first day he went into rescue. And it's alien to him not to be responded to with anything but pure love. So Horton didn't know what to make of this woman. She tried to get near him but he backed away. Hopefully he wouldn't have been able to understand what this new word meant, but he knew something wasn't right there and kept his distance.

I had a few people visiting that day and Horton was racing around getting pats and giving kisses. People had to bend down for a kiss because I never liked new people picking him up in case they handled him the wrong way and also, Horton is not a toy. He is a living, breathing, beautiful little being. It wouldn't have been fair on him to be passed from stranger to stranger. If he approached somebody and wanted to be cuddled then I'd go over and lift him up and instruct them on how to position his body so that he could sit comfortably on their knee. But Horton wouldn't have a bar of this woman. He was going from person to person receiving multiple pats but when he got to this lady's chair he stopped dead in his tracks. He must have been able to sense the negativity. I'd never seen him do this before. He tilted his little head and looked at her for a few moments then pushed his body backwards, all the time keeping this woman in view, then when he was a safe distance away he turned and scooted off. He stayed clear of her side of the room after that. One of my friends who spent a lot of time with us picked Horton up and he spent the remainder of the visit asleep on her knee.

What this woman said left me speechless at first. I mean, a burden? No! A blessing? Yes, indeed! She said that I'd probably need an extra pair of hands when dealing with him and I said an extra set of eyes in the back of my head would be better so I can see what he's getting up to when my back is turned. When she used the word burden it hurt my heart. Horton is so easy to look after; she had no idea what she was talking about or perhaps the little extra care that is needed for Horton's life to run smoothly would have been burdensome for her. In that case I was glad she didn't have one like Horton to look after. It'd be tragic for him to have to spend his life with a person with such a damaging opinion of him. Luckily, he came to me. Luckily, she wasn't the one who got to be his mother. What a terrible existence that would have been for him. Horton would never have thrived in her home. He would have picked up on the negativity, known he was not fully loved, not fully wanted, and quite possibly given up. That's why it was so important to me to not have Horton sitting alone at the vets with time on his hands to allow sad and unnecessary thoughts to enter his head. Also, it made things a lot easier for David and me. We didn't have the added worry of being apart from Horton any longer than we needed to be. I think if we'd been made to leave Horton longer he would have been in quite a state before he was put under and I believe that may have made things worse for him. If his little body was already in a state of stress before being sedated it could have had an effect on how well he handled the anesthetic. God bless our vet for not making Horton go through that. He knew us well enough to know that we wouldn't feed him anything before bringing him in so he would be okay to be operated on right away. Personally, I think the reason vets get you to take your dogs in early is because they need to have them in their care for a few hours so they know for certain that they haven't eaten. I'm sure there are a lot of owners who swear blind they haven't given their dogs anything to eat, but in reality have sneakily given a few morsels because they think it isn't going to do any harm. They do it because they love their pets and don't like saying no, but if they thought things through they would realize how much worse they are making it for them.

When we took Horton in for his operation our vet was in the waiting room having a cup of tea and talking to a sales rep. There were no other patients in there. It was almost as if Horton was the only one having an operation that day and they were waiting solely for him. David carried Horton and I carried the nappy bag, his bed and a blanket. I'd also written a note with special instructions for Horton's care. Our vet and the nurses knew him well, but I just wanted to make sure he was extra specially taken care of. Also, if a new nurse was on who hadn't seen Horton before, well, I just wanted her to be able to know what he needed when I wasn't around to tell her. We did think about sitting in the waiting room while the operation took place, but they suggested that we may like to go to the shopping centre nearby and have a cup of coffee. Perhaps the thought of us sitting in the next room may have unnerved them.

Our vet always has a few dogs stretched out in beds behind the counter. One is a surgery dog and the others belong to the vet nurses on duty. It's like 'bring your dog to work day' every day there and I always liked that about them. But when we walked in, the dogs behind the counter began barking loudly and that seemed to be making Horton uneasy, so I told David to put him on the ground. I knew that once he was out of their sight they would go back to snoozing and that's exactly what they did. As soon as David let Horton go he scooted off happily. He went over to our vet and the rep to say hello then did a few laps of the waiting room having a good look at everything as he went. Once everything had been properly sniffed, he went back and sat in front of our vet. I think he was hoping they were having a biscuit with their cup of tea because he was real hungry by this time. The sales rep had never seen Horton before so he got the usual stranger reaction from her. She patted and gushed and Horton lapped it all up then scooted off back to his dad. He glanced up at David's face and once he was acknowledged, shot off round the surgery again. Horton was having a ball. Clearly, he had no idea what we had brought him in for. He was under the chair, stalking the vet's legs when the sales rep walked out. I turned my back to sign the usual paperwork that goes with operations then turned round just in time to see the vet scoop Horton up. He had his empty cup in one hand and Horton in the other and I completely lost it. I burst out crying.

Seeing the vet standing there like that with Horton made it official and I just wanted to race over, grab Horton and walk out the door with him. I cried because I didn't want to put my little special needs pup through an operation, I cried because I was leaving Horton with somebody other than David for the very first time and I cried because in the back of my mind was the worry of something going wrong. I think I could have stood there crying like that all day long but it wouldn't have done anybody any good. I trusted our vet so I just had to turn and walk out as quickly as I could, otherwise I may have done what I really wanted to do and walk out of there with Horton. Horton was about to go through an ordeal. I didn't want him having to wait around while I composed myself so I walked out the door without looking back because I knew one look back would have changed everything. I had to be strong for Horton's sake and just keep walking and let the team do what they needed to do.

I believe the operation was harder on me than it was on Horton. I think the hardest part for Horton was not being allowed to have breakfast. While I fed the other pugs, David took Horton to another part of the house, but it was no use; he knew exactly what was going on and cried like crazy for his food. David was talking to him and playing with him but it didn't distract him one little bit. He just sat there and cried because he wanted his breakfast. He was well aware of our daily routine. He knew where the others were and what they were doing because he was usually out there doing it with them. Horton's first meal of the day has always been his favourite because he's spent the night time sleeping and is always hungry as soon as the sun comes up. I knew how hungry he was going to be this morning. Horton loved eating and to deprive him of that was the worst thing in the world to do to him. But we knew that later in the day when he was recovering from the operation quickly and easily that he would no doubt be glad we didn't let him eat. We just had to promise him a special dinner when he came home and leave it at that. We couldn't give in, couldn't let one bit of food pass his lips otherwise he would have been ill during recovery and that wouldn't have been fair on him. He'd never vomited once in his life and he wasn't going to today either. So I just kissed his head and said, "Sorry, baby. No food for you this morning. You'll have to wait until you get home."

While Horton was having the operation, the last image of him in the vet's arms stayed clearly in my mind. David had something to eat but my stomach was a mess so I just sat with my mobile phone in my hands, waiting for it to ring. The vet said he'd ring us as soon as the operation was over. Ninety-nine percent of me knew Horton would be okay but that one percent doubt was playing havoc with my mind.

I had been asked by my friend in rescue to make sure the operation wasn't performed until Horton was twelve months old. She was worried that the drugs used would have a negative effect on his body and wanted to make sure he was fully developed before being sedated. I understood this. I certainly didn't want Horton to be in any danger so we waited. A few people couldn't understand this as most dogs are de-sexed at three months old. The younger the better some say, but Horton was not a regular dog so normal rules didn't apply.

The reason we de-sexed him at all was due to his size. There was simply not a lot of room left in his nappy once he started developing and it got to the point where we felt it was getting a little uncomfortable for him. Horton was a tiny pug but in that area he was just about as big as a regular-sized male pug. Also, one vet I spoke to worried about infection. This vet came out to the farm a lot to see to the livestock and he knew how Horton lived his life. When I told him my concerns over sedation he said he was more worried about Horton cutting or grazing the area when he was nappy-free. The best thing to do was to have him de-sexed. We all knew it had to be done.

As I left Horton at the vets that morning I did feel good that we'd waited until he was older before booking him in. I felt by doing so we had given him the best chance of coping with everything involved with being operated on and that was the one thing I had real peace about.

Harper wasn't feeling very well that day so when David finished eating we decided that instead of sitting in the car waiting we'd make a mad dash to the farm, check on her, then come back and wait for Horton to come round. I didn't like leaving Horton – being up the road in a coffee shop was about as far away as I wanted to be from him – but Harper was on my mind so we headed home to make sure she was okay. I figured whether or not we were some distance away or just up the road wouldn't have made much difference to Horton, and Harper needed me too. I hadn't been happy about leaving her for so long either. I felt torn that day. I desperately wanted to be in two places at once but that was impossible. Sadly, Harper passed away a week after Horton was de-sexed. He hadn't even gotten his stitches taken out before she was gone.

Our farm is about an hour away from our vet. He used to be in the same street when we lived in suburbia. When we moved to the farm we kept going back because he's always been so good with our pugs. To travel all that distance whenever one of our pugs was sick didn't seem like an unusual thing for us to do, but our friends all thought it was. They told us we were mad actually and that one vet is as good as another. But when it comes to the health and happiness of our pugs no distance is too great to travel and most of our pugs are old and he's brilliant with older dogs. He has a special place in his heart for rescues, too, so he is definitely the right vet for us.

We only got halfway back to the farm when my phone rang. The vet said Horton had been done, that all was well with him and everything had gone perfectly. He said Horton was sitting up looking around and that we could collect him any time we wanted. I asked him how long Horton had been knocked out for and was told that it was just ten minutes. I thought that was brilliant. He wasn't out for too long, which meant a lot less stress on his little body and a faster recovery time.

David was driving and I was so excited that as soon as I hung up the phone I shouted, "Turn around! Turn around! We're going back! Our baby's ready!"

David's face lit up and I've never seen him spin the car around so fast in his life. The trip back to the vets seemed to take forever because we just couldn't wait to have our little one back in our arms. We burst through the door almost knocking each other over in the process. We were both so anxious to see our son, we looked like those folks who get up early when there's a sale on and the first one through the store door gets a prize. We needn't have rushed, though, because there was nobody behind the desk when we walked in. We had to wait for what seemed like half an hour, but in reality was only about five or six minutes, for the nurse to come out. We were peering through the door, watching her come down the hall. She saw our noses against the glass and smiled. I was glad when she walked past the room where the dogs are usually held and happier still when she turned into the room nearest the end of the hall. It meant they had put Horton in an area closest to them, one where he could be heard and checked on regularly no matter how busy they became. It meant they understood his individual needs and were taking extra special care of our son in our absence.

I watched as she carried Horton out of the room. He was sitting up in his bed, which we had left with him because we wanted him to be able to smell a piece of home while he was away. He was sort of balancing in the middle of the round bed as she brought him out. He looked like a little shipwrecked pug floating in a dingy out at sea. His eyes were bright and he was looking around but he didn't see me until he came through the door. His eyes fixated. We said hello and he acknowledged us not so much with his entire face as he would normally do; it was in his eyes. You could tell he recognized his mum and dad but was too groggy to go nuts. David took the nappy bag and bed while Horton was handed to me. I kissed his beautiful face twice. He was a little unresponsive, no kissing me back and I understood fully. He adjusted himself as I put his head on my shoulder. I glanced sideways at him to properly say hello but his eyes were closed. He was out like a light, fast asleep as soon as his little face made contact with my shoulder. We thanked the nurse for all she'd done and asked her to thank our vet for us when she next saw him. Then we gently carried Horton to the car with all the care and pride and love new parents do when taking a newborn baby home from the hospital. David fussed around getting Horton and me safely in the front seat without waking the little fella up. When he'd succeeded at that he went and put all of Horton's belongings in the back. I don't think we needed to take as much care as we did because Horton was just completely out of it and snoring away loudly. It was like he knew he was safe as soon as he was put on my shoulder, so flaked out. The drugs were still in his system and he just couldn't stay awake a moment longer. When I adjusted Horton's position making sure he was comfortable, I noticed he was wearing a clean nappy and they'd put it on the right way round.

We had food in the car, a special treat for the other pugs to have when we got home. We always bring them a treat when we've been out and although today was stressful we didn't let them down. I knew they would be waiting by the door wondering what we had for them and if we'd just carried Horton in and forgot about them some little pugs noses would definitely have been put out of joint. So, delicious smells filled the car but Horton wasn't for noticing. Most of the way home he slept on my shoulder exactly where he had been placed. He had a little stretch and yawn halfway home but that was about it and he didn't even open his eyes when he did it. He'd had a big ordeal, he was exhausted and again I was glad he hadn't been out of our care for too long. I was thankful to our vet for not making him come in early. Everything had worked out beautifully for our son and I was grateful. A lot of people were praying for Horton that day and it seemed all those prayers had paid off. Things couldn't have gone more smoothly for him. When we got home David took Horton inside while I stayed outside and gave the pugs their treats. I remember how much Harper loved the treat that day, and I gave her extra because she loved it so much. That was one of the last memories I have of Harper. A week later she was gone and I mourned her loss greatly.

When I came inside David had changed Horton's nappy and he was asleep in the middle of our bed. He hadn't even stirred when his nappy was changed. That's the first time he'd slept right through it. I would have liked him to have stayed awake long enough for me to get some fluids into him, but that wasn't going to happen till later in the day so I just lay on the bed beside him, curled my body gently around his and stayed there watching him sleep. It was late when Horton finally lifted his head. He woke up and licked my face then sat up properly. When I knew he was fully awake I left David with him and went into the kitchen to start getting the pugs' tea ready. Horton must have heard the bowls hit the bench because David said he shot across the bed and started bouncing and calling out to me. Clearly he wanted his tea: the special treat tea we had promised him. He'd missed out on two meals today but be dammed if he was going to miss another one. He ate his dinner fast. It was only small because we didn't want it to be brought back up. Once he'd eaten and been changed, he sat and played with a few toys. We gave him another small meal just before we all turned in for the night, mainly to get more fluids into him than anything else. It was a sloppy watery meal but he sucked it down anyway and looked around for more.

He slept soundly throughout the night. I checked on him a few times but he was always fast asleep. When he woke up in the morning he was back to normal: eating, playing and scooting along the veranda barking. He couldn't have his nappy off, though, due to the risk of infection. There was also an added worry of the area becoming infected due to the lack of airflow. It was a two-edge sword really. So we would feed him, change him and let him have a little play outside so he wouldn't become bored. He hated to be inside all day long. He lived for being outside on the veranda. Then we put him in the middle of our bed, on a thick layer of towels, nappy-free for airflow, with every single toy we had in the house to keep him occupied. This went on for ten days until the stitches came out, but it worked. He didn't end up with an infection in the area. David took time off work to be with Horton during this time so he had the added bonus of having his daddy's attention all day long and he loved that.

The Letter I Wrote To Our Vet When Horton Was De-sexed:

"Horton last ate at 9 o'clock last night and it was only a light meal so if he's first up to be operated on he will be fine. Because he didn't eat this morning and wasn't in his usual routine he hasn't had a drink either. I tried to get some fluids into him as I don't want him getting dehydrated but he wasn't interested, so he will need a drink at some point. You may need to hold the bowl up to him as all the water bowls are raised here. It makes it easier for the older ones with arthritic necks to drink.

I've sent along one of his spare Tinkle Trousers with a napkin already in place. I've also added a few more spare sanitary napkins in case he needs them. His nappy is only good for weeing. If he has a poo it will just fall out the back, so be warned. lol. Also he does a little jerky bouncy movement when he's pooing, so you'll have some warning and be able to grab a bit of toilet paper.

I've sent along one of his beds so he can be propped up when he's in recovery. Horton won't be able to get himself upright if he is laid fully on his side and he will panic. He thrashes around and freaks out whenever it happens at home and coming out of the anesthetic and being in a strange place, he may panic even more.

He's always been like this. I thought as he grew he would have developed more of a pug-type shoulder and be able to lift himself up, but due to his back problem I feel he will never be able to do this. Other than that he is a pretty tough little guy and very little bothers him. I think he panics because he feels vulnerable in that position. It doesn't happen all that much but if he gets knocked over by one of the other dogs I just gently place my hand under his shoulder and bring him back up again. At first I used to leave him just to see if he could get himself right. It was agonizing to watch but I felt I had to give his mind time to try and figure out what to do and how to work his body round so he could conquer the problem. This is not a real issue as it happens so rarely, but if you can think of any way I can help him in this area I am open to suggestions.

Please take good care of Horton. Please don't let him die under anesthetic. He is very precious to us. Thank you."

CHAPTER EIGHT

Names are Important

I believe the names we choose for our animals are important, which is why such care is always given here before settling on a name. I adore beautiful-sounding names and love names that have beautiful meanings. I have four baby name books in the house and when I have the time to read a newspaper I always have a look in the birth columns to see what's popular. I also like to use the names of my two-legged family members and friends for my four-legged family members as way of honouring them. Mainly, I'll use it as a second name although there have been a few times when the pug, horse or sheep looks so much like the actual person that I just had to use it as a first name. Of course, I never tell them why I'm doing it; they just think they're privileged, but it can be pretty funny when you get a photo of the two of them together. The human namesake will be doing their best smile and trying to get as close to the animal as they possibly can and all the while I'm looking through the lens thinking to myself "Twins, twins". I don't often keep the original names our pugs come with unless they came from a wonderful loving home and the owners had to give them up purely because there was absolutely no other option available to them. Normally, I'll change their names as a way of breaking the association with the past. The way I see it, it's a new life and a new name. Sometimes I'll go for something similar sounding and sometimes I won't. I find that no matter how old a pug is when they come to us they never seem to have any trouble getting used to a new name when it's spoken in love or said with a great deal of enthusiasm. When I'm having my quiet moments alone with our newest furry family member I'll use the new name repeatedly as I sit stroking them on my knee. In those first few weeks, they are getting used to so many different things: our house, the farm, new beds, new diet, their new brothers and sisters and the routine of their new life. Once they know they are loved and wanted they tend to settle down. I talk to my pugs all the time so they become familiar with my voice and the meaning of my words very quickly. They soon get to realize who I'm talking to when their new name is used. It's lovely when you say the new name and their little head shoots up and they come running to you for the very first time. In your heart you know all is well. They have accepted the name they have been given and we can all start moving forward together as a family in this happy little life on this quiet little farm.

I'm terribly fussy with pug names because these beautiful souls are the most important things in the world to me. I'm less fussy with the sheep; there's just too many of them to become picky, but the horse names I also put a bit of thought into because horses are my second favourite animal in the world. Somebody pointed out to me a few years back that perhaps I spend far too much time than is really necessary choosing a pug's name. Up until that point I hadn't really thought about it, but they were right. I do. I think it's because our pugs are members of our family. We've always thought of them that way, so I guess I spend as much time as any new parent does when choosing a name for their baby. That's probably why we'll never have any of the common dog names in our house. No Ladies or Princesses, no Maxes or Dukes. Although there could one day be a Shadow. I know it's in the top ten most popular names for a dog, but I love it. Not for a pug, though. I think it suits a giant breed more: a Dane, a Mastiff or a Wolfhound perhaps. So I guess there will never be a Shadow here because I couldn't have a large breed knocking around my elderly pugs. It wouldn't be fair on them. They deserve tender, loving care when they come to our farm and that is what we always give them.

I have a long list of names ready for when a new animal arrives on the farm. I like to be prepared, although there have been a few times when I wished we'd left the pug nameless for a few weeks and gotten to know them better first. Once a strong personality comes through you sometimes think another name may have been better suited to that particular little soul. Most times, it doesn't really matter. By that time you are used to the name and they are used to the name, so you let it go and move on. There are far more important things in life to worry about. And it would be hard, I guess, having a pug here for a few weeks without a name because the use of the name is all part of the settling-in period.

The reason we change their names is because most of the pugs we take in come to us old, unwanted and unloved, and we don't want to have them living here in these beautiful surroundings dragging that old name around with them. I reckon it would hold them back, make it harder for them to heal and some have enough trouble in that area as it is.

There are also times when we have wanted to choose a name that suits a pug when it first arrives here, but haven't. We couldn't because we knew that in a couple of months they would no longer look the way they first did. We've had a few that have been very overweight when they first came to us. I have a real soft spot for chubbers and can always think of half a dozen cute names that would suit a chubby little pug beautifully. But you have to force your mind ahead and try to picture how the pug is going to look when he or she is thinner and go with that name instead.

There was one occasion when a name was changed a few months after the pug arrived. This has only happened once in all the years of having dogs mind you, so I suppose it proves that most times we've gotten it right the first time round. It was with Steffy actually. She is deaf so there was no confusion to her. She can't hear her name being called so when David wanted to change it I told him that if it meant that much to him he should go ahead, although at first I didn't like the name he chose or, should I say, the reason why he chose it. I had called her Gillian. It's an old-fashioned name but I liked it back then for some reason. I don't like it now but back then I did and thought the name actually suited her face. Gillian means 'youthful' and I loved that because I thought every time I used it I would be reaffirming her status and putting positive energy into the room not only for Gillian but for the other pugs as well. They were all so old. Gillian was our youngest at the time and the other pugs had years on her. I figured calling out something that meant 'youthful' a couple of times a day would be wonderful for my little old pugs to hear. I think words are powerful and I'm all for keeping the atmosphere in our home loving, positive and nurturing. I always live in the hope that by putting positive affirmations out there, my little old sweethearts will grab onto them for dear life and it will help them live longer. That is my life's aim, to get every pug that comes to the farm to live in great health for as long as they possibly can. It's something I spend a lot of time thinking about and that's why the name Gillian was chosen, but David didn't like it. He was against it from the start, hated it actually, and because I always signed her for the re-call I stopped using it when David was around. I doubled up on using it when he was at work, but used the hand signal only when he was at home. That way, I didn't have to hear him going on about how horrible he thought the name was. He wouldn't even use the name. He started calling her Steffy instead. Not Steffy as in Stephanie; Steffy as in 'Steffy the Deafy' was what he used to call her. At first I thought he was belittling her and told him how mean he was being, but over time I saw how much he loved that little pug and she in turn loved him back enormously. He'd sign for her by lowering his hand to the ground and shaking it about to get her attention and call out "Steffy, Steffy the Deafy" and she'd run and jump into his arms. You couldn't possibly watch the two of them together and not see the amount of love there, so I let him have his way. Besides, he wasn't doing it out of malice. There was no spite or unkindness there, Steffy was the first deaf dog David had ever come across and he took great care in looking after her. If anything, he thought he was being funny and Steffy didn't much care what he called her. All she was interested in was the amount of times he rubbed her tummy and scratched behind her ears. I figured she was all right with it, so I just let it go, but I told David that next time Steffy was at the vets he was the one who had to explain the reason behind the name change.

I don't think David was too taken with the name Horton when he first heard it. He certainly didn't hate it but he said he thought we could come up with something better, and by 'We' he meant 'He', because I was already sold on the name I'd chosen. So he went off and had a think about it and I dreaded what he was going to come back with. Sometimes his names are brilliant, but most of the time not so much. He is always trying to sneak in a Star Trek or Stargate name in somewhere and as much as I've tried to put it off, I do believe we are going to have a sci-fi pug name in the future. David had Deanna, as in Deanna Troi from Star Trek, picked out for Sarah thirteen years ago, but I didn't like it back then. Now I do so that has been put on my names list. I think David knew Horton was special and just wanted to get the name perfect. David is also into Egyptology, so Ra, as in the Egyptian God, is also on the list, so is Ethon, as in the giant eagle in Greek mythology.

A lot of our pugs have two names. I'm big on them having middle names, but Horton was given more. His full name is Horton James Sparky Comer. I chose the name Horton because I loved the sound of it. I'm always on the lookout for nice names and make a note as soon as I hear one. A few months before Horton came into my life, they kept advertising a movie, Horton Hears a Who! I've always liked Dr Zeus because he puts wonderful life affirmations into books for children and you've got to love someone who does that. "Horton hears a who! Horton hears a who!" I'd hear it over and over again and loved the name more each time I heard it. I had lambs due in a couple of weeks' time and assumed I'd use it for one of those. I thought it'd make a great name for a ram lamb. But the lambs came into the world all beautiful and healthy and none of them looked like a Horton to me, so it stayed on the names list. I have read many Dr Zeus books over the years but never the one called Horton Hears a Who! so I had no idea who Horton was. I actually thought he was one of those funny little Dr Seuss men in the books. I didn't realize he was a big blue elephant at the time. So I went out and bought the book to find out all about him. The book was lovely and the Horton character was lovelier still. He wasn't mean-spirited or spiteful, he wasn't one of the bad guys; he was a nice elephant, kind, considerate, helpful. He helped save a village and I liked that.

The name James was added because I liked the sound of the name. It's David's grandfather's name for one, but it's also a good, strong, solid name and although Horton's amazing personality had not yet been revealed to me, I figured a good strong name would be beneficial to him. But honestly I reckon I could have called him anything and he still would have soared. It wouldn't have mattered because Horton was going to be who he was born to be and no name was going to make any difference to that.

The name Sparky has a lot of sentiment behind it. It was the name of a pug that had hemivertebra and was euthanized because of it. It was special to the lady who brought Horton into my life and that was the reason I kept it. She had met the original Sparky. She has the same heart as I do when it comes to pugs and her heart, like mine, was broken when that pug was put to sleep unnecessarily. That's what was so heartbreaking about it. Either one of us would have gladly given this pug a home and looked after her for the remainder of her days. There are options available for pugs born with hemivertebra. Just because they have the condition does not mean their lives have to come to an end. It always haunts me when owners make these decisions because a lot of the time they are based purely on the fact that they themselves do not want to put the extra effort in and think because they don't want to do it nobody else will either and that's definitely wrong. There are so many of us out here who will. There are loads of people just like me who want to do it, who love to do it and because we sometimes find out after the dog has been euthanized, there is nothing we can do and that's the thing that truly rips your heart out. Sometimes I'll be going about my business, doing chores around the farm and my mind will wander to these pugs: the lost cases, I call them. I often think about how their lives would have been different if the owners had rung a rescue group instead of walking into their local vets.

When Horton first came I would kiss his forehead whenever I changed his nappy, I'd gently whisper in his ear, telling him to fight hard to grow strong and to live a long life. I'd tell him to live for all those who had gone before him and been put down. I'd tell him to live the best life possible and to enjoy all this world has to offer. He didn't know it but he was carrying many lives on those little shoulders of his. That's another reason I spread the word about Horton. I felt if people knew dogs like Horton existed and lived happy, healthy lives, it may prevent others from being unnecessarily euthanized. I felt if telling Horton's story saved just one pug then it'll have all been worthwhile, but my heart hopes Horton's story will end up saving a lot more than just one.

I'm glad I chose the name Horton for this wonderful little soul. It suits him. I'd never heard of a dog called Horton before. I have since because a few pugs have been named in his honour, which is nice. I couldn't think of a more perfect name for the little guy. I like that in a house full of pugs with human names it is unique to him. He was a special little pug and deserved a special name and I believe he got it. I couldn't imagine him being named anything else, and all you have to do is begin saying his name, not even get the full pronunciation out, and he's there by your side. He stops what he's doing and scoots over in seconds and when he arrives I always pick him up and give him a hug. Honestly, I think I could spend the entire day hugging and kissing Horton. I don't do it because he deserves to be getting on with his life, playing and discovering things instead of being carried around in my arms all the time. But it'd be so very easy to idle the day away kissing and cuddling Horton, holding him close and sniffing his fur. He always smells delightful. I'm not sure what it is but it's always nice, even when he needs a bath. I guess it's just his own special smell of lovely. When my friends have been here hugging him, and believe me everybody wants to hug Horton (well, apart from the ones who think they may hurt him, but once they are shown how to hold him properly they make a beeline for him as soon as they get in the door), you'd think I'd never spent any time hugging him, but when they've gone and I'm snuggling him or changing his nappy I can smell their perfume on him. He is so used to getting kisses now. I plant little kisses all over his face whenever I change his nappy and he'll just sit there, face tilted up, eyes closed, absorbing it all. When the nappy's done and he's wriggling because he wants to get going and I'm still kissing, I'll say to him, "Hold still. Mummy isn't finished showering you with love yet." Then I'll quickly put him down as I feel guilty for spoiling his fun when he wants to go off with the others.

Basically, Horton is just an all-round, easy going pug. It takes little effort to look after him but you do have to keep him in the back of your mind all the time. I'm always aware of the last time his nappy was changed, so I know when to check it again. He is reliant on me for everything and I can't have him sitting around in a wet nappy, getting a rash because I'm on the phone or a visitor has dropped by unexpectedly and I'm having a good chat. You should never take on a special needs dog if you don't have it in you to continue giving the care required day after day after day. If a special needs baby touches your heart, by all means do it, but what you need to do first is have a good think about the years you will have the dog in your home, the routine you must abide by, the cost of care, the time, the patience, the understanding. If you can't say one hundred percent that you are up for the job, can't meet all of the dog's needs, then in all fairness you should walk away, leave it to be adopted by somebody who can. A fast decision made because your heart strings have been pulled, tugged on, or very nearly stretched to breaking point is not the right reason to take on a special needs dog. The worst thing you can do is act on a whim. This is a breathing, living, feeling being. You don't want to muck the dog around. He or she has a right to be treated with the highest respect and thought given to how it is feeling. I'm not telling you not to take on a special needs dog; I'm just telling you to go away and have a real good think about it first, ask questions, do research, talk to somebody who has a dog with similar needs. There are always plenty of people to help and support you. And if, after having done all of this you still want the dog, still believe you can make a difference in its life, then I encourage you to grab the opportunity that awaits you with both hands. Because I can tell you from experience that you are in for one of the most beautiful, most precious, most memorable and most rewarding rides of your life and it is so well worth it. Also, the research you'll have done, and the questions you'll have gotten answers to will be an asset to you in the long run. But never feel guilty if you are not the type of person who can do this kind of thing, day after day. It isn't for everybody, but there is something everybody can to. You can foster, you can walk dogs that are in the pound or in foster care, you can knit blankets or coats, donate food or help raise money for the cause. There are so many little things to be done; you just have to find something that suits you and fits into your lifestyle. The needs are many and every little bit helps. And if you feel it in your heart to do any one of these things, well, all I can say is God bless you and thank you for that.

As a way of getting Horton used to his new name I used to say it over and over again during the day, whenever I picked him up for a snuggle or changed his nappy. And at night time, when I gave him his massage, I used his name as I stroked and caressed his little body. In no time he knew his name and responded with eagerness every time I used it. If he was facing the other way when I called, he'd spin around with such speed to see what I had called him for. His eyes would dart all over the place, firstly to my hands in case they held a treat then to my face to try and figure out what I was saying to him. He'd rush over to me when I held out my arms. If I had a clean Tinkle Trouser in my hand he knew it was nappy-change time and after a few weeks would scoot over to the chair I changed him on. With so many other pugs in the house and pugs being the curious little souls that they are, I found it easier to have Horton up off the ground when changing him. If he stayed on the floor he drew a crowd and when the others gathered he thought they'd come to play with him and there was no way he was going to let me change his nappy if he thought he was going to miss out on play time with his siblings. He'd wriggle and squirm and his brothers and sisters would stand between me and him, kissing me, kissing Horton, lunging at me for a snuggle or pawing at my arms for a pat. Others would try and sit on my knee. A few would actually climb on and stay there so I'd end up stroking them while Horton chased Emily round and round in circles, weeing as he went. It was just impossible to get the job done if Horton was on the ground, so he had to come up. I mean, don't get me wrong, those times were wonderful – any time spent with all the pugs gathering round were fantastic happy family moments – but if I was having a busy day or if Horton had just had a big wee it was unfair to leave him wet no matter how good a time we were all having. And on the odd occasions I did manage to get the job done while sitting in amongst all the fuss, Horton would be so excited at having everyone gathered round he'd end up weeing again as soon as the new nappy was on and so the whole thing had to be repeated.

I remember the very first time Horton had his nappy changed in the house; all the pugs came over to see what was going on. I held the new nappy out so that everyone could have a good look and sniff at the unfamiliar item I had in my hand. It was so new to them. It was new to me too but I at least had been told he was coming wearing one. The pugs had no idea what was going on.

They were so curious. A pile of flat noses sniffed and sniffed at the nappy for the longest time before finally wandering off. And although they all got used to the nappy in no time, the changing of it always held their interest, probably because of the way I carried on. If kisses were being given, everybody wanted to be a part of it.

Massage time was different. It was done at the end of the day when everyone was tired out. There was never any interference from anybody else at massage time. I could even massage Horton right next to a sleeping pug without his sibling waking up. I looked forward to giving Horton his nightly massages. I think I loved them more than he did, but he sure did love them a lot. I believe touch is important to the general wellbeing, for us and for the four-legged friends we share our life with. Touch conveys love and love conveys security. Touch connects you with one another. It lets you know you are not alone in this world. It doesn't matter how old you are, whether you've been born with skin, feathers or fur, touch is important to you and essential to your general wellbeing. I believe that's why elderly people with pets live longer than those who don't have them, especially when a spouse dies. I also know that our pets are a lot better at asking for touch than we are. Human beings put up barriers. They don't like to ask for that which they need in case it makes them appear weak or vulnerable. Dogs don't do that; they'll come and put their nose under your hand. I think we humans can learn a lot from our dogs. Touch brings comfort, not only in the body, but the heart and soul as well. Touch has a way of calming. It's reassuring. It lets you know somebody cares, somebody is there for you, that you are an important part of their life and I wanted Horton to feel all of this, to know he was no longer alone in this world, that he was now part of our large loving family. He was one of us. He was no longer an unwanted little puppy. He had a whole lot of family members, both two-legged and four- who thought he was marvellous and loved him with all their hearts. I was constantly telling him that I loved him but now I wanted him to feel it as well, and loving actions speak volumes to our fury family members. Those nightly massages not only helped his little body, I believe they helped his soul as well. I wanted him to develop into a strong, healthy pug. I wanted him to have a healthy immune system and I felt that if he was wrapped in love, felt secure, felt happy, well, all this would go towards helping him have the best shot at life. But mainly I started those massages to benefit his little body, keep him limber and supple and because I just couldn't stop touching him if I tried. Any amount of time with Horton was a wonderful experience.

If he was in a playful mood at the start I'd chase him around the bed with my hands a couple of times and when I caught him I'd tickle him or kiss him and he'd squeal and race off again with my hands running over the covers after him. After a few laps, all the giddiness would be out of him and he'd then come over and settle down so I could start with the long slow strokes. His little seashell feet were my favourite parts to massage. I loved them. They were so tiny, so beautiful, so perfect. They were so lovely and he was so lovely. Horton liked long massages but sometimes he'd fall asleep halfway through, which was a good thing because by that time my arthritic hands would be killing me. Other times, I'd think he was asleep and stop only to have him open one eye and then the other. If I wasn't back massaging by that time his little head would shoot up and he'd look around to see where I was and why I had stopped. If I was doing something for one of the other pugs he would come over and start tapping my arm with his paw. I think he thought it was all about him and I don't blame him because basically it was. He knew when it was 'his' time and he didn't appreciate his mummy being taken away. He wasn't naughty or demanding; it was more a gentle pat, as if to say, "Come back to me." And of course I never said no to him. As much as my arthritic fingers were screaming for a rest I'd start massaging again until he began snoring, then I'd only stop when I was positive he was fully asleep. But I couldn't just stop suddenly. That would wake him, so I used to pull one hand away and keep going with the other one. The strokes would become slower and slower until I felt he wouldn't notice if I stopped. Most of the time, this worked. Other times, I'd be about to pull my hand away when one of the other pugs would start barking at something and Horton would spring upright, fully awake, and start looking around the room to see what all the fuss was about. Sometimes, he'd join in and start doing little woofs and then of course all the lulling would have to begin all over again.

CHAPTER NINE

Horton Makes Some International Friends

I can clearly remember taking Horton's second birthday photos. His first birthday photos were done in a rush and although they were incredibly cute – I mean, how could they not be? Horton was in them – once I printed them out I realized just how mismatched they were colour-wise. Horton was big-eyed and beautiful but he was sitting there in a blue party hat with his green and yellow Tinkle Trousers on and there were two different coloured blankets on the chair with him. We had him sitting on a deep pink blanket that was folded over a few times to make him higher so he could reach the cake and a pastel pink blanket was slung over the chair behind him so that his little face would show up on the photos. The office chair was black and he was black and once I noted this I remember running back into the house and grabbing something pale to make his face stand out. In hindsight, I should have thought things through. With everything being so mismatched, I thought it made the poor soul look like a little orphan. Not that Horton minded any of that. His eyes were glued to his cake. It was a banana and blueberry muffin with a glob of mascarpone icing on top (not enough icing to make the pugs sick but enough to hold the one single candle in place). He was so happy when I brought that cake out. David was standing next to him so he wouldn't fall off the chair and when he saw me coming he started bouncing up and down. If David hadn't been there to keep hold of him I reckon he would have bounced himself right off the chair. I've never liked putting hats on dogs and before Horton came I'd never done it, but Horton was so special and I wanted to make the biggest fuss when he turned one. I think that party hat was on his head for only about thirty seconds, just long enough for me to take a few photos then, due to my feeling guilty about putting him through the ordeal, it came off as quickly as it had been put on and our one-year-old baby dived face-first into his cake.

I never lit the candle because I didn't want Horton lunging forward and singeing his little whiskers off. I suppose I could have done without the candle all together, but I put it on for show so that in later years, when looking back over the photos, we would know what year we were celebrating.

The other pugs were all on the ground gathered around Horton's chair, waiting for the muffin to be cut up. They each got a piece and so did our Clydesdale Gerald who was grazing near the veranda's edge and came over for a look at what all the excitement was about. Horton didn't seem to mind sharing. He got to have his piece of muffin first and also licked the crumbs off the plate. That was enough for him and to be honest, I don't even think he knew that all the singing and excitement was because of him. He probably thought the pugs were just having a special treat. Everybody always got in on the treats and today was no different.

Looking back, I'm glad we celebrated Horton's birthday the way we did. We always do something for the pugs on their birthdays but normally it's just a special meal that they all get to participate in and the pug whose birthday it is determines what the meal is going to be. You get to know their likes and dislikes so the meal is made up of what is special for them. And everybody loves joining in on birthday treats. Because our pugs are rescued it's impossible to know when their real birthdays are, so each year we celebrate the days they came into our lives. Those days are special for everybody in the house. They were the times when we got a new son or daughter and the pugs got a new brother or sister. Over the years, a few pugs have come with paperwork so their dates of birth were recorded, but that's a rarity for us.

Horton's second birthday photos were very different to his first. Much thought and effort was put in on my part because I made sure I had more time to plan. I felt really guilty about the previous year's rush and vowed to make Horton's second birthday one to remember. The green hat was bought in advance and I flipped over one of my pale green cake stands to bring the cake higher so it was easier for Horton to reach. Also, folded over the back of his chair was a cream-colored blanket that I thought made both Horton and his hat stand out. Black pugs are always harder to capture on film than fawns. I've taken some photos of my black pugs that I thought were perfect only to have their facial details disappear when I got them printed out. With blacks, the light has to be hitting their faces at just the right angle otherwise you get nothing. You especially get nothing if they happen to be asleep because then it's just an all-black face and you're left trying to guess where their nose and eyes are. I reckon I take more photos of my pugs sleeping than when they're awake. I just physically cannot walk past a beautiful sleeping pug and not creep back across the room to grab my camera. I just can't do it. They are so incredibly cute when they're asleep that I have to stop what I'm doing and take the shot. My house is overflowing with framed photos of glorious, squishy-faced pugs in different stages of slumber. They take forever to dust but I don't care because as I clean I stop and admire their beauty and recall the memory of taking the photo.

Horton's second birthday photos were so wonderful and I was so proud of them that I wanted to share them with everyone. I wasn't on Facebook at the time but I sent them to everyone I knew, everyone who had met Horton and loved him, everyone who had never met him but fell in love with him regardless. I was just so proud of both Horton and the photos because I thought they were perfect. I was proud of Horton for everything he had achieved in the past two years and the photos because I thought they were the best pug photos I had ever seen. The true personality of my son was captured perfectly by the lens. His mischievous spirit, his beautiful, squishy, velvety face, his slight head tilt that he did when he was thinking; it was all there, captured beautifully for everyone to see. So, being the proud mum that I am, I wanted everyone to see it. The lighting was ideal, although to be honest that was just a fluke because in concentrating on Horton and how cute he was, I'd not given the lighting a second thought, but we lucked out in that area regardless and I was grateful for that because it meant Horton's little wrinkles and black whiskers were in full view, not concealed like they had been so many times before. I just think we were blessed in that moment with the most perfect amount of light and sunshine. And again it was only for a few precious moments because I didn't want the hat on him any longer than it had to be.

This year, Horton seemed to be more involved with what was going on. He had been with us long enough to know when we were talking to him or, in this case, singing to him. He heard his name in the birthday song and seemed to acknowledge that I'd said it. He sat in his chair eyeing up the cake, but he did look up at me when I sang his name.

Below is the email I sent out to everyone when Horton turned two.

"Thought I'd send you a few photos of Horton's second birthday. We took the photos on Saturday as David is away on business all this week. Horton loved all the attention when we were taking the photos, not that he's ever short of it, mind you, but the cake, the singing – he seems to know it's all for him and loved every second of it.

Can't believe he's two already. It's just gone so fast and the time we've had him has been so special. Honestly, I think I could write a book on the many joys of Horton; well, if not a book, definitely an essay and a long one at that – the happiness he's brought into our lives, the love, the laughter at his antics, the courage he's shown in overcoming obstacles. The extra work with a special needs dog is minimal and the rewards ongoing. We consider ourselves lucky to be his parents, to be able to watch him grow, to have witnessed his small body get stronger and his personality develop into the confident little soul that he is today.

David and I count our blessings every day. We wonder what we did to be so lucky to have Horton in our lives. There is just something very special about him. I know I'm his mum so I'd be saying it anyway but other people see it too. He has an effect on people. He can bring a smile to even the most miserable face in the street. He gets people in with his huge eyes and multiple expressions. He has all the regular pug expressions and more.

Horton is a little dynamo, a real live wire who enjoys every aspect of living. He has two speeds – full-on and sleeping – or maybe it's more like one speed and a snooze button. He's curious, into everything and looking around for more. If one of the others barks, no matter what part of the house Horton is in, he's there in half a second, pushing his way to the front to see what's going on. If one of his sisters runs around the house with a soft toy, Horton is not far behind, scooting along the floor doing his funny little bark. And when they drop the toy he'll pounce and shake the living hell out of it before running off to find something else to do.

Speaking of his bark, it's so wonderful to hear. He still barks like a puppy. We think it's due to his condition. He'll never have a big boy bark and we are kind of glad. We've seen him change a lot from when he first came and we used to say to one another how sad it will be when he grows out of his baby bark. Previously having all old dogs, his puppy bark was precious to our ears, a real novelty that we hadn't had the joy of hearing for a good many years. We'd stop and listen to it in the early days, trying to soak it in in the hope of embedding it in our hearts and memories forever. We said we'd record it and never got round to it but it doesn't matter because he still has it and it's lovely.

Changing his nappy never gets boring, no matter how long I've been doing it. I thought it may but it hasn't. No matter how busy I am it's still a pleasure, an honour, a privilege. It's what enables Horton to live life. When he came I told him that if he could take in and expel nutrients on his own that's marvellous because his dad and I would take care of the rest. Nappy-change time is also a chance to have a little talk to him, to kiss his ears and tell him I love him. Then the nappy is done and he's off again until next time.

I wake up happy in the mornings because Horton is in my life, and with my other pugs my cup overflows. I just wanted to share Horton's special day with you. Oh, and about the essay, I think I just wrote it, lol. But he's so wonderful and to think he was scheduled to be put to sleep at twelve weeks of age.

Regards

Horton's Mummy "

I got a lot of response from sending this email. People responded to the photos by saying it was like they could just reach out and touch him and they loved hearing about his year as well. In fact, the email was sent on to a lot of other people that we didn't even know, because friends and family thought Horton was the most beautiful little thing and his story should be shared with as many animal-loving people as it could be. And because of that email, out of all my pugs here on Grace Farm, Horton is the most well-known, the one I'm most asked about. His name is always remembered above the rest and that's because he has become special to a whole lot of people. Really Horton is the reason I started writing about my pugs in the first place. Before Horton, we had never put birthday hats on pugs, partly because in the back of my mind I thought it was kind of cruel. A lot of dogs don't like it.

It isn't a natural state for them; it's more a hoot for the owners really. But with Horton I just had this incredible urge to make a bigger deal out of his birthdays, to record them in every way possible and to have a row of Horton's birthday photos on the wall behind my desk. I figured in the end I'd have at least twelve. A dozen beautiful happy photos that recorded Horton's life, our life with him and the way his little face was changing over the years. There is a huge difference between his first and second birthday photos. Horton went from a round-faced, chubby pup to a mature, chiselled-looking boy. A year can make a big difference in a little pug's life. In the future, each photo will have a different coloured hat, there'll be more and more unlit candles on each cake and every year the photos will be taken in a different part of the farm. As I held his beautifully framed first and second birthday photos side by side I started planning what I was going to do for his third birthday and how great that was going to be.

I had a lot of questions asked about Horton after the email was sent out. It was nice that strangers had taken him into their hearts, so I sent a backup email telling them all a little bit more about my special boy. Below is my response email to the second birthday questions.

"Thank you for your interest in my lovely boy. Horton is a special needs pug, although Horton himself isn't aware of it. He was born with hemivertebra, a curving of the spine, which prevents him from using his back legs the way other dogs do. He also needs to wear a nappy as his condition causes pressure on his bladder so he can't be housetrained, but in spite of all of this he does beautifully. He just gets on with life regardless of his disabilities. He is a fighter with a will of steel and he's overcome

many obstacles to get to where he is today. If love could make Horton walk he would have been upright a very long time ago, and once walking I'd say he'd be the fastest little pug in the world if, like I said, love could make it so, but it can't and I have come to accept that. It doesn't worry me, though, because Horton is just fine; well, much more than fine actually. He is fantastic just as he is. He is amazing and such a light in my life I could literally write page after page about little Horton's early struggles, his antics, his love of life and the enormous amount of happiness that dwells inside this little pug's body. Please don't feel sorry for Horton because he doesn't need it, but if you are the praying kind I would appreciate it if you kept him in your prayers.

Thank you.
Take care
Andrea Comer"

When Horton turned one I was going to write a long email telling my friends how he was going, but Ruby was sick at the time and I just didn't get round to doing it. I shot a quick email off saying he had just turned one, he received a few birthday wishes back and that was it, over and done with. We didn't even get round to taking his one-year-old birthday photos until much later on. It was just one of those busy times in a house full of elderly pugs, so the poor little soul had to be pushed aside for a while until things settled down. I felt awful about it but Horton for his part didn't seem to care. He just enjoys his life no matter what's happening in his day. He throws himself into life at full speed. He's like one of those pull-back action cars; if his legs are the right way round when putting him on the floor he zooms off as fast as lightning as soon as he makes contact with the ground. Then he's off exploring and is just about the happiest little pug anyone ever met. I think people look at Horton, at his awkward-looking body, his funny back legs and his curved spine, and feel that his disability should be reflected in his nature somewhere. But Horton doesn't see himself the way other people see him. He was born into that body, it's the only body he's ever known and so he worked out what to do with it, figured out how best to maneuver himself so he could keep up with the rest of the pugs and off he goes, no looking back. It's as if he was dealt a blow, blew it out and got on with life regardless. When people hear about Horton they start to feel sorry for him and I say don't; he doesn't feel sorry for himself at all so why should you? I also tell them they can come and meet him if they want to because nothing changes a person's mind about Horton faster than Horton himself does. I also tell people to leave negative feelings at the front gate because dogs can pick up on emotions so quickly. We have elderly and special needs pugs living happily here and I won't allow anybody to dampen our spirits. That is why when Horton turned two I made a real effort to make it special, to kind of make up for the previous year, and put the time aside to sit down and write a bit about Horton to send off with a few birthday photos. Well, Horton's second birthday email and the backup email I sent out made their way onto Facebook and after that they took on a life of their own. At the time I didn't even know what Facebook was. I had heard the name and been asked a few times to join but being techno-challenged I didn't take it any further. It was all a weird unknown world to me and I was happy to leave it that way. Strangers who Horton and I had never met got to read about our life and to be honest, that really freaked me out.

Here I was sitting on my little farm with my sweet pug family and suddenly people all over the world were finding out who we were and that panicked me. I think I was a bit naïve about the power of the internet. But the folks who wrote to me were very nice so I decided to join Facebook, but when all these people started asking to be my friend I'd have to walk out onto the veranda and deep breathe. It was all so new to me and a little bit scary, but people loved Horton so I just tried to concentrate on that. People who were having a bad day got to read the email as did dog lovers and rescuers who needed to hear some good news. Animal lovers all over the world got to read Horton's story and wrote back to me, saying how he had touched their lives. Horton was already a well-known and popular little boy amongst friends and family but that email changed everything. I was a bit shocked at the reaction Horton received. For a long time my friends in rescue kept saying to me that Horton's story needed to be told, but I was reluctant. I think in the back of my mind I wanted to shield him or I thought to broadcast his progress would somehow demean all the effort he had put into becoming the pug he is today. I suppose I didn't want to make a spectacle of him, didn't want to draw attention to the fact that he was different. I suppose in my mind doing this was my way of protecting him. Then again, maybe I was merely putting my own feelings first. Perhaps if I was in the same position I wouldn't want attention drawn to me, but I don't think Horton sees it that way. He loves being talked to, acknowledged, doted on. I prefer blending into the background, but Horton doesn't mind taking center stage. And I think it would be wrong of me to deny him these things just because I'm a shy person. If I go to a party I'll spend my time hiding in a corner avoiding the crowd, but if

Horton could talk I think he'd be sitting in the middle of that crowd telling a joke or two. He'd be holding court, drawing people in with his magnetic personality. Well perhaps not sitting in the middle of the room because he doesn't like loud noises or loud people but he certainly would be out talking to folks and enjoying the party, not hiding in the corner praying for the night to end the way I have done so many times in my life.

From the feedback, I came to realize that it would be a mistake not to share Horton's story with other people. It would be selfish of me not to let him touch other lives. He's touched mine and made it better, richer, happier; it would be unfair of me to keep Horton to myself. In a way I believe David and I are merely Horton's guardians. He is not our possession. Horton belongs to everyone who was born with love in their hearts for the animals of this world. He belongs to everybody who has loved a dog and lost them, to everyone who has read or heard a story of animal abuse and cried. He gives hope back to those people who've suffered loss and brings a smile back to the faces of those who have forgotten how to. Horton belongs to everybody who loves him and is a part of every life he has ever touched. I'm not saying that he's a miracle worker; he is really just a little black pug who was born with a disability and has not allowed his condition to hold him back and that in itself seems to have an impact on people.

I became aware of this when a friend of mine (well, more of a friend of Horton's actually, because she loves him a lot more than she does me, I'm sure of it) told me one day that Horton was a little bit hers. I think she was unsure of how I'd react being so in love with him and all, but I just looked at her nodded and said, "Yes, yes he is," and I meant it. I got it. I knew what she was saying and it was a turning point. It was then I realized that Horton touched people. Once you've met him or read his story he stays with you. There is a lot of sadness in this world we live in – people have to cope with so much in their day-to-day lives; there is sickness and loss and heartache and sorrow – and if Horton's story can bring a bit of relief, bring a bit of happiness, put a smile on somebody's face then I shouldn't be trying to stop that. That same friend had a dog that was a little bit like Horton, not anywhere near as bad she tells me, but she lost her dog too soon and mourns him to this day. She had my heart on hearing that because I have been in her shoes a few times over the years. When Horton came into her life I think she saw a little bit of her dog in him and it touched her heart. I believe with Horton she was getting back a little bit of what she had lost. She felt connected to him and I understood that. And for his part he loved her from the very first second they met and I was glad he took to her so quickly and easily. Perhaps Horton sensed she was in pain and needed to be loved.

I get a lot of people talking to me about their dogs and I like hearing their stories. They may be sad at times but I believe it helps to share with a like-minded soul. As animal lovers, we should be there for one another so that's what I've always tried to do.

CHAPTER TEN

Personality Trumps Legs Every Single Time

Although Horton's legs get a whole lot of attention, the truth of the matter is that they are not the biggest part of him. They are an important part of him because he does need that extra care, but there is so much more to him than the fact that his back legs don't work properly. Actually, his spine is where the issues lie. If it wasn't curved the way it is he would be able to walk upright, but because people can't see his spine clearly and his little legs are kind of out there, this is what people are drawn to when looking at my son. I wouldn't say it annoyed me when people used to focus solely on his legs but I did think it was a great pity because it meant they overlooked the true essence of what made Horton Horton. I mean, I got it; there aren't too many paraplegic dogs out there, they're not the sights people see all the time and I suppose if I was only seeing glimpses of Horton not living with him every day I also may be a tad too preoccupied with his legs. But I thought it was a real shame that people allowed those sweet little back legs of his to overshadow everything else about him. And you can't go drawing people's attention to the fact that he has a mischievous personality, is incredibly intelligent and super adventurous or has more determination in that tiny body of his than anybody else I know. These are the things people will discover for themselves should they be lucky enough to spend a lot more time in Horton's presence. But once they put that which is obvious out of their minds, they get to witness the real Horton and how much he loves life. They also get to see his playful, fun side.

And then you'll get the people who say the only reason he enjoys life so much is because he nearly lost his at twelve weeks of age and I guess that's part of it, but I think Horton is enjoying life regardless of the fact that his back legs don't work as well as they should. After all, this is the body he was born with. He doesn't know how to be any other way. I think he just knows he's got one shot at life and is going to enjoy it regardless of his situation and I believe we can all learn from that.

Still, I've not come across anybody who's gotten to know Horton properly who hasn't agreed that the one best word to describe him is joyful. Pugs are a cheerful bunch, they're a fantastic little breed, but Horton has a way of taking it to an entirely new level. He is just the happiest, most joyous little being there ever was. From the time he wakes up to the time he goes to bed he's happy – happy discovering new things, happy watching everything that's going on, happy with farm life, happy with his large pug family and happy to kiss every face that comes within a few inches of his own, whether it be me, one of his siblings or a visitor to the house. People say he's happy because he's grateful to be alive but really, shouldn't we all be grateful to be alive regardless of our circumstances, regardless of where we live, what we do for a living or who we share our life with? We've all only got one shot at this life, we'd be pretty stupid not to make the most of it. Also, if we don't like something we do, have the ability to change it, even if it's only one small step at a time, that's what makes us lucky to be born human. Most animals in this world don't have a choice, don't have control over their circumstance, but we do. That's why it always annoys me when people start complaining about their lives. It's like, "Buck up will you?" It could be worse. At least you weren't born a steer whose life will be cut short for beef, a battery hen, a pig, a sheep, a goat or a dog or cat born into a world where dumb asses don't de-sex and where pounds overflow.

I firmly believe Horton is joyful because that's just the nature that was born in him. Joy was the first word I used when emailing my friend in rescue the night Horton came. When I finally got on the computer to let her know Horton had arrived safely and was doing well there were three emails waiting for me from her. I think she was worried about him, worried about how he was doing, worried about what we thought of him. Perhaps she thought, having now seen Horton in the flesh, we may have been having second thoughts. Maybe we thought he would be too much to look after, but she needn't have worried because I loved him from the start. "You had me at hello" doesn't even come close to how I felt about Horton and how quickly, madly and deeply I fell in love with him. I believe the first sentence I wrote to her was that Horton was pure joy, just pure pure joy, that I loved him and that he had puppy breath and I was ecstatic because I hadn't been blessed with puppy breath in the house for a good many years. She wrote back saying only a true mother would be that excited about puppy breath. I think the way I was gushing about Horton and how wonderful he was must have put her mind at ease and calmed her heart because she didn't email me again to see how he was doing for well over a week.

Maybe you think I overuse the word joy, but this little pug just exudes it. He delights in everything this world has to offer. If he sees a puddle he'll paw at it then squeal with delight at the splashing sound he's just made. He'll circle round, all the while stopping to make the splashing noise again, then when he can't hold off any longer he'll jump right in. He loves having a bath, licks at the water while I'm washing him and when he hears me filling up the sink he'll bounce on the floor by my feet and practically leap off the ground when I bend down to pick him up. I always wash him in the kitchen sink because he's so little he'd end up getting lost in the laundry trough. Horton likes the hose, the sprinkler and even my water feature. Water in any form appeals to him, but he's always gotten overly excited at the sound of running water because he knows there's a whole lot of fun to be had there.

The day he discovered ants will be embedded in my mind forever. He was on the veranda in the sun with a few of the other pugs and I was inside doing the dishes. When I'm inside and he's outside I've always got one ear listening out, making sure he's all right. This day I heard a high-pitched squealing. It didn't even sound like Horton, but I knew it wasn't Steffy our resident high-pitched screamer. Horton squeals and Steffy screams and there is a whole world of difference in those two sounds, believe me. I took off my rubber gloves and headed for the door. It wasn't quite the scream of a pug that'd hurt itself but it wasn't a noise I was comfortable with either. The two pugs that'd been inside snoozing on the couch leapt down fast and were at my heel in no time. I couldn't see Horton at first which made me start to panic then as I turned the corner, there he was, sitting in the sun along the front of the house yelling his little head off because he'd discovered a trail of ants. It was the first time in his life he'd seen one ant, let alone hundreds of them, and his eyes were enormous with excitement.

A few of the oldies wandered over to have a look at what all the fuss was about and on realizing it was just a trail of boring ants, walked off in disgust. It was like they felt they'd been tricked into being made to get up and wander over at their delicate ages, tricked into thinking there was something much more interesting over there for them to look at. I think their little brother's enthusiasm fooled them. It took a lot to get Ruby on her feet once she was comfortable and she stood giving Horton one of her long slow irritated looks before finally waddling back to her comfy cushion.

Horton sat watching the long line of busy, marching ants going about their business. He was fixated, totally mesmerized, couldn't take his eyes off them for very long. He'd glance over at me and in his expression acknowledged I was there. His ears shifted and his little face softened when he saw me but then it was back to his fascinating find. Not wanting to miss out on what they were doing he shuffled his body a bit closer then closer again. I think the fact that I was now out there with him gave him the confidence to go have a better look. He peeped round the side of the post to see if there were any more ants round there. There was. I watched his head go from side to side then up and down as he followed the line along the front of the veranda then up and down the post. His little eyes were alive with excitement. He looked to me like he was following one or two particular ants only but would then lose sight of them in the assembly line or when they got too high up the post. His head would bob around a bit until he found another couple to watch then he'd zero in on those. I could see by the tilt of his head that they were where his main focus lay. He'd watch closely as they came down the post and began marching along the veranda's edge. Sometimes he'd scoot along after them, follow them along until once again they got lost in the crowd. I began to wonder whether he was fascinated to see where they were going or just happy watching them move. I didn't know what was going through his mind at the time but I sure wish I did. I would have given anything to know what Horton was thinking in that moment. I stood watching him watch the ants for a while and he was lovely, just a sweet little puppy who'd discovered something new in the world he was living in. That moment will be with me for the rest of my life and to think if I was preoccupied with what was going on inside the house I would have missed it. Sometimes we can get caught up in what we think is important only to miss out on the real joys in life. Yes, the dishes and the housework could wait but that moment with Horton couldn't. I'm so glad I paused. I'm glad I watched and I'm glad I got to witness something so beautiful.

It made me realize just how important saving Horton's life was. He was so easy to look after and asked for little in return. If things had gone the way the breeder planned he wouldn't have been out there discovering ants and squealing with excitement, he wouldn't have been around discovering the ladybirds, grasshoppers, dragonflies and Christmas beetles that followed. We would never have known how much he loved water and splashing in puddles, that he falls asleep halfway through his night time massage or that he likes to chase the sheep and actually thinks he can catch them. Or that he seeks Emily out when he wants to chew on somebody's tummy and one of the old nana pugs when he wants comfort and a peaceful presence after a big day. All these things would never have been if that beautiful big personality of his had been allowed to be extinguished at twelve weeks of age. This life of his that I'm telling you about would never have happened. You wouldn't be reading about him now. David and I would not have been allowed to love him as a son and his siblings would never have known the joy of their little brother. All this would have been taken away from so many purely because a breeder considered him useless.

Horton and our others pugs have always been involved with everything David and I do around the farm: gathering wood, dishing out hay to the livestock; if we're planting a tree they are right there beside us, even when digging a hole they are with us. Of course caution is taken so that Horton or one of the blind ones don't fall in, but unless the job we are doing is dangerous for them they are all there with us enjoying what is going on. It's the way we have always lived our lives. It's incredibly important to us that our pugs be involved in our activities. I think it's good for them to keep their minds and bodies working and nothing keeps these things in top form better than living full and interesting lives. Nothing is ever done around here unless it's done as a family. If we are going to be outdoors for a while blankets are brought out for the oldies to lie on so that they can be near us in comfort. The deaf ones come out and have a look at what's going on and the blind ones all get up close for a sniff. We like to let them all be involved as much as they can be and there are always two sets of eyes on all of them, making sure nobody is in harm's way. We always take precautions. In fact, we are probably overcautious if anything. We're always on the lookout so that nobody ends up getting hurt. If David is using the spade I'll take Horton and the blind ones off to the side so they don't walk in the way and get hurt. And I'm proud to say that in all the years we've been doing this we've never had an accident. Of course this means that jobs do take a lot longer than they normally would, but we're okay with that. We figure, why rescue all these pugs only to leave them inside when we're outside doing something? That wouldn't be fair, not to them, not to us. I have to admit that a lot of our farm jobs aren't the most exciting things in the world to be doing, but doing them with a pile of curious pugs and everything changes. They love it and we love it.

Most of the pugs that come to Grace Farm to live out their lives are elderly. Horton was the first puppy we've ever taken in. Our hearts lie with these poor elderly souls tossed out of their homes because they have done nothing more than grow old. But I feel the cruelness would continue if we brought them here to live lesser lives. I feel you can get a longer life out of an old dog if you give them something to wake up for in the morning. And, no, I don't just mean breakfast. As much as food is an important part of every pug's day, I believe their daily walks, their interaction with the livestock and their involvement in everything that's going on here on the farm makes life more interesting for them. They have a routine and they love it. I know they love it because if we have a day where the routine is altered, even by a little bit, a pile of old flat faces look up at us with disgust. We can't even cut a walk short if we're pushed for time because they know, they always know. We can't get anything past them. You may think at times they are old and maybe a bit cloudy minded because of it, but they react as quick as a whip and have no trouble letting you know when you try and take something they like doing away from them. Ruby especially won't tolerate her walks being cut short. She'll stand in the middle of the paddock and won't even turn round to look at us because she knows if we catch her eye we'll end up calling her back and she doesn't want to come back. She wants to finish her normal walk so she'll stand there and wait until the walk continues. I've even turned and walked back to the house. The other pugs eventually follow but not Ruby. That little old girl stands her ground. I'm always the one who goes back. If she's been left for a while she'll eventually get tired and sit down but always with her back facing the direction she knows I'm coming from. And she'll listen for me too and knows full well when I'm approaching. She'll then stand up and scurry off as soon as I get close. She'll even walk in the rain. I don't really like my oldies getting wet. I like to keep them warm, safe and dry but sometimes it's easy to misjudge the clouds and end up caught in the middle of a paddock in a rainstorm, but still Ruby refuses to take a shortcut back to the house. Rain, hail or shine, she wants her full walk and will make sure she gets it, so I keep a stack of towels by the back door to dry them all off as soon as we come in. I believe that's why I get some of the pugs to live longer than they normally would, because they are kept active and their minds are kept active. They are loved and they know they are loved and who wouldn't want to stick around for more of that?

I think as owners we have to be constantly looking at things from our dogs' point of view. Some people don't give this much thought and I believe we need to in order to make our dogs as happy as they can be. If we don't pause and think about what our dogs' lives are like how will we know if they are enjoying them? Some have come here on their last legs and gone on to live a few more decent years. You give them time to settle in, adjust to the upheaval that has just become their lives and that's it; they begin to trust you, start to fall in love with you, start to feel at home here and begin looking forward to their days. It's pretty simple really. No magic formula, just a whole lot of love and a pile of understanding and they come good. I like spending my days in their company. They make me laugh all the time with the things they get up to. Pugs are just about the most curious breed that ever lived. They are inquisitive little beings that love getting in on what you are doing. If I'm in the garden they're right there with me, sniffing and digging at the dirt. If I'm busy in the shed they all lay in the entrance where the sun has warmed up the concrete. Whatever I'm doing they're always there beside me seeing how they can get involved and this little farm of mine is ideal for them because, regardless of the season, there is always something happening here.

Horton used to worry me at times with those little back legs of his; before he started kicking them they used to get so cold. We'd always make sure to do the jobs in decent weather, but you can't always pick it as much as you try to. Sometimes when it clouded over I would feel Horton's legs and they'd be really cold, so I'd carry him inside. I'd change him then rub his legs until they were warm and set him up in a bed beside the window so he could watch us while keeping warm. I'd go back outside and carry on with what we were doing, but keep looking up at the house, making sure he was all right and every time he would be bouncing up and down and pawing at the window wanting to come back out. Although I couldn't hear him, I knew he was crying because his little mouth would keep opening and shutting. He hated being locked up, hated missing out on the fun. He had a few of the oldies in with him because it was too cold for them to be out there but that didn't seem to settle him down. They had all gone to sleep but he was there watching everything and wanting to be involved. I hated seeing him like that. Some days I left him and we'd finish up the job quickly so we could all go back inside and be together. Other times, David finished up while I went inside to be with Horton, but most times I went and got him, put him inside my jacket and brought him back outside. Horton used to love that, but the truth was I loved it more. He'd then watch the job being finished with his little head peeping out of the zipper. His body would be warm as toast and he didn't have to miss out on a thing. He smelt so beautiful and his fur was so soft but the most important thing was that he was warm and he used to warm me up too. It was like having a little hot water bottle strapped to me and I could feel his heart beating against my chest. I'd put my hand underneath and cup his little legs up so they weren't dangling down because that would have defeated the purpose.

Sometimes, I'd do this on the walks as well: carry him around the open paddocks under my jumper when he'd tired himself out. It was skin on fur and a lovely time of bonding with him, a special time for mother and son. The other pugs carried on walking and sniffing but Horton was cold and when he was cold the sniffing game no longer interested him. His little face would be peeping out inches from mine. I'd kiss his ears and talk to him, telling him how precious he was to me. I'd just talk to him about anything really while always keeping an eye on where his brothers and sisters were and what they were doing. Sometimes he'd fall asleep. If he was warm and particularly comfortable his little eyes would shut and I'd feel him snoring. I didn't even have to look down; I could feel his breathing changing and eventually the vibration of his puppy snores against my chest. At night, Horton snored so loudly that we could hear him above all the others. He could even out-snore his dad and that's saying something. I mean they all snore (well, Harper never did; she just gave little breathy huffs in her sleep), but in this house the two black pugs are by far the worst snorers we have. Not that it matters really because I believe I am at a point in my life now where I don't think I could sleep without a chorus of snoring pugs in the background. It's music for my dreams. At night, Horton gets into such a deep sleep that he sounds like scrap metal being put through a wood chipper, but in my arms it was more of an idling truck type of snoring and it was lovely that he felt so at ease in my embrace that he would fall asleep.

CHAPTER ELEVEN

Grace Farm

I have always been in awe of the way Horton handled himself around the farm. He was courageous in so many ways. The boldness with which he scooted up to the fence to look at the livestock amazed me. By pug standards, Horton is a very small pug. At his heaviest he barely hit 6kg. The sheep weigh 80-120kg and the horses so much more, yet he seemed to love them all and held no fear in his heart for any one of them. He would scoot towards them with such speed and sit by the fence watching their movements for hours. It was like he couldn't get enough of them. He must have thought they were the most fascinating things he had ever seen. Sometimes he'd do little woofs, especially if they were grazing in the distance and he wanted them to come over. Other times, he'd be content to go up and down the fence-line sniffing with the other pugs. When he got tired of sitting up, he would lie beside the mesh and watch everything that was going on. Gerald, our Clydesdale, weighs over 600kg and he was one of Horton's favourites. For some reason he loved him more than anybody else out in the paddock. Maybe it's the smell or the way he looks. Gerald is striking. He is a Clydesdale crossed with a Welsh

179

Mountain pony: my two favourite horses. He has the Roman nose and the white splash on the belly, the socks, the feathers, everything a normal Clydesdale has only he's not as tall. He looks like a miniature Clydesdale actually, just a shrunken down version of a regular Clydesdale. Then again, perhaps it had nothing to do with looks. Maybe Horton just connected with Gerald's calmness. Gerald has the lovely, quiet, peaceful nature that the giant horse breeds are all blessed with. Horton singled Gerald out very early on as somebody he wanted to spend a lot of time with. He was so taken with him that after a while we just started calling Gerald Horton's horse. I'd say to Horton, "Come on, let's go see what your horse is doing today," and we'd go out and see if Gerald was in view. Horton knew what I meant because as soon as I said Gerald's name he would rush to the back door and wait for me to take him outside. If Gerald was down the back he'd come flying up as soon as he saw us. I think Horton thought he was galloping up solely to see him, not for the carrot I had in my back pocket, and would almost bounce out of my arms until he was on the ground.

Gerald could be a tyrant around the sheep; he has no trouble displaying his dominance, likes being the king and bosses them terribly at times but he was never like that with the pugs. Yes, he liked some more than others but for a horse who didn't like dogs when we first rescued him I think he's done pretty well for himself. Of course due to the size differences the pugs, Gerald and the sheep are never in the same area wandering freely, there is always a fence between them as my main priority here on the farm is to keep everybody safe at all costs.

The pugs are fascinated with the livestock when they first land on Grace Farm. Most have never seen or smelt a sheep or a horse before so they are always drawn over to the larger paddocks at some point during the settling-in period. Some are more adventurous than others and go over right away to have a look, they've been here less than an hour and they are over by the fence peeping through the mesh, whereas some take a while to discover there are larger animals living on the property. Our blind pugs take the longest. Obviously, they smell the livestock faster than the seeing pugs do because their sense of smell is heightened, but I guess they figure it's just another one of the many different smells associated with their new home. There are smells of hay and roses and Cypress trees and sounds of Kookaburras and other native birds, just so very many different bird calls to get used to and so the sounds of the paddock dwellers seem to take a backseat sometimes. For obvious reasons, in all areas our blind pugs tend to be more cautious, not just with approaching the fences but with everything around the farm. Although there have been a few who've gone over to the fence-line for a wee and seem to have no idea there is a huge horse standing on the other side of the fence peering down at them. I guess they would sense Gerald's mass and they'd definitely be able to smell his hair and hear him breathing, yet they seem oblivious to it. Maybe empting one's bladder is very important to a little old pug. Maybe it's the only thing on their mind at the time or perhaps it's because of the fact that Gerald is so calm they are able to sense there's nothing to fear. Either that or they simply have no interest in horses and are happy enough to live their lives here without giving the largest family member a second thought.

Gerald is always funny when he notices a new pug in amongst the pack. I guess he can smell them as much as they can smell him and comes running down the paddock. The sheep can tell when there's a new pug on the property, too, but are nowhere near as interested. They are aware but don't feel the need to meet face-to-face right away. I suppose they feel there's plenty of time to make acquaintances when their bellies are full. Gerald is more curious. The sheep look up then carry on grazing. It would be different if they thought the pugs were a threat to their lambs, but they know there's no threat there and carry on with what they're doing. Gerald, on the other hand, wants to know everything that's happening on his farm. If something is new, be it a pug or a newly planted tree, he's right there watching it all. Gerald comes trotting up then stops midway, snorts a few times then starts picking at the grass, all the while slowly creeping up on them. He likes to check them out from a distance first in case they go all 'crazy pug' on him, which has happened in the past with a few pugs that have no idea what the hell a horse is. When he's observed them for a while he'll wander over, bend his head down and sniff. If the pug is still calm then he'll poke his nose through the small square holes in the mesh and sniff some more. He can only get the tip of his nose through but on occasion he has given one of the new pugs a lick. To date this has only happened with two pugs, Horton and Arthur. Horton saw it coming and was a little bit taken aback. He didn't really know what to make of it but he didn't try to move away. He wasn't scared; he just sat looking up at Gerald with a perplexed look on his face. The size different between the two of them was amazing. If I was as little as Horton and was sitting beside something that huge I think I'd be pretty terrified. But Horton displayed no fear. He was more mystified I think. I don't know if it was the size of Gerald's nose Horton was most impressed with or the fact that his tongue was so long it reached through the fence and curled around his chin. Arthur, on the other hand, is blind and had no idea what had just happened to him. He stopped suddenly, paused for a few moments trying to figure it out then carried on walking. I think its Gerald's way of welcoming the special needs pugs to the farm. It's like he is saying, "I know all is not right with you but I'm letting you know you are going to be okay here."

Somebody once told me that I shouldn't put human feelings on animals because they don't feel emotions the same way we do, but I think that's wrong. It can't be a coincidence that a horse has singled out two special needs pugs to kiss, and if that did happen by chance then I have dozens more stories of similar experiences taking place. I think people don't give animals nearly the amount of credit they deserve. Maybe because it's easier to say they are unfeeling and unintelligent, then they don't have to feel bad about neglecting or abusing them. Gerald once lived in a riding school. He was subjected to a terrible life there. Horses have incredible memories. They never forget mistreatment or the face behind the hand that struck them. We can't for certain know what is going on in the minds of the animals we share our life with, but what I do know for sure is that they are more like us than most of us will ever know. They feel hurt and pain just as deeply as we do, they feel elation too, and happiness and love and they grieve, I've witnessed them doing it, and that's why it's so important for each of us to do all we can to bring joy into their lives.

When Gerald came here he was unsure of men but David's kind loving spirit and his calm quiet nature worked wonders on him. He won him over in no time. Gerald has healed nicely during his time on the farm and I believe this is why he connects with some of our pugs more than others. It was a learning curve for David as well; he had never been around horses before. He'd been to a riding school once as a kid but that was where his experience ended. Yet he took to them beautifully. I sort of threw him in at the deep end. If he was scared he didn't let on so I don't think he was, which was a good thing because horses can sense fear and insecurity. They are super-intelligent beings. I think he was more uncertain of what they were going to do because he'd never been around horses before so had no idea what was going on in their minds. I just told him to use slow movements around Gerald, no sudden or unexpected moves, otherwise it'd unsettle him. No waving your arms around; let him see where your hands are at all times and if he was reaching out to stroke him to do it nice and slowly, all the while talking in a calm voice as he went. I've found most of the abuse suffered by larger animals, big dogs, big horses, is done by weak men trying to prove their masculinity. You can tell a lot about a man by the way he treats an animal. Well, that's the way I've always judged them anyway and it's a pretty accurate way of assessing somebody.

One morning after Gerald had been with us for about four weeks I was busy doing something so gave David the halter and sent him in the back paddock to bring Gerald up. He'd never seen a halter before and wasn't sure how it went on. I thought, well, he'll either come round the corner in a while empty-handed or he'll be leading Gerald. Next time I looked up from what I was doing there was David and Gerald standing together in the entrance of the shed watching me. I've never seen a guy looking more pleased with himself in my life. I smiled both on the outside and the inside that day I can tell you. After that, I would watch my husband out in the open paddocks with Gerald and Pride. Sometimes he'd take the slow movement thing a little too far and end up looking like somebody doing Tai chi. I could have laughed real hard and loud at that and believe me I really wanted to at times, but he was being cautious and respectful to the horses, so I didn't say anything. I just kept a close eye on him in case I needed to go in. But I never once had to intervene. The horses trusted him. They never flinched or backed away. They could sense who he was and knew he was never going to hurt them. David is a natural with horses. He's a big man in stature but has the most calming nature and the horses pick up on it and it soothes them. He's been a real asset to me over the years because of that. The horses love him and time and time again it's been a beautiful thing to see. Pride wasn't the easiest horse to be around. He was a bugger of a thing who played up for me and was even worse when he knew his handler was inexperienced. Ponies can be like that. He was a bugger for the Ferrier too, didn't want to stand still and didn't want his legs touched. You'd pick his hoof up and he'd pull it out of your hand again and sometimes give a little air kick. Pride wasn't scared, just if he saw an opportunity to play up he would take it. He also didn't like to have a halter on and wouldn't let you worm him without making the biggest fuss. Everything you did with him became an ordeal. He wanted to be out in the paddocks all the time, running free and would only let you catch him if you had a big bucket of food in your hand. Gerald was the complete opposite; once you earned his trust he'd let you do anything with him. He was quiet, calm and trusting. Once he knew you were all right that was it; he loved you. All in all, Gerald is one of the best horses I have ever known.

I never rushed Horton into meeting the livestock. I never rush any of the pugs actually. I just let them wander over whenever they feel the time is right. The vision-impaired babies usually get used to the house and the rest of the farm first. It's a big thing coming here and not being able to see properly, and there is so much for them to get used to that my heart goes out to them. Sometimes I take them on a lead when I'm out walking. I do that for a couple of days and sometimes a full week depending on the pug. I find it helps them to get to know the way we go on the walk. Both morning and night I always walk the exact same track every time. I do this so that if somebody wanders off and loses us they'll know where to go to reconnect. If I zigzag all over the place, uncaring and unthinking, it's not fair on those who can't see. Life is hard enough; they don't need me wandering off in whatever direction takes my fancy on the day. A path is trod and once they learn it life becomes easier for them.

First, they learn the layout of the house, the rooms and where the furniture is, that sort of thing. Our house is tiny so it's no big deal. They have it sorted in no time then the path and direction of the walk is learnt and imprinted. Then, once all is good in their minds with that, they gain confidence and begin searching out what else is going on around the farm. In time they discover we have livestock here.

Horton got used to seeing the livestock from the safety of the veranda and I always pull a partition across so all the pugs are safe. They are used to being able to go off the ramp at the end of the veranda whenever they like, but when the livestock come on the front paddock everything changes. Precautions have to be taken. A vet said to me once that dogs have to learn to respect horses, their size, their feet and their ways, but I don't agree with that, not when it comes to my pugs anyway. I think it would be pretty irresponsible of me to bring slow-moving, elderly pugs here and ask them to deal with these huge, fast-moving and at times unpredictable animals. Because we rescue, we never know what temperaments we are getting when a new animal arrives. Not all of our horses have been as placid as Gerald. We lucked out with him, yet as docile as he is he is still a horse and I would never let him near the pugs unless there was a fence between them. Accidents can only happen if there is a way for them to happen and I am always over-cautious. I take the chance away. I feel it's my job to be on guard and alert at all times. It's no use being heartbroken and sorry after a bone has been broken. Wishing you 'Had Of' doesn't take away the pain you've caused one of your dogs through your own stupidity. Yes, it would be lovely if all the animals on Grace Farm could live side by side in perfect harmony but I think that's what heaven is for. Ruby with her bandy legs would find it hard to move out of harm's way. She doesn't do anything fast. She can't. Oh, she thinks she is moving quickly when she's running. You can see it in her eyes and on her face. Her little head is down in a determined manner and she's going for it, really going for it, and it is fast moving for her, well faster then she normally moves anyway, but she would have no chance of avoiding a long-legged horse. Not many of our pugs would and as much as I would love all the occupants of the farm to be respectful to one another, the truth is that due to the size differences accidents can and will happen. I love my pugs too much to put them in danger. Even Gerald on windy days can get a little bit silly – most horses do – and you never know what he's going to do next. You can't predict his movements. I always call Horton away from the fence on windy says; Gerald deserved to have a play, of course he does, but I never wanted Horton or the other pugs anywhere near the fence-line at this time. If Gerald pushed a sheep into the fence in rough play and Horton was sitting close, peering through as he normally did, he could have easily gotten kicked in the face. Sheep legs are spindly and have no trouble poking through the fence when a game is on.

Most of the other pugs came away when they were called and a few real sensible ones would see the goings-on and not want anything to do with it. Most of the oldies were content to stay by my side and bark at the livestock from a safe distance, but not Horton; he wanted to be part of everything that was going on and the faster and more vocal the livestock became the more he was drawn. He'd hear me call his name and know I wanted him to stop then he'd look around, seeing how close I was, then floor it over to the fence because he knew he'd be able to make it there before I got to him. He'd glance over his shoulder, do his cheeky grin, then be scooting off towards Gerald as fast as he could go. Everything was a game to Horton and I think he was playing with me. Or maybe he was just being naughty and I was too in love with him to see it. Either way, he never got hurt by a sheep or horse, and that's the main thing.

If we were about to go out I'd take all the pugs over to the fence for a wee before we left. Horton wears a nappy so he wouldn't really need to be out there with the others but because we always made him one of the pack he did everything they did. So we'd take his nappy off and let him follow the others as they sniffed about, but when Gerald happened to be near the fence Horton didn't want to come back in. If he'd realized we were going out on an adventure he would have shot inside the house in no time, but he just assumed he would be able to stay outside and linger a while because Gerald was there.

I have the most beautiful photo of Horton looking over his shoulder at me with Gerald by the fence in the background. It's one of my favourite photos and I'm glad I was able to capture that moment of him being mischievous and doing his cheeky face. I carry my camera with me a lot of the time, shove it in my pocket as I walk out the door, because some of the best shots I've ever gotten are when the pugs are out and about on the farm doing their own thing. Staged shots never work for us; there's too many to get sitting looking up at the same time. I'm always trying for that one perfect photo of the pugs in a row looking up, wide-eyed and beautiful. It's the one pose I've been trying to capture for many years and I'm still trying now, but I doubt I'm ever going to get it. The most I've been able to photograph sitting together looking up is five. Sprawled out, lying down in the sun, I can get all of them in the frame but the sitting up all perfect and pretty shot evades me still.

CHAPTER TWELVE

Not the New Boy Anymore

Horton had been living on the farm for about a year or so when I decided it was time to adopt another pug. Harper had died a few months earlier and I felt the time was right to bring another needy soul into the fold. This new pug's name was Arthur and he had suffered much neglect in his previous life. He had no third eyelid so was unable to ever close his eyes fully. His eyes dried out because of his condition so he needed help in that area. His previous owners hadn't even realized he had the condition. They failed to lubricate his eyes which resulted in scarring of the eyeball and loss of vision. It always saddens me when I hear about such cases. Arthur has the most beautiful big eyes and his vision could have easily been saved if eye drops and Optimune had been administered daily. That's all it would have taken; a quick routine morning and night and he would be able to see today. To his credit, Arthur came in and settled down to life on the farm nicely. He took his time when first meeting his new brothers and sisters, took in each different scent and got to know the differences in shape and size of each new sibling who came over to say hello. Horton was in amongst the pack looking at the new boy. I think it tickled him that he wasn't new anymore. He was one of the pack now and it was his turn to scoot over and check out the newcomer in the same way he had been checked out when he first arrived. Horton was kind of showing off a bit, like he was saying, "Hey man, I've been here for ages." Regardless of the pompous attitude, Arthur didn't seem to take much notice of Horton at first. He was too busy getting to know the others who bobbed about in front of him. After a while Horton got bored with it all so went off to play with a toy leaving the others to get acquainted. It was a bit of, "Well, if you're not interested in me then I'm not interested in you." I don't believe he was upset at being ignored; I think it was a relief not to have somebody preoccupied with his legs. That was new to Horton. A first, actually, although he had no idea at the time that Arthur couldn't see his entire body, let alone his legs. I watched Arthur standing in the middle of the pack. He couldn't see the others circling but he would have been able to sense they were there. He didn't seem to mind in the slightest that he was surrounded by so many and didn't care at all that he was being sniffed. He was an easy going pug and just took everything in his stride. He was cool and calm no matter what situation he was in. When the older pugs got their fill and wandered off, Arthur went over and had a drink then set off discovering the lounge. I suppose he was mapping the place out in his mind. He bumped into a few things, the side of the couch and a table leg, but carried on discovering. When he came across his new little brother chewing on a toy he stopped and gave Horton's body a good sniffing over and the little prince wasn't too happy about that. Horton never liked being sniffed. He was okay if the dogs stayed on his face but when they went on to sniff his body he didn't like that at all and because Arthur couldn't see, he lingered longer on Horton's body than a fully sighted dog would do. I don't think it was because Horton's back legs were placed differently and he was discovering that; it was more the nappy that Arthur lingered on. It wasn't wet – it was clean and dry and freshly changed – so it didn't smell of urine, but it did smell differently to what the other pugs smelt like. Most pugs don't smell like dry sanitary pads and Arthur's new brother did. Horton sat up and watched every move Arthur made. If he realized the new addition couldn't see he wasn't letting on. When Arthur came round for another sniff at his face Horton sniffed him back. Over the next few months, as they got more used to each other, if Arthur lingered too long sniffing, Horton would give him a little yap to let him know it was time to move on. And if Arthur didn't get it the first time Horton would follow up with a dive forwards, lunging at Arthur's face. I don't think he ever bit him but he came pretty close, especially on the days when Arthur took no notice. It was like, "Dude, enough already," or "Seriously, blind bro, you're being rude."

Arthur does sniff a lot at the other pugs. He does it over and over again all day everyday so they do tend to get annoyed by it sometimes, especially if he wakes them up, but as it's the only way he can tell who is who he has to continue doing it. If he's been sleeping, the first thing Arthur does is get up, have a little stretch then go from bed to bed making sure all his brothers and sisters are accounted for. When he gets to Horton it's like, "You may not be able to see me but I can see you perfectly, so move on, okay?" and Arthur does. He never stays on Horton long because he knows he's going to be told off if he does. But there was certainly no malice between the two of them, so I just stood back and allowed them to get used to each other, get to know one another's likes and dislikes and sort it out amongst themselves. All my pugs are going to be living in close harmony with one another; they have to get used to what is and isn't okay for each different personality. It normally doesn't take long for the new pug in the house to get to know who is okay sharing a bed and who isn't, who likes you in their face and who doesn't and also who is going to be up for a play and who is happier to just sit and watch.

I remember the day Horton discovered that Arthur couldn't close his eyes. I knew it was coming and I also knew how smart Horton was, so I knew it wouldn't take him long to figure it out. All the pugs had been on the morning walk and were in their beds resting. Arthur had lost the pack a few times so his walk had been doubled as he ran backwards and forwards trying to locate us. He'd come inside and collapsed into the nearest bed. The older pugs all found their own special beds and were sound asleep in no time. Ruby and Grace were asleep together in the big bed, Tommy was up on his special chair, Emily and Steffy were on the end of the couch and Sarah was all the way over the other side of the lounge. Sarah was really missing Harper, mourning her little mate; she used to go over and sleep in the bed the two of them shared when Harper was still alive. Horton, as usual, was full of energy. He was in no way ready for a nap. He'd scooted along after the other pugs then sat watching as they all settled down. When they started snoring he went over to the stash of toys and began searching for his favourites. He was lying in the middle of the pile chewing away and looking out the window. I knew he would be

busy for a while so I went to the kitchen table to write a letter. My
uncles don't have a computer so no emails for them. Everything is
handwritten on a nice card when I know the pugs are going to be
asleep for a while. Every now and then I'd look over to see how
everyone was doing: not much movement at all from the sleeping
pugs and whenever I looked at Horton he had a different toy in his
mouth. He'd chew a toy until it was wet then spit it out and get a
dry one. But he must have seen something interesting outside
because he spat his toy out quickly and scooted off to get a better
look from one of the side windows. He sat and barked for a while
and kicked his little back legs out. His bark was never loud so
there was no fear of him waking anybody up. Horton only ever
barked a series of small woofs at any one time. He sat at the
window woofing for a few more moments then lost interest in
whatever it was and turned to go back to his toys. I always love
watching Horton move. He was beautiful and it never got old for
me. I always stopped what I was doing and watched him. He was a
lot more interesting than anything I was ever doing anyway and he
was just a joy to see scooting along with such ease. He could move
pretty fast these days and was so full of energy and excitement for
life and I never wanted to miss seeing any of it. As Horton passed
the sleeping pugs he looked in each bed. Perhaps he was looking
to see if anybody was awake and up for a play or another walk.
They weren't, so he carried on. He sped past Arthur's bed, only
glancing in slightly, but then he stopped suddenly and backed his
little body up, pushed himself backwards as fast as he could, and
sat in front of Arthur's bed for a few seconds, staring. He then
leaned in closer for a better look. His head was on the side and he
had the most unusual look on his face: sort of serious, sort of

curious and sort of mischievous all at the same time, as if he
wasn't sure if there was something wrong with Arthur or if he was
just playing silly buggers and was about to jump up and pounce.
Horton wasn't taking any chances. He positioned his body so he
could get away fast if Arthur decided to chase him. They used to
chase each other a lot when they were playing and I think Horton
thought Arthur was trying to lure him in then jump up and get him
once he was off guard. Horton always had the upper hand in these
games anyway and poor Arthur was left to roam the lounge
searching for him. Horton would be either under a chair or the
coffee table waiting and jump out at Arthur as he passed by and
Arthur would be there all bug-eyed and super hyper, just waiting
for Horton to reveal himself so the game could carry on. Perhaps
Horton thought Arthur was trying a new tactic. He sat and watched
him for quite some time and his expression kept changing. It
showed me that he was really thinking things over. Horton always
showed everything he was thinking on his face and I would have
given anything to be able to know what was going through his
mind at that particular moment. Arthur wasn't aware of any of
this; he just kept on sleeping. I figured, blind or not, he would
have woken up with somebody sitting a few inches away, staring
so intently at his face. He would surely have been able to feel that
presence, feel that breath on his face, but Arthur's snoring never
missed a beat and after a while Horton must have decided that was
just how his new brother slept and so scooted back over to his
toys, his Tinkle Trouser strap tapping at the floor as he went. I
loved the little sound the Tinkle Trousers made because they were
uniquely his. No other pug in the house made that sound so I
always knew when Horton was on the move. He used to come up

behind me and seem startled that I knew he was there. It was like, "Mummy, I was being sneaky. How'd you know I was here."

Wherever I went in the house a little tap, tap, tapping sound followed me about and it was a beautiful sound because it belonged to Horton. I think Horton's Tinkle Trousers are the best little things that have ever been invented for paraplegic dogs. They make caring for him a breeze and his life ran so smoothly because of them. We get them sent over from the USA and would work with using four at a time. Usually we'd order them every six months and tried to order the four in one go to save on postage costs. I think a less active dog wouldn't have gone through them quite as quickly as Horton did but he loved his life and went at it full speed. The Tinkle Trousers kept up with him beautifully considering they weren't designed for life on a farm. For a dog kept indoors I reckon the Tinkle Trousers would have lasted two or three years but we didn't mind that Horton destroyed his so quickly. It showed that he was enjoying life. I think a normal nappy-type of thing would have been no use for Horton. He would simply have shot out of it as soon as he was put on the ground, left it sitting on the floor at my feet most likely. Normal nappies are great absorbers but they simply aren't any good for dogs that drag the lower part of their bodies around. But the Tinkle Trousers were fantastic. They came up over his shoulders and once they were on they were on for good. Horton never once came out of them and that's saying something because he sure put them through hell on a daily basis around the farm. Four worked best for our needs. I'd have one on him, one drying, one in the wash and one ready for when he needed changing. But in the warmer months when he spent hours on the veranda nappy-free, I could wash and dry all four in one go. Winter was a little harder but with the fire always blazing the Tinkle Trousers would be dry within the hour. They arrived in perfect condition but within a week of being attached to our little rough-living boy they looked like we'd gotten them second hand.

They didn't have a huge variety as far as boy colours went. I mean, they had a few different colours – green with a yellow trim and purple with a yellow trim, plain black and an olive coloured one – but my favourite was khaki. I thought he looked so handsome in it. The colour suited him perfectly, went well against his black fur and made his amber eyes pop. However, we used to order the ones that didn't stand out too much as a way of not drawing attention to him. The olive greens and khaki just blended in. Half the time people didn't even know he was wearing a nappy. I think they thought it was one of those trendy dog harness things and I liked that. I liked the fact that he could go out and not have all this attention brought on him by having to wear some brightly coloured or neon garment. He wasn't a council worker, he didn't need to be seen, he was a little paraplegic pug wanting to get on and enjoy his life and the Tinkle Trousers helped him do just that. It meant he could go about his business without a pile of people staring. He could go into my friend's antique shop, stalk the customers and play the little games he loved so much without alerting everyone that he was there. I never feared anybody stepping on him because he could move pretty fast – forwards, backwards, sideways, any way he liked – and because he was in such an interesting place he sped off at very high speeds. He just pushed off with those powerful front legs of his and he was gone. Blink and you'd miss him and people usually did. They had no idea this little black pug was going from one display to the next, following them, watching their legs, ready to pounce if he was in a pouncing mood that day. He could move faster on the wooden floorboards at home but even on the carpeted floors of the shop he still got up quite a speed and the Tinkle Trousers prevented him from getting carpet burns. They offered wonderful protection for little male dogs. Horton used to go underneath the display tables and wait for legs to go by. Just as he used to hide underneath our kitchen table waiting to jump out at Arthur, he would do the same with people in the shop. But if the shop was overly crowed we didn't put him down. It was too hard to keep him safe and he didn't understand that. He didn't know why he couldn't go down and play and he used to try and wrestle out of David's arms. He was upset when he wasn't lowered, so in the end we only took Horton there at times when we knew they wouldn't be busy. That way he could go down on the floor and have a ball. He never chewed anything in the shop and never made a mess. He did get his leg caught in a low-hanging display one time and brought a pile of old-fashioned aprons down behind him, but he wasn't scared. He just sat there looking around for his dad to come over and help him, and David was beside his son in a second. Horton half-turned around, watching what David was doing, then fully turned and pounced on the pile of aprons once he was free. He started doing his puppy bark and pawing at the frilly edge of one of the more flashy-looking aprons and we ended up buying that one, not because he had torn a hole in it or anything like that, because he wasn't being rough, but because we wanted the memory to keep with us forever and figured if we had that apron hanging on a hook in the kitchen we would always remember that day. We would always remember the look on Horton's face when his eyes were searching the shop for his Dad to come help him and the way he turned and barked and pounced once his leg was untangled. It was as if he was having a go at the pile of aprons because he thought they'd had a go at him. That was pretty comical to see; a real cute thing to witness.

A few people in the shop came over and were watching the scene and they all thought Horton was the most adorable little thing. He got loads of pats that day and welcomed each one. But that wasn't always the case with Horton. He was selective over whom he would and wouldn't allow near him. He just didn't like some people touching him. I believe dogs can sense more about people than we can and I never pushed him to go near anybody he didn't want to meet. Even if that meant offending someone, I didn't care. He was so precious to me and I took my cue from him. He knew best, so I shielded him from them. Horton loved most people and if he was backing away he was doing it for a good reason. I think if we as human beings concentrated more on our instincts and went solely with them we could avoid a lot of unpleasantness and heartache for ourselves. But we tend to feel bad about offending people or hurting their feelings. Dogs don't do that. If something isn't right it isn't right and you can't change their minds.

I was out with Horton one day when a man approached us in the street. He was tall and wide but I knew by the way he looked and acted that he had special needs. He was harmless, just a little boy in a big man's body really, but he made a beeline for Horton as soon as he saw us. He yelled out something to his mother then came flying across at us pretty fast. Luckily, we were in the middle of the county and there wasn't much traffic going past because he didn't even stop to look if there were any cars coming. He just saw a puppy and raced across the street to say hello. One car honked its horn and shouted something nasty out the window, but he just turned and waved like the person driving was an old family friend. As he got closer, I saw that he was about fifty years old and his poor elderly mother couldn't keep up with him. She looked to me to be totally worn out. He got right in our faces, far too close for comfort, something he was obviously used to doing; personal space didn't seem to bother him, but it was bothering me and I thought it would bother Horton too, but it didn't, not in the slightest. I think Horton knew the purity of this man's heart and he licked the big heavy hand that reached out to him. "Pat gently and slowly. He's only little," I told the guy and thankfully he softened his pats right away. He stayed with us for a while and asked a few questions. When I understood what he was saying I answered, when I didn't have a clue I just talked to him about Horton and he seemed happy with that. I was glad Horton hadn't rejected this man. He seemed as if he'd had a good load of that in his life already and I was happy my little pug not only accepted him but liked him enough that he leaned over and licked his face. The man was delighted by this act. When his mother finally got to us she apologized for her son's behaviour, but she really didn't have to; there was absolutely no need and I smiled and told her so. I had a feeling that she'd spent a lot of her time apologizing for him.

CHAPTER THIRTEEN

Horton's First Christmas

I think the Christmas of 2008 will stay in my mind forever. It was Horton's first Christmas with us and it was the first year my Mum had been well enough to come to the farm. Before that I had only been able to sit beside her bed and tell her about it, describe the green hills and wonderful countryside as best I could and hope her mental images lived up to it. She'd seen my farm animals in photos but now she was actually coming to meet them in person and I was very excited about that. We'd planned a family Christmas earlier in the year, before we even knew Horton existed. Horton hadn't even been born when the plans were being made and in the back of my mind was the constant worry of whether Mum was actually going to be well enough to make it this time or if she was going to have to cancel again. Then, once Horton entered our lives, I had concerns about how he would be with so many people in the house. I didn't want him getting accidently stepped on. My mum was using a walker now so that worried me as well, both for her safety and the safely of all of our pugs. A lot of my elderly babies were slow moving and I worried that Horton may get his back legs run over by one of the wheels. At this point, Horton hadn't started moving his back legs and he hadn't been with us long so the muscles on his front legs weren't fully built up yet. He could move sure enough, but he wasn't up to the speeds we were going to see later on in his life. When people came they used to walk around the house real slow, like imaginary ice skaters. They were used to doing this with my old blind pugs and when Horton came, a special effort was made to look down the entire time they were walking around.

I knew my family was used to me having multiple pugs and pugs with special needs but with so many dogs and so many people I feared for the worst, and seeing as Horton was our most needy one my thoughts were entirely on our new little boy. I did think about having him go stay with a friend while the family was here. She lived just around the corner and I figured he'd be safer there than he would be here. She was on her own for Christmas and desperate to have some one-on-one time with little Horton and I thought it'd be nice for the two of them. I didn't want him to go and be away from his new family for Christmas, but I thought it'd keep him safe, so was considering it.

When I broached the subject with David he was dead against it. "No, no," was his quick reply and he wouldn't be swayed. Horton was our son and he was going to spend Christmas day with his family and that was it.

"But what if I drop Horton off just before the family arrived then get him once the meal is over and people are more subdued?" I figured there'd be less walking around then, Mum would have already seen the property and after eating Christmas dinner all most people do is sit around and talk. I figured that would be a brilliant time to bring Horton home to meet my Mum and my friend who was looking after him could come and spend the rest of the day with us so she didn't have to be in an empty house. But David wouldn't have it. I don't think he could bear to be parted from Horton and told me firmly that he didn't think it was fair on Horton to be away from his family at Christmas time. He said we'd work things out. I think he was even considering uninviting certain family members so there wouldn't be as many people in the house. David's way of thinking about it was that this was Horton's home and if the family didn't think they could come here and be respectful to not only our special needs boy, but his elderly brother and sisters as well then they may as well not come at all.

I did think about setting up one of the baby playpens and putting Horton, Harper and Ruby in there. That way they could see all that was going on, be close to us, but out of harm's way. I did a trial run when I had a few friends over for lunch and it was a disaster. Harper kept getting her legs through the bars and her head also got stuck in the corners once or twice. And all Horton did was bounce up and down on his nappy and cry. Ruby was fine. She sniffed at the bowl of water I put in there just to make sure it held no food then simply shuffled onto the bed and went to sleep. Horton wasn't a crier. He never cried and to hear this just broke my heart. I couldn't bear the sound of him being upset. I just couldn't bear to have Horton spending the day crying. That was no way for the little soul to spend his very first Christmas on earth, so the play pen idea went out the window as did a few other ideas I had running round in my head. Instead, I just rang each person who was coming and explained how Horton was. Most had only seen him in photos, and Horton in photos and Horton in real life were two entirely different things. They all agreed to watch their feet and that put my mind at ease a little bit, but not completely. So I started thinking of ways to make Horton safer on the day.

I did think again about the play pen, thinking that if I put Horton in it for an hour a day he would be well used to being in there by the time the twenty-fifth rolled around. We have a few wooden baby play pens that we use to feed our blind pugs in. I like the play pens because they can eat side by side with their siblings, feel their presence around them, listen to them all happily tucking in, yet be able to eat their own meals in peace and safety, knowing that one of the full-sighted ones isn't going to swoop across, bump them out of the way and steal their food. I thought, if I set the play pen up in the middle of the lounge Horton would be able to see everything that was going on and feel part of it. He'd be safe yet wouldn't be missing out on any part of the day. I knew he wouldn't feel left out or lonely. People would be going across to meet him, give him a pat and say hello without a single foot going anywhere near his body. David didn't like that idea. He said Horton would still feel isolated. He had only been with us a short while, but we had all become extremely close during that time. We bonded fast, developed a deep deep love for one another so quickly. He said that Horton had been rejected enough and he wasn't going to allow him to be cast aside on such a special day of the year. I told him that as well as putting a blanket down and some water I'd throw a pile of toys in there for him. Horton loved his toys. He played with them for hours. Harper and Ruby would have no interest so they'd be all for Horton. I even suggested getting him a few new toys to make his time in the play pen a bit more interesting, but David still wouldn't be swayed.

Yet again, my mind started ticking over. I thought of ways of alerting people to the fact that Horton was nearby and as it was Christmas, my mind went to bells. I figured if I attached a little Christmas bell to Horton's Tinkle Trousers he would look festive and everybody would be able to tell where he was at all times. Well, unless he was still and if he was still he was safe wasn't he? Then when he started moving again everybody would hear and know to pay special attention to where they put their feet. David didn't mind this idea. He thought it was a good one actually, so that's what we did. I began searching for the right size bell that made a decent tinkling sound, but until you start looking you have no idea how many bells are for show only. They are beautiful in appearance but that's as far as it goes. They have nothing inside, they make no sound, so for us they are useless. But the search continued and eventually I found a fat, chunky little bell that was loud enough to alert, but not so loud that Horton was afraid of it. It was light in weight too so it was perfect for the job. The bell would be attached to the top part of his Tinkle Trousers so it wouldn't get in the way of his movement and wouldn't hit the ground as he went along as I figure that would annoy him. Well, it would annoy me if I was him so I was sure he wouldn't like it either. Also, being on his back meant it wouldn't be obvious to the other pugs, as I did fear one of the most curious ones – Emily – spotting the bell and trying to pull it off. That would have freaked Horton out big time.

The only way I could buy the bells was attached to a wreath, but I didn't mind. Sure there were way more bells than I needed, but they were such beautiful colours and being a real fan of Christmas decorations I figured I'd use the other bells over the years to make the table or the tree look pretty. There were jade green, shiny gold, bright red and deep purple bells to choose from. I thought I'd have Horton wearing his bright green Tinkle Trouser and put one gold and one red bell on the top. I was only going to use one bell at first as I didn't want him to have too much weight or annoyance attached to his little back. That wouldn't have been nice for him. He was only little and his body wasn't anywhere near as strong as it would one day become. Sure, I thought four bells would've looked great and very Christmassy, but figured that amount would upset him. He'd definitely know they were there. One bell would have been best for him. He wouldn't have been able to feel that at all; he'd hear it but maybe not even know where the sound was coming from. Then I thought, "Well, these bells are a bit cheap," and cheap means crappy, and crappy means that things don't always work. I thought two bells would be best. If one failed then the other one would work and our little guy would be safe from harm. Naturally, I checked both bells worked before I set them aside and during the week I rang the big bunch of bells on the wreath. In fact, I shook the living crap out of them a few times a day so that Horton and the others could get used to the sound. If the sound was new it'd set everybody off barking. I imagined poor little Horton on Christmas day just going about his business then one pug would bark then another and another, then they'd all go rushing towards the windows like they always do when hearing a strange sound. Horton would be over there with them, bouncing and barking out the window. And the more he'd bounce the more the bells on his back would ring and the more they'd all bark and I knew it could go on all day once they were in the mood for barking.

On Christmas Eve, before David arrived home from work, I sewed two bells onto Horton's freshly washed, bright green Tinkle Trouser and put it on the chair ready to pop on him once the first family members began to arrive. Because the family was coming I was up late making sure the house looked perfect and did extra bits of cooking as well making sure we didn't run out of food. I mean, you never run out of food on Christmas Day do you, but it's always in the back of your mind that the shops will be closed and you'll have extra mouths to feed, so you buy enough to feed an army and shove it in every available space you can find. Your cupboards are full and your fridge is full and yet you are still going out of your mind with worry in case one of your guests goes home hungry and you're labelled a bad hostess. Of course, men don't worry about these things. David couldn't have cared less, but I did, so extra bits of everything were stocked up on to put my mind at ease. I mean, my Mum was finally coming to the farm and I just wanted everything to be as perfect as it could possibly be. I normally go all out with Christmas decorations anyway but this year I took it up a notch. I love shiny, glittering, sparkly things. David says I must have been a magpie in a previous life. I'm that obsessed with them, I collect them in a frenzied fashion actually. If we lose one another in a shopping centre David always knows where to find me because I'm drawn. The year my Mum came to the farm I outdid myself with the decorations and the tree and the lights looked beautiful. It was the first time Mum would be seeing my house so the feather duster and vacuum cleaner got an extra workout as well.

David got up with the pugs early on Christmas Day. He knew I'd been up late and would be fussing about in a state all day long, so he let me sleep in and took over doing everything for the pugs. He walked them, fed them and changed Horton's nappy, then he showered and got dressed. He also put the turkey in the oven for me. He must have been quiet because I'm a light sleeper and I didn't hear a sound. The only reason I knew he was up was because every now and then a wrinkly little face appeared at the side of the bed. They all thought it was weird that I was still asleep and so kept filing in to check on me from time to time. I'd pat the head of whoever was peeping up at the time then fall back to sleep. I was exhausted. I thought David was wonderful for doing all that for me, but I couldn't help thinking he was doing it half to be helpful and half for his own sanity. I think he had been creeping around the house quietly all morning because he knew once the 'Christmas Monster' was up the peace would be well and truly shattered. I would be going nuts, making sure everything was going to be all right for the day.

I do think people put too much pressure on themselves at Christmas. Most miss out on the joys because they're too busy making sure it's going to be the best Christmas ever in people's minds. I wish I didn't do it; I loathe myself for succumbing actually and yet most years it's the same, even though I swear it won't be.

When I finally woke up I couldn't believe I'd slept in so long. I opened my eyes and glanced across the bed to find Horton lying a few inches away from me. Normally, as soon as he sees my eyes open he'd be straight on me, jumping on my pillow, kissing my face, wanting to be hugged, or positioning himself in the nook of my arms then leaning right back so I can massage him, but this morning he just lay there. I ran my hand across the bed trying to engage him but he barely glanced my way.

"What's wrong with Horton?" I asked David, becoming concerned.

"Nothing," he said.

"Then why is he acting like that?" I asked, knowing it wasn't his normal state. David told me that Horton didn't like the bells. "What bells?" I asked, forgetting about the ones I had sewn on the Tinkle Trousers the previous night. I was half-asleep. I thought maybe Santa had come round the streets on the fire truck waving to the kids. This happened every year when we lived in the suburbs. It wouldn't work too well out here on our country roads with only one or two lonely farm houses dotting the hills in the distance. But I thought maybe the tradition had finally reached the country and that they had been ringing the bells really loud in order to gain everybody's attention. Horton didn't like loud noises of any kind so this would have definitely upset him.

I sat up and had a closer look at Horton. It was then that I saw he had a pile of Christmas bells hanging off the Tinkle Trouser he was wearing. It wasn't the bright green one I had sewn two bells onto either. It was one of his purple and yellow one and there were so many multi coloured bells attached that Horton would have certainly felt their weight. David, in trying to do everything for me to help out, hadn't seen the two-belled Tinkle Trousers I had sitting on the chair, so had taken it upon himself to grab the Christmas wreath, find a large safety pin and attached a pile of bells to Horton's little back. I think he was really proud of himself for doing so as well. He couldn't see that there were far too many bells for Horton to be comfortable. I think he was just making sure Horton got heard by everyone in the house. But by the amount of bells on his back I reckon he would have been heard two towns over. If Horton hadn't been so put out by it I probably would have started laughing, and we did laugh afterwards and have laughed about it so many times since, but in that instant all I could think about was my poor little baby lying in the middle of the bed in such an unhappy state. I clipped the Tinkle Trousers open, didn't even take the safety pin off, just got the entire thing off him as quickly as I could. Horton was ecstatic right away and began charging around the bed giving his normal amount of good morning kisses. He went from miserable to joyful in about two seconds flat. He also left a trail of wee all over the bed so the bedding had to be changed quickly before it soaked through to the mattress. Horton was so happy to be out from under all that weight, he wouldn't let me put another nappy on him right away. I had to chase him all over the bed and as he ran he was so excited at me chasing him and so happy to be away from all those bells that he urinated big time.

After that, we couldn't put the two-belled tinkle trousers on him. He wouldn't have it. It was nowhere near as heavy as the last one, but he just heard the bells and that was it; he slumped and sulked. It took almost a week before he settled down and trusted us again. We couldn't sneak anything by him. He was aware and suspicious of everything we did for days afterwards and watched our hands with an eye of mistrust. But he was safe on Christmas Day and that was the main thing. He spent the day either in his Daddy's arms or on his knee. He met all the family members with great excitement and never came to any harm because he was so well looked after by David. I think he felt bad about the bell incident and more than made up for it by spoiling Horton even more than he usually did. Horton sat at the head of the table on his Dad's knee and looked down his nose at everyone else. He seemed to know he was special and that he and his Dad had pride of place. But if he was being a brat about it nobody seemed to notice; they were all completely under his spell. They all thought he was beautiful and just about the cutest little thing there ever was.

After dinner, we all sat in the lounge. Once everyone was down and out I knew it was safe to allow Horton on the ground. David took him off to change his nappy while everyone found a seat. When Horton re-entered the room he was on the ground, not in his Dad's arms and everyone was amazed at his speed along the floor. He scooted into the room well ahead of David and did a few laps of the lounge then came and did a few smaller circles in front of everybody's chairs. Once the clapping finally stopped and he knew his moment of glory was well and truly over, he dived onto his stack of toys and played quietly by the window while we all talked. Horton was the one thing we most talked about and he looked up whenever anybody said his name. Every so often he'd come over and sit in front of somebody's chair, looking up at the new faces. He didn't do it with me or David or anybody else he was familiar with, just the family members he'd never met before. He'd shoot over and pause for a few moments, take their faces in then scoot back to his toys. He was particularly taken with my Mum and went and sat in front of her chair for a long time, and he bounced up and down on his nappy whenever she glanced down and spoke to him. He also went and stuck his head in her handbag and pawed at the strap, he could smell she had treats in there for the pugs and was so excited when she dished them out.

It was a very special Christmas, one of the best Christmases I've ever had. Mum loved the farm and thought it was beautiful, Horton and the other pugs stayed safe and we didn't run out of food.

CHAPTER FOURTEEN

Food for Thought

Like all pugs, Horton loved his food and I used to love watching him tucking in. It would make me happy preparing nutritious meals for him and his brothers and sisters. I believe elderly and special needs dogs need to be given the best quality food. It has to be fresh and loaded with vitamins and minerals: no wasted mouthfuls, and by that I mean everything they eat should mean something. It should be benefiting their bodies in some form. Bones, heart, joints, teeth, the list goes on and on and if it's not doing something to aid them then you shouldn't be giving it to them. All dogs need good nutrition but some of the pugs I take in come to me after living their lives on bad diets. Special care has to be taken with what I feed them once they get here because I'm not only feeding my pugs to nourish them, I'm more often than not trying to undo years of deficient eating.

Horton would sit beside, and sometimes on top of, my feet whenever I was doing anything in the kitchen. He'd paw at my legs or bounce up and down on his bottom when he smelt something he liked and he liked a lot of things so he was always bouncing. When he first came I used to enjoy seeing his reaction to different taste experiences. I'd feel a scrape of his claw or the softness of his nappy as he bounced and look down to see these two huge bright eyes looking up at me with anticipation. Horton had a way of making every experience happy for me. If I was tired at the end of the day, just knowing the health benefits from the extra effort I put into preparing the pugs' food made it all worthwhile. I loved seeing their eyes light up at mealtimes and knowing every bite was filled with pure goodness and loads of vitamins and minerals to make their coats shine and their immune systems healthy and strong. I've never understood how anybody can just open a can or put a cup full of cheap, dry food in a bowl and think they've done all right by their dog. I mean, just the smell of it tells you everything and if that doesn't convince you that you could be doing a lot better by your dog then the sight of it should. It's colourless and to me, colourless means it's lacking in nutrition. Our pugs have always eaten a wide variety of fruits and vegetables – the safe-for-dog ones, of course, and you need to check this out because not all fruits and vegetables are safe to feed to your dog. But I firmly believe that to get a dog living to a ripe old age you need to feed them as much goodness as you can. Mine all eat raw carrots. They love them. Each one lines up for their bit of carrot then off they'll go to various areas in the lounge so they can eat in peace. And neither David nor myself can eat a banana, peach, strawberry, pear, mango or apple without a pile of bug-eyed babies looking up, pleading. We are careful with the seeds because, really, you have to be. Pips are poisonous for dogs and we can't have them coming to any harm.

One blazing summer night a few years back, we all sat outside under the peach tree and made a meal out of that. We put the stones in our pockets so the pugs couldn't accidently get at them and we all sat in the shade enjoying ourselves. I love fresh spinach and eat it every day and because I eat it every day so do the pugs. My pugs love blueberries too. We've only got the one bush so they disappear pretty quickly, but we keep talking about putting more blueberry bushes in. So far we haven't got round to doing it, though. But I'm good with the strawberries and year after year their little bellies are full with the most delicious Grace Farm grown strawberries, and each year I find myself planting more and more strawberries to keep up with the demand. I have them in vegies patches, in pots all along the front of the veranda and a good many in hanging baskets as well. I love watching them growing and when they are in season our morning routine is to have our walk around the farm, then as we are heading back to the house we stop by the vegies patches and each pug gets one or two each, depending on how many are ripe.

In winter, I cook pumpkin and add that to their meals as a way of bulking them up without adding too many calories. We all like a warm, nutritious meal when it's cold and our animals are no different. Also, they tend to get a bit hungrier in the winter months so the pumpkin seems to satisfy them nicely. Again, I have to stress that not everything we eat is okay to give our dogs. Our dogs are very different to us and we must never forget that. Onions are definitely no-nos. Do a quick search on the internet for a list of what your dogs can and can't eat then stick it to your fridge so you don't forget. But please make sure to start adding more nutrients to your dog's diet because it's important. If you're time poor you can just cook up a big casserole once or twice a week then freeze it in daily portions. All you have to do then is take it out of the freezer the night before and warm it up in the morning. There are a lot of ways you can make your dog's diet better and if you go for seasonal veggies then it can be done quite cheaply. To me, there's no excuse good enough for not feeding your dog a better diet. Supermarkets are full of vegies that are already sliced and diced. All the work's been done for you. Even if you're the busiest person in the world, the least you can do is open up a bag and pour out the contents. And believe me, putting that little bit of extra effort into your daily feeding routine will help lessen your vet bills, too. Keeping our four-legged family members as healthy as possible should be our number one concern. You can be the laziest owner on the planet and still be able to give your pet better nutrition because it takes the same amount of time to open a can as it does to tear the seal on a bag.

All pugs love dinner time and with having so many pugs living in our house it's a grand event here. We've got separate areas to feed them in and once we've worked out who is all right eating with whom everything runs pretty smoothly. When a new pug enters the house everything shifts but things quickly return to normal once they've all figured out the slightly different routine. Some prefer eating on their own because they've been used to eating that way in their previous home. Some like eating inches away from the ones they came here with, so we keep doing that for them. It'd be mean to separate them when they've been eating together all their lives and there's no need to really, because they eat calmly side by side then sit waiting patiently for the other one to finish before checking out each other's bowl. There's never once been anything left in somebody else's bowl but it doesn't stop them checking because today could be the day that their eating buddy has left something for them. Tommy and Lilly always ate together and even though there was a massive size difference between the two of them, everything went beautifully. They were always polite and respectful of one another's eating space. Ruby and Grace are so lovely to watch when they're having their meals. It's a case of heads down, bottoms up until one of them finishes then they'll glance over at each other and swap bowls. Steffy is a fantastic little girl. She can eat with any of the other pugs and there are never any problems. She finishes her meal then sits by her bowl watching the others eat. It doesn't matter how long they take either. Steffy doesn't care; she'll just sit patiently until they wander off then she goes over for a look in their bowl. Emily, on the other hand, can't be near any of the others at mealtimes. She's a real problem child in that area. A lot of it is how they have lived in their past lives and you can't alter the past, so we just find it works out better to be respectful of their eating history. I suppose I could put a hell of a lot of effort into training so they all eat side by side, like little guzzling angels and really it'd be quite a feat pulling that off with so many pugs, but eating times are generally where pug problems lie and I just find it quicker and easier to feed them separately. The effort in training I leave for other times, times when it is needed in order for a multiple-pug household to run smoothly.

So the blind ones don't get their food stolen, they go in little wooden pens. That way they can hear the others eating, know their brothers and sisters are close by and that the family unit is still together, but they get to eat in peace, at their own pace. You can't allow the blind ones to have their dinner pinched. That wouldn't be nice. Eating is such a pleasurable time for pugs and not all pugs eat at lightning speed either. I mean, a lot do, but not all of them, so the pens come in handy for making mealtimes work. I have three doors that go off the living area onto the veranda and once the pugs know the bowls on the countertop have been filled they all file out into their separate eating areas. Some days it's done easily with a hand movement. I started doing this years ago with the deaf ones and now everybody knows what the hand movements mean. They're not watching my hand in case I've got food in it for them; it's more that they're waiting to see what I want them to do and the blind ones just file in behind everyone else.

Horton has always eaten indoors on his own. He's so little and I wouldn't want him getting knocked around. The others are a lot sturdier than he is and would use that to their advantage to get more food. Pugs lose their manners when there is food around so you have to remember that. Also, I don't want Horton outside dealing with the others when he's trying to eat. I believe mealtimes should be peaceful experiences that aid digestion and that couldn't happen if he was outside. He feels the cold too, so it works best if he's fed inside. I mean, I could put him out in a pen so he's protected but because he gets changed as soon as he's eaten, I find it best to feed him in the house. That way I can put a clean nappy on him right away while he's on his own, then he can join the others and have a sniff in all their bowls when he's clean and freshly changed.

Horton knows feeding time well. He knows what's going on, who goes out what door and from the way his head moves, he seems to be counting them as they go. He sits near the kitchen bench watching them file out. I don't think he's so much guarding all the food; it's more that he knows that as soon as the last of his sisters and brothers are outside then I'm going to turn and come back past the bench and grab his bowl for him. Horton gets fed first. It's the way I've always done things and I figure he knows there's no point in going all the way across the lounge only to come back again; he may as well wait there and make things faster. Sometimes that works; other times, not so much. If somebody gets confused or is playing games and not wanting to go out of their normal door things tend to take a bit longer. But when a hungry little pug is waiting to be fed seconds can seem like hours and Horton quickly comes scooting across the room to find out what's going on. He peers between my ankles to see which one of his siblings is holding everything up. He can hear me using my stern voice and looks up at me as if he knows I've had enough because he's had enough too. He's not normally impatient, but he's ruled by his tummy I guess because his little face is by my side in no time seeing what the holdup is. Most days everything runs smoothly; I'll put the other pugs out then turn and look at Horton and he'll be off running to his eating place before I've even crossed the room. Some days he'd make eye contact with me before he turned and scooted; other times, he wouldn't. When he first came and was unsure of what to do he'd follow me from door to door or sit halfway across the room, looking around for what was coming next. The look on his face told me he didn't realize it was dinner time. He was too new to know, so I'd turn and say, "You go go! You go go!" and he'd head into the kitchen then look back at me as if to say, "Is this where you wanted me to go?" As he got more used to things he'd go all the way through the kitchen, up the hall, into our bedroom and wait there, or he'd be waiting in the entrance of our ensuite and keep peeping back, looking for my feet to come round the corner. When he was really hungry, which was usually in the middle of winter, I'd turn quickly just in time to see a flash of black whizzing across the floor. He knew the putting-out routine, knew which pugs went first, second and third and when the third door closed he knew it was his time to be fed, so off he'd scoot. Blink and you'd miss him. Our ensuite was the best room in the house in which to feed Horton. It was quiet and I could close him in so he could be alone with his food. He seemed to like being on his own when he ate. He'd look over his shoulder to make sure I was closing the door before he began eating. He used to eat in his foster mum's pantry when he first went into care and I think he just got used to doing that. Eating in a small confined space seemed to make Horton feel safe. We don't have a walk-in pantry here so our ensuite is the next best thing. It's only a small room yet big enough that he could whizz in then back up and position his body comfortably to eat. On overcast days I'd leave the light on in there for him so he could see what he was doing and in winter I'd put the heat light on so that he'd be nice and warm. By the time I'd put all the other food bowls down Horton would be finished eating so I'd change his nappy and off we'd go to let the others pugs out of their eating pens. Some days I'd hear him banging on the door wanting to get out. He knew that once he finished he could go outside and check out everyone else's bowls and was always in a great hurry to do that. As Horton gained strength he was able to open the sliding door and get himself out and come scooting back into the lounge looking for me before I had a chance to grab a clean nappy for him.

When Horton was a pup we put him on three mini meals a day as it was important not to overload his stomach. Because of the way his body was we couldn't have him over-full, but we couldn't starve him either. He was a growing boy and needed good food put into him. But it wasn't like there was any fear of him getting fat; he was never still so burnt the calories off in no time. Puppies are always growing and always hungry and this seemed to suit his needs just fine.

When Horton was eighteen months old I did think of cutting it back to two meals a day, like the other pugs had, but it didn't seem to sit right with him. He used to wake in the middle of the night crying for food, so the three mini meals continued. It made it easier actually because he ate his last meal, the smallest meal of the day, just before bedtime. I'd take all the other pugs outside for their final toilet break and once the last shuffling old body had cleared the doorframe David would put Horton's food bowl down and come outside and join us. The nightly wee is a special time at our house. Being on a farm in the middle of the countryside, there's no light pollution so the star show is amazing. David and I both stand looking up at the night sky, pointing out Orion and the others. Orion is my favourite. I had never been into star gazing until I met David. I'd learnt about the stars at school but that was where it ended. When we were first going out we used to lie on our backs in the middle of an oval and he would point each constellation out to me. He knew a lot about the stars and was so enthusiastic when telling me that I became interested too. How could I not? His passion was infectious. We were in suburbia back then so he had to make do with pointing to an area and telling me that was where certain stars should be. We always wanted to live in the country, not for the star show – that was an added bonus – just for the way of life really. We knew we could rescue more animals if we lived on a farm, so from the time we got married that was our goal. Actually, it was my goal long before I met David and luckily for me my husband understood the imprint on my heart and decided to share my dream with me. And what was even luckier was that I didn't have to drag him kicking and screaming because he loved animals too.

On our first night on the farm, neither of us could get over the amount of stars we could see. The gatherings I'd only been able to view in books were twinkling right down at me now and it wasn't even that clear a night. David was ecstatic. He said, "Wait till summer, baby. Wait till there are no clouds in sight." We felt like those stars were shining solely for us, as if they had been put there as a welcoming sign, a sign that everything was going to be all right. We felt they were blessing this little farm of ours and the decision we had made. On the ride to the farm, we were driving down the winding country roads, four cars behind the truck carrying all our belongings. As we drove further and further away from the side-by-side houses and up into the hills, I felt incredibly calm. There was perhaps a five percent doubt in my mind, but the biggest part of me knew we were doing the right thing. We sold a beautiful, double-story home on the edge of a lake to come all the way out here, and at the time very few people understood why. They thought we'd lost our minds, but they didn't understand what was in our hearts. When we said the stairs were getting too hard for Ruby's old bandy legs they looked at us as if we were stupid. I mean totally insane. Enough to be locked away kind of insane. They said, "Then just get rid of the dog." It wasn't only the stairs, though; with the arthritis in Ruby's neck and back she was finding it hard to have a harness on when going for a walk and she loved those twice-a-day walks along the water's edge. We knew we had to find a place where all the pugs could walk free of leads and harnesses and free of pain.

This little farm with its tiny two-bedroomed house was perfect for us. Sure, we would have liked bigger but it was all we could afford and besides, it had a really nice harmony to it. That sat right with me, and it had a ramp at the back door. We needed one for the front so David built another as soon as we moved in, but that ramp was a sign for me and the first time we brought the dogs down to look at the farm before signing on the dotted line Ruby got out of the car, staggered around a little bit to get her legs moving after being in the car so long, had a wee, then made a beeline for the ramp and ran straight into the house. And the guy who owned the place just stood there watching her go. She found her way to the kitchen and was standing swaying beside the oven when the rest of us walked in. It was as if she was saying to us, "I like it. Let's buy it." She always swayed by the oven when she was hungry. It didn't matter to her whether there was food cooking in there or not; she knew ovens meant food and so swayed until she got given something. She also never minded whose house she was swaying in either. Whenever we went visiting, Ruby would always find her way to the kitchen and stand swaying until somebody gave her something to eat. And I think the cute little face she does when she's swaying gets her more food than it probably should have; well, that and the fact that she generally won't move on until her wish has been granted. Ruby sways because she can't stand in the one spot for very long without it becoming uncomfortable on her little awkward body. She'll be there shuffling from one foot to the other, looking up at us with that beautiful old face of hers and she is so gorgeous that we just end up giving her a little bit of something and subtracting it from her next meal. Due to her body and its unusual gate, Ruby has to be watched with her weight, but when she's happily shuffling off to the nearest bed she has no idea her next meal is going to be smaller by a few mouthfuls. All that's in her mind at the time is, "I got me some! I got me some!" Half the time I believe she stood her ground because she thought if she moved out of the kitchen that would be the one time the food got dished out and I think she feared missing it. So she stayed and she swayed. And the man selling the house gave her some cheese that day from memory. He'd made some banana muffins for us to eat while the paperwork was being signed, but they were disappearing fast so he went to the fridge, got out a block of cheese and cut a bit off for Ruby and the rest of the pugs.

When Horton finished his last mini meal of the day he would scoot to the back door as fast as he could go. All our doors are glass, sliding doors and he'd sit watching us until we came in. Sometimes he'd get impatient and start pounding on the door with his paw, telling us to hurry up and come back in. Sometimes it was David and I and the stars that kept us out there so long; other times it was his elderly sisters who made him wait. Tommy would walk outside and be lifting his leg in no time, but the girls always had to sniff every patch of weeds and every blade of grass before carefully selecting that special area to squat in. And Horton all the while would be pounding. He had eaten his tiny dinner, now he wanted his nappy changed and to be put into bed and a blanket placed over him. He used to eat his last meal so fast some nights that David would barely have time to get outside the door before he was at his heels. Sometimes he'd want to come out and join us; other times he was contented to stay inside where it was warm. In the middle of winter he never once pounded on the glass. I think he thought it was funny watching all of us standing out there shivering while the little old ladies of the pack made their special selection of grass. The colder the night and the stronger the wind, it seemed like the longer they took choosing and I'd look back at the house and see Horton sitting there all warm and cosy watching us and envy him like you would not believe. When we came inside again Horton would turn and scoot back up the hall. He'd beat every single one of us into the bedroom. He loved getting in bed at the end of the day. It was the only time he actually enjoyed going to sleep. I think he knew at night time everybody in the house slept and there was nothing going on, nothing to miss out on, so he used to settle down to sleep very quickly every single night.

CHAPTER FIFTEEN

All Babies Need a Pram

As soon as it became evident that Horton needed to have a pram I set about trying to find him the perfect one. I'd never had a dog in a pram before and was really excited at the prospect. I knew Grace would have liked a pram because she wasn't overly interested in walking, but I just had it in the back of my mind as a thought for later on in her life and left it at that. She was such a tiny pug, so I found it easier to tuck her under my arm and stride back to the house with her whenever she pawed my leg to tell me she'd had enough walking. Besides, every day differed with Gracie. Some days she'd walk all the way, some days half and others only a quarter of the walk had been done before the pawing began. The weather had a lot to do with it, but until there was some consistency I just held the images of pretty pink prams with lacy frills in my head as something to be gotten at a future date. It would've been useless getting a pram and just carting it along for the ride on the off-chance Grace wanted to get in and I felt it would hinder being able to go in certain parts of the paddock and I'd have to be constantly looking down, making sure I didn't run into anybody. With Grace, until she or one of the other oldies needed a pram full-time there was no point in getting one. But of course all that changed as soon as Horton arrived on the scene. If we were to be able to stay together as a group on the longer walks then he needed some help doing that. I mean, I could have let him scurry along a bit then pick him up like I used to do when he was a puppy, but I worried about Grace and didn't want her feeling left out. She was used to me being able to pick her up when she got tired. I couldn't just shun her because I had a new special needs son who needed looking after. Grace was here first; she needed me still being there for her, looking after all her needs. They all did. I have never rejected one pug because a needier little blessing joined the clan and I wasn't going to start now. I have always felt sad when a family gets a new dog and the old dog is left out. That just doesn't sit right with my heart. No dog should ever be cast aside because you've gone out and bought yourself something shiny and new. There are ways to enjoy your new dog while still letting the old dogs know they are important. A lot of fights with new additions are done out of jealousy and if you work it right, double up on your love and attention, then nobody is going to feel left out. I get annoyed when I hear somebody saying that they had to take their old dog to the pound because it was picking on the new one; of course it's going to start fights. Wouldn't you fight too if your partner brought in somebody new then acted like you weren't even there. I'm not advising you not to get another dog; I'm saying that you need to put some thought into it and everything will run smoothly. Put yourself in the old dog's shoes.

Give some thought to how it would be feeling at this time and use your common sense.

When David was home, everything on the walks was easier. He'd take Horton and I'd take Grace, but he was only able to walk with us on the weekends, so I had to work something out to enable everyone to be happy on those five days a week I was walking with them on my own. I did think of trying to juggle things, leaving Horton down and carrying Grace, then when she'd had a little rest popping her down and starting to carry Horton so he could do the same. I also thought about carrying both of them. I had two arms didn't I? In my mind it was a breeze but in reality, not so much. I knew one day I would probably end up dropping one of them and if by some miracle I could avoid doing that then picking up one while holding another would no doubt be uncomfortable for one if not both of them. I couldn't be juggling my two babies like shopping bags. Grace was old and needed to be handled with care and Horton had special needs and needed thought given every time he was picked up or put down. A pram would be easier and keep things running smoothly and once the others learnt to walk in harmony with the four wheels I knew things would work out pretty nicely for all of us. All it'd take was a bit of training and we'd be set.

With Horton being a boy I knew I wouldn't be able to get the pink girly pram I'd dreamt of, but I wanted to get something big enough for both Horton and Grace to fit in. I looked at a lot of second hand prams to find the right one. I was going for a human baby's pram because, basically, at the time, I had no idea they made special prams for dogs. And I went for second hand one because I didn't know if Horton or Grace would take to it. I figured if they didn't like it I'd simply drop it off at the nearest opportunity shop and start thinking of another mode of transport. Plus, second hand prams come with a few dents and scratches, so it wouldn't bother me as much when my babies added a few more. I started looking on eBay and was outbid a few times because I couldn't believe how much second hand prams were selling for. I had my heart set on an old English pram, the ones with those beautiful high wheels, but I figured a jogging pram would have better wheels for handling the uneven ground out in the paddocks. The wheels on those things are thick and chunky and I wanted to keep the jerking around to a minimum. I couldn't have Horton's little head and neck bouncing around all over the place. I wanted the wheels to take the impact, not my son's body and a jogger would be ideal for that. But the beautiful blue and yellow jogger came and Horton hated it. He sniffed the chunky shock-absorbing wheels and quickly backed away. It was even worse when we put him in. I didn't realize there was a downwards slant on those things; we used blankets to level it out so he didn't fall forwards, but he still didn't like being in there. The jogging pram was wrong in all manner of ways. It had to be modified so he wouldn't slip through the bar at the front and it wasn't secured at the back. Basically, it was made for a human baby and no matter what we did to it it was unsuitable for a dog. So it had to go.

Next came the most beautiful royal blue pram I had ever laid eyes on. Small for a human baby, I thought, but it was perfect for both Horton and Grace to fit in comfortably together if that's what they wanted to do. The lady we bought it off was totally disgusted that it was going to be used for a dog. Apparently, it had been in her family for years. With a look of horror on her face, she glared and said, "A dog? Are you serious? A dog?" She spat the words at me like venom. I think if it hadn't been purchased on eBay and already paid for she would have refused to let us take it. I truly believe she would have had a good old cry once we were out the door, she seemed that upset about it. Luckily, I had left Horton at home with David when I went to pick up the pram. It was a long drive and I didn't want to put Horton through that, so he stayed home with his dad and my sister came along with me so I had some company. The woman's husband didn't much care who the pram was going to be used for; he just wanted the money, but I feel he would have had quite a job on his hands calming her down when we left, so I guess he'd earn every cent. I am glad Horton wasn't there with me. Thankful he wasn't around such negativity. At least he was spared that.

As I drove home in the dark I wondered what Horton would be doing now. He loved his daddy time, all the pugs do. I imagined him being spoilt rotten while I was away. David always makes every second of his time with the pugs count and I was happy Horton was home enjoying himself. The hostile woman could cry all she liked; my baby had a lovely blue pram and I was ecstatic about it. But that pram proved to be as unsuitable as the first one. The reasons were entirely different but it was still just as unsuitable. I worried about telling David because there was already one perfectly good pram sitting in the local op shop and here was yet another one I'd gone and spent a lot of money on and now it was not up to the job, but once he found out it was unstable he didn't seem to mind. To be honest, I don't think it was actually meant to be for a human baby; well, not for when they started sitting up it wasn't. It seemed to be more for a newborn, although they didn't say so at the time of sale, probably because it's a waste of money to buy a pram merely for the first few months of life. It was a really lovely looking pram, though. My sister thought so too. We talked all the way home about how beautiful it was and when I rang and told her it was no use for Horton, she said she'd give me what I paid for it so I could go out and buy him a more suitable pram. Now it sits in her home holding her antique doll collection and looks beautiful doing so. Whenever I'm at her house I go over and give it a little push and think of what might have been. I sure did have my heart set on pushing Horton around the farm in that little pram, but I would never put him in danger so it had to go. Well, they say three times is the charm and for Horton's pram it was the case. The third one came and I reckon would have stopped traffic when it was brand new. It was that beautiful. I loved the size of the wheels. Big, chunky and white they were, but they didn't stay that way for long. I used to wash the mud off the wheels every time I brought it back inside after our winter walks, but after a while there were more important things to do, so I kind of got over it. I figured they'd only end up getting muddy again, so I parked it on a towel to drip and went off to do something else. If it was particularly caked up I'd wash it, but if it was just speckled I'd leave it be. The third pram was blue on the bottom half and white on top and the navy against the pure white on the body really set it off. The ribbed plastic on the handle was cracked and its body was a bit scratched and damaged, which made me smile. I could see the irony in it, not in a nasty way, more that the pram was meant to come to us, as if it belonged here somehow. The hood had a tired bit of old discoloured lace gripping onto it and I really thought the first strong wind out in the open paddocks would have seen the last of it, but it held on for dear life every time the winds came and is still attached today. That too would have been glorious to look at when it was brand new and would have framed the faces of chubby-cheeked babies beautifully. As I pushed my baby along I thought about the other mothers who had done exactly the same thing, stood in the same position I was in, held onto the handle like I was doing now, thinking their babies were the most perfect little things in the world too. I liked that my pram had history; well, not just history but a history of love. No heart loves quite like a new mother's heart loves and I liked thinking that all that loving energy was being passed onto Horton as I pushed.

The pram opened up a whole new world for Horton and for all of us as a family. People thought I was stupid – well, at least looked that way – for pushing a pug around the paddocks in a pram, but I didn't care. I wasn't put on this earth for them. I was put here for my animals. I truly believe that I was born to love and care for these beautiful creatures and give them the life they deserve and I love doing it. If folks looked at me and thought I looked silly pushing a pram around the farm well that was on them. I had nothing to do with it and besides, their opinion of me wasn't what was important. My aim was to show Horton the world and not let him miss out on anything. I wasn't about to leave my little sweetheart inside the house because somebody might have thought less of me for doing what I do. What did I care about that? All that was on my mind was that my baby was living a full life. He loved those pram rides and I loved pushing him. I was in my element. To be honest, I think I loved it a lot more than he did, but David says that is debatable.

What I liked about the pram was that it allowed Horton to get real close to the action of life on a farm, yet be out of harm's way. It not only got him off the ground, it got him up higher than he normally would have been and gave him a fantastic view of all that was going on. He loved his vantage point; you could see it on his face. He loved being right in the middle of things and I never had to worry about his safety when he was in his pram. I think he would have liked to be on the ground sometimes; he loved to be upfront and touching everything either with his mouth or his front paws, but without the pram there was no way of keeping him one hundred percent safe in certain situations. It put my mind at ease.

It took Horton a while to get used to being in the pram and we didn't push him. We just sat him in there a few times a day without moving the wheels and let him have a little sniff of everything and get used to being so high off the ground. At first Horton just sat there too scared to move. I would stand close to him so he didn't feel alone then as he relaxed he started moving around in the pram, discovering all corners, sniffing the sides and pawing at the ratty old lace. I'd walk a few steps away then a few more and a few more. I wanted him to be able to look down and see the ground so he'd know he was up high and he couldn't do that with me blocking his view. Once being up there and me not being right by his side didn't faze him, I started pushing him around. Nothing drastic; no more than a few slow steps at a time. Once that didn't worry him we went round the lounge a few times and eventually out the back door. His front legs were so strong which was a good thing because the back ramp being on the angle it is really altered the way the pram leant, but Horton took that in his stride too. After the first time he knew what to do; he looked down, saw it coming and braced himself beautifully and down we'd go. I did used to hold the pram as upright as I could, but with all the other pugs being excited about the walk and jostling for prime position, my mind would be on avoiding them and Horton just realized what he had to do when going down the ramp and did it.

Maybe I took the getting Horton used to the pram thing a lot slower than I needed to, but I didn't want to scare him. That would have put him off for life. In the end he loved that pram because he associated it with being out and about. He'd beat me across the room to get to it. He knew the routine; he knew when it was time for a walk and the ground in winter was too wet to have him down, so he got to see everything from the warmth and comfort of his pram while his brother and sisters ambled about on the ground, sniffing and weeing on everything in sight. Sure, Horton missed out on a sniff but he used to enjoy watching them going about their business and shot from one side of the pram to the other keeping an eye on the seven of them wherever they went. They used to come over and check on him regularly. Their stiff old legs would wobble on over and their little old faces would glance up to see what he was doing then wander off and continue with their walk. Some of the more able-bodied ones would jump up at the sides for a closer look at their baby brother and that was fine because there were a lot of scratches on the pram already. A few more weren't going to hurt. Besides, Horton loved it when they did that. He made it into a game. Tommy, being so big, could get really close to Horton and he'd try to paw at Tom's head. Or he'd bounce forward and do his little playful bark over the side then bounce back, flip round and do the same at the other side of the pram. I never had to worry about that pram tipping over because it was solid. Even if Tom jumped up while I was away helping Ruby to her feet I knew his weight wasn't going to send Horton down the hill or crashing to the ground. Once the brake was on, that pram wasn't going anywhere. I was glad I had chosen a human baby's pram because those brakes are tough. They're made to withstand more than dog prams are I think, because they're designed to prevent a human baby rolling onto the road. Products for dogs and products for human beings are two very different things. Not too many people sue over a dog but they sure do when a human baby gets injured and so manufacturers tend to put more effort into their products for that reason.

I don't think Horton felt like he was missing out on anything by being in his pram. I think he used to like lording it over the others to tell you the truth. Horton liked having the higher position and would peep over the side, looking down on them in more ways than one. I believe Horton thought he was getting special privileges with that pram and I think it made him feel superior even; well, it certainly didn't make him feel like he was lesser than they were that was for sure. He was great at sharing too, which was a good thing because Grace wasn't the only sibling who decided they'd like a ride in the pram with him. Harper and Ruby hopped in too from time to time. If they got tired or weren't feeling well on that particular day they'd come over and let me know they'd had enough and so into the pram they would go. The most I ever had in there at one time was four. That's the most that could go in at the same time as Horton without squashing him. I probably could have fit five or six in there at the one time as long as one of them wasn't Horton, but that's the most it could take. Four did get awfully heavy and hard to push on the unevenness of the ground and it was the ride uphill that most needed help with, so that's when they all hobbled over for a lift. Still, it gave me a good workout and they all ambled out and scurried off as soon as we got to the top of the hill.

But the pram wasn't just handy for family walks, it changed Horton's life. His world became bigger once his four-wheeled vehicle entered the house. It meant I could show him more of this earth he was so interested in discovering. If I was going to help one of my friends with their animals it meant Horton could come with me, not just wait in the car or in their house watching us from the door but actually come right where we were and get involved; well, as involved as he could be and remain safe. There were two things that were always on my mind with Horton – his safely and his happiness – and it was a constant juggling act getting the two right. I didn't want to have him living a lesser life in any shape or form, but his safety had to come first. His health and his safety were the two most important things. After they were sorted, the fun could begin and as far as Horton was concerned, life was all about fun.

I'd take him with me when I was helping move livestock. Just little livestock: sheep or goats, never cows or horses. I'd find him the perfect spot, in the shade if it was sunny; under a tree with a breeze was ideal for Horton. Being a black pug, he needed to be kept cool, and I'd pop his pram against a shed or in the entrance of a shed on windy days. I'd put the pram brake on, make sure he was comfortable, bring the hood up so his ears wouldn't get cold (I didn't want him getting an earache) and then off I'd go. I'd put him as close as he could be so he'd see what was happening but far enough back so he wouldn't get hurt. Although he was never in the same paddock as the livestock he needed to be in my full view. I needed to be able to glance over and see what he was doing at all times. I'd be unsettled if I couldn't see his squishy little face. Horton used to love watching the show and would bounce up and down on his nappy. He'd be doing his puppy bark and really getting involved with what was going on. I'd glance over and see his little mouth open and his eyes would either be as big as saucers or closed with his head tilted back in a long, slow howling woof. He had the most beautiful eyes and I loved watching them taking in the world. He'd be completely worn out by the time we got home and fall asleep as soon as I put him in the car sometimes. He seemed to be more tired than I was but he'd had a good day and that's what was important to me. He'd be barely able to lift his head when David got home. Normally he'd be shoving the others out of the way in order to reach Dad first. David would walk in and be bending down giving multiple pats then look up and ask where Horton was. I'd point to a bed and there he'd be, sitting up, wide awake but too tired to get out. He'd be hoping Dad would come over to him and be doing everything in his power to make that happen: bouncing, shouting out, anything that didn't involve actually having to leave his bed because he was too worn out for that.

On his big outing days Horton would be half asleep, even when I was changing his nappy. He just couldn't manage to keep his eyes fully open throughout the whole thing. I'd prop him up so I could get the nappy under him and he'd be there all sleepy-eyed and swaying. If I didn't have my hand holding him up he would never have stayed upright. He was simply too exhausted to do so. I've always adored changing Horton's nappy; it's just one of those loving tender mother and son moments of closeness that I got to enjoy. He was so good about it, too. Even though he preferred being nappy-free he would always come over to me when I called his name, even though he could see the new nappy in my hand.

I remember the weekend the power went out; it worried me because Horton didn't do well when he was cold. Luckily, it didn't happen in the middle of winter. It was towards the end of October from memory; not freezing but still cold enough to bother Horton once the sun went down. You always think you have enough candles in the house for times like this, but you don't and we were running out fast. Having no idea when things were going to be restored I began rummaging in places I hadn't rummaged for years and began finding items I hadn't seen for years. A few dog toys got tossed on the floor and I could hear them squeaking in the darkness. Eventually, I found some tiny tea-light candles in the back of a drawer and set them up in the bedroom and the entire family settled in there. It was a fun night. All the pugs gathered on the bed with us and David and I sat talking while they slept. Horton was fascinated with the candles and took the longest to go to sleep. The older ones settled down quickly but he sat doing tiny woofs at the flickering flames. He was totally mesmerized. He'd never seen candles before. For safety reasons the ones on his birthday cake never got lit so the glow of candlelight was a whole new experience for him and he loved seeing new things. First he began barking at them while I was trying to change his nappy. Horton didn't like dark rooms so I got David to bring him in once the candles were all alight. David put Horton on the bed where most of the light was centered and as soon as his nappy was off he shot over to the other side for a closer look at the candles. He didn't even give me chance to put the other one on and because the candles were exciting for him I thought he may have had a little accident on the bed but he was more interested in the candles than weeing. He climbed over his sleeping siblings to get a better look. They were high enough to not be a danger to anybody and he sat watching them for the longest time. When I came over and put his nappy on he barely looked at me. He just shifted positions when my head got in the way of his view. He was like that for ages, just sitting there looking up, taking everything in.

It was going to be a real long night without any TV, computers, CD players and no phones. I thought it may have been boring, but it wasn't. David and I sat and talked about the pugs and the farm and our lovely life together. We talked well into the night while the pugs soundly slept. It was nice just sitting together like that without any distractions. You forget just how long it's been since you had time to sit and talk without any interruptions. We vowed to do it more often and we did, but not nearly as often as we should.

No power meant no heat. We have a log fire but the fan is electric so all the wood in the world was useless to us because we couldn't afford to chance things and set the whole house on fire. It meant no hot water bottles either and I worried about keeping Horton warm. When he finally got tired of woofing at the candles he came shuffling over and began pawing at my arm to bring him up. I kept him asleep on my chest throughout the night. He always liked sleeping in that position whenever I was reading a book or watching TV. He could hear his mummy and daddy talking but that didn't keep him awake. He was comfortable so he stayed put and we kept each other warm all night long.

CHAPTER SIXTEEN

Other Breeds

Although our main passion in life is pugs we do occasionally take in other breeds. Only the small ones, though, as I can't have my elderly or special needs pugs being knocked around by dogs twice their size and weight. David would prefer it if we stayed with pugs and I have a real hard time getting him to let me bring another breed into the house. David and I have been very lucky in our relationship; we've rarely argued about anything from the first day we met. I think we are probably one of those happy couples that get on other couples' nerves. My sister calls us freaks and says we're not normal and I suppose in a way she's right because I don't know too many other couples who are exactly like we are. I think we have just been very lucky to have found one another and I feel blessed to have David in my life. We just really seem to like one another, respect one another as human beings and are extremely compatible in a lot of areas. We never argue about money, we never argue about what TV shows to watch, what movies to go and see, what we want to eat or any of the other trivial things in life, but if we're going to disagree on something this will be it. He wants to stick purely with pugs but my opinion on the matter is that it doesn't hurt to bring a small elderly non pug dog into the house to live out its final days. And when there is a little dog in a pound somewhere in Australia and we're the last hope that's when I know in my heart that we have to act and it's also when I know I am going to be in for a few rounds of heated discussions with my husband. Personally, I don't like arguing with David and he says the same thing about me but when I feel this strongly about something I just have to put up with a little discomfort in order to get what I want; well, not only what I want but when I want it or should I say before the dog's time in the pound runs out, which, more often than not, leaves me with only a day or so to change my husband's mind. Don't get me wrong, David isn't a horrible person. He pays all our vet bills without complaint. Time and time again he pays them, regardless of how hefty they are. And he has never once taken the cheapest option when it comes to our dogs health. It's always, "Save the dog, do what you need to do to make them well again. We'll worry about the cost later." He loves each one of our pugs with a true father's heart and will do anything for them. With other breeds, though, I think he worries that if he says yes to me all the time then we'll end up with a pile of different breeds of dogs running about the place. I guess you do need to have one level-headed person in the family to keep things sane and running smoothly. I have much to be grateful to David for because a lot of husbands don't share or support their wives' interests as much as David does with me. David is a keeper and I'm well aware of how lucky I am to have found one as good as he is.

I do understand how David feels about pugs because they are the breed that truly has my heart but I love all canine species regardless of what they look like and have a huge amount of admiration for them. I have a list of dog breeds that I know I'm never going to own. They're on a wish list inside my head and I know that's probably where most of them are going to stay. Basically, I was born loving dogs, all animals really, but dogs have a special place in my heart. I adore everything about them. I think they have the biggest hearts. No person is ever going to love you with the kind of love a dog does. They don't just love, they live it, totally, and one hundred percent pure love and devotion is bestowed on their owners. I like their antics as well. I think they are the funniest little creatures God ever created. I also like their intellect, how their minds work and love watching them going about their day-to-day lives. And the best sight you are ever going to see in my book is a dog peacefully sleeping. Some lie flat, others contort, twist, wrap themselves around things, yet seem perfectly comfortable sleeping that way. Large breed or small, in my book, you can't surpass a dog sleeping for all-out cuteness. I also like the differences in the breeds, not just size and shape, but the different personalities that reside in each one. I love the slow, graceful gait of the huge breeds and adore the deep bellowing woofs that come straight from those large abdomens of theirs. I also love the natures of the tiny breeds. You'll find a world of quirky characters there. I appreciate each specific canine breed we have. Cross breeds can be a whole lot of fun too because you can get some crazy-looking dogs coming out of cross litters and their siblings don't all end up looking the same either. I find that adorable. It's always interesting to see what they'll end up looking like as adults. I love all stages of a dog's life and I take in the oldies because I like looking after them. I'm a natural born nurturer, so it suits me well, but I love watching stumbling, unsteady, giddy puppies as well, especially when they're playing. That's a great sight to see. A pile of puppy siblings rough-housing is magical to witness. I don't often get the chance to see these wonderful sights but when I do I'm never in a rush to leave, I reckon I could watch them for hours on end.

If I didn't share my life with pugs then I wouldn't just settle on one particular breed. Pugs to me are perfect, so I like having a lot of them around, but because no other breed comes close to a pug for me, I think I'd have to have a few different breeds to make up for it. This last line could get me into a bit of trouble because dog lovers are very loyal and very protective of the breed that has their heart. And I like that about them. I really do. All breeds need to have somebody in their corner batting for them. I think it's important that people love different breeds. It would be heartbreaking if we all adored the same one. It'd mean so many wonderful dogs were being left out and what a truly sad thing that would be. I've never argued with anybody who feels the need to stick up for their breed. I think, "Good on you for being so passionate and loving of that particular breed that you're getting hot under the collar about it." I mean so many dogs are ill-treated in this world that I can never be anything but supportive of a person who deeply loves their dog. Personally, I have never felt the need to push a pug onto anybody. I figure if they can't see how wonderful they are for themselves it's okay. Pugs have plenty of people who love them. I have, however, been able to change a few people's views about the pug breed merely by having them spend time in my home. A lot of people make up their minds about the pug breed without ever having met one. Once they spend a few hours in their company and see how wonderful they are, opinions change.

I think terriers are a fantastic, lively and just all round good fun and they can go from deep sleep to alert in about two seconds flat. They'll be lying there resembling a soft toy then be up with ears pricked, barking in less than a heartbeat. Terriers, pure or mixed, are about the best value for money you'll ever get fun wise. Shih Tzu's have lovely shaped faces. They remind me a lot of pugs. I like that they look like plush toys. The little trotting along they do is adorable too. Pomeranian's are cute and Pekinese are perfect. I mean, how could they not be? They're basically just fluffy pugs. If I could share my life with a large breed it'd be the English or Neapolitan mastiff or an Irish wolfhound, deer hounds are beautiful, too. When I was a teenager I saw a photo in a glamour magazine of a woman in front of an old stone house with thick columns. She had six Irish wolfhounds with her, it was a fashion magazine and she was no doubt a model wearing beautiful clothes, but I didn't see the clothing or the woman I just saw the dogs and that image has stayed with me all these years. I think it would be great to have so many huge hounds to wander around the grounds with. Perhaps that'll be me in my next life or perhaps it is the life I'm living now. She was tall and slim and her dogs were tall and slim. I'm short and chubby and I have pugs. I guess me and my pugs are just squat down versions of her and her dogs.

I think basset hounds have unique bodies and they just draw me in. I love their ears, snouts and eyes. They always look depressed to me but I think that makes them even more appealing. For over twenty years I've wanted a basset hound. I've even got a name picked out – Breeze – but I don't think there will ever be a

Breeze in my future. I'd also love to have a Chihuahua or Chihuahua x sharing my life again: white, short coat, female. I've had a little pink winter jacket sitting in the top drawer for about eight years now just waiting to keep a little body warm. The white Chihuahua is the wish list dog I think about most of all. Almost every week I wonder if this is going to be the week she will enter my life, but so far I'm still waiting.

I've had a few mixed breeds here over the years and I've enjoyed loving and sharing my life with all of them. One little guy stands out clearly in my mind. His name was Miles. Miles's name was Golden Ledger when he came. We called him Miles because it just seemed to fit in well with that little face of his. He was a pure-bred Shih Tzu and only weighed about 2.5kg. He was mostly blind, too, but none of that seemed to matter. He made himself at home here right away. The only problem we had with Miles was that Horton thought he was the boss of him. Horton had never seen a dog smaller than himself and I guess it was just too tempting for him not to act on it. I suppose being the boss of somebody was far too enticing for him to just scoot away from.

Horton had never tried to boss any of the others around, but he wouldn't let himself be picked on either. Once his health and strength improved he had no trouble at all letting the others know if they were getting on his nerves. He never started any arguments. He'd rather put his energy into playing with Emily, his toys and farm life. He was happy to fall in with the pack, not be in charge of it. Horton was not a bossy pug but it seemed that having somebody in the house that was smaller than he was just went to his head. He scooted along beside Miles wherever he went and hardly slept the first few days after Miles entered the house. He was that excited to have this funny-looking creature living here. When Horton first set eyes on Miles he shot over from the other side of the room and began circling him. If he'd been able to walk on four legs he would have been stomping about trying to display his power. He got real close to Miles's face and you could see from his expression that he knew Miles was different. You could almost see his mind ticking over, as if he was thinking, "Hang on a minute. You're not like us are you? You're not a pug." He tilted his head to the side and was looking at Miles like he was kind of defective. I don't think he'd ever seen a different breed of dog before; well, not close up anyway. He's seen a few different breeds in the vet's waiting room but they were either in a carrier or sitting high up on their owner's knee. But little Miles was here on the floor standing right in our lounge and Horton thought he was the best thing ever.

Once Horton got used to having Miles around he began getting a little bit rough. It started off as playing but when he knew Miles wasn't up to telling him off it got a little bit more forceful. For Horton's part, he was in his element. He loved being the boss and Miles had such an easy-going nature he didn't seem to bother about it too much, so I let it go for a while hoping the novelty would wear off and when it didn't I decided to step in. The power of thinking he was in charge of somebody turned Horton into quite the little monster. He was having so much fun with his new chew toy and wasn't for stopping on his own, so something had to be done about it for poor Miles's sake. I don't like dogs being harassed in their own home. It's not fair. All of us, whether human beings or dogs, have the right to a little bit of peace in our own homes. It was around this time that Horton learnt the meaning of the word no. Up until then there'd really been no reason to tell him off. He was such a good little boy and hardly put a paw wrong. He knew the word stop. I used it all the time when he got too close to the gravel driveway. He knew that the tone of my voice would change when I meant business, so he'd sit by the edge of the gravel and wait for me to catch up and carry him across. Of course there were a few times when he'd ignore me. If he saw Gerald over by the fence he'd forget about everyone and everything around him and would shoot over to see his friend as fast as he could go. I never told Horton off when I caught up with him, because by the time he reached Gerald he would have completely forgotten I'd told him to stop and also because I think we all need something in our lives to get so excited about that we break the rules for.

People thought I was cruel telling Horton no. They didn't think he was doing much harm to Miles but they weren't here all the time. They only saw part of it. And besides, Horton was just like any other one of our pugs; he had to learn what was and wasn't acceptable behaviour. My sister couldn't bear to hear me telling Horton off. She hated seeing the face he did. She'd get really upset about it and have to leave the room. She thought because Horton was born with a disability it gave him some sort of free pass to do whatever he wanted to do, but it didn't. It couldn't. If we were treating Horton as normal in every other way then he had to be treated normally with discipline as well.

He was a very intelligent boy and he knew what he was doing was wrong because after the first time I told him off he wouldn't go near Miles if he thought I was watching. But as soon as my back was turned he was straight onto it. He'd even pounce on poor

Miles as he slept. I'd hear the noise and turn quickly to catch Horton in the act. He looked bewildered by this, as if he couldn't figure out how I knew what he was doing if my back was turned. He was good, though. He'd stop right away. Sometimes I didn't even have to utter a word; I'd just turn and point my finger at him and he'd stop.

Horton got pretty sneaky when he wanted to break the rules. He'd be dying to have some fun, chew on Miles's ears, and would go to all manner of lengths to make sure I didn't know what he was up to. He would sit watching Miles sleeping and little old Miles sure did sleep a lot. Horton would sit across the room watching the rise and fall of his tiny old brother's chest then, as soon as he woke and went over to have a drink, Horton was beside him.

Because Miles couldn't see very well and his little old mind got confused from time to time sometimes he'd walk all over the house, go in and out of every room until he found his way back into the kitchen and the water bowl. Horton would see him leave the room and quickly scoot after him. He'd get level with him in the hallway and start biting at his ears as he walked around searching for the water bowl. Horton was always only ever playing. He never got nasty or bared his teeth or anything like that, but he did get rough and to poor little Miles there wouldn't have been a great deal of difference in the two. It took a while but in the end Horton realized that Miles had somebody in the house that was always going to watch out for him. It wasn't fun if he was getting told off all the time so he went back to playing with Emily. He could be as rough as he liked with her and never once got reprimanded for it. Thing is, it was the same with Horton; I would always be there to make sure none of the others played too roughly with him. It was a case of whoever in the house needed protecting the most would be the one I would constantly look out for. I think Emily was glad to have her little rough playing brother back. She seemed to have missed him when he was off harassing Miles. As soon as she realized he'd lost interest in his fluffy brother she bounced off the couch and began engaging Horton in play. He'd spend hours scooting after her then she'd let him catch her and he'd be so thrilled he'd start doing his little puppy barks and bite into her tummy. She loved it and he loved it and little Miles peacefully slept right through it all in his bed on the other side of the room. And when he got up to get a drink nobody noticed any more so he was able to quench his thirst and go right back to sleep again; well, as soon as he found his way back to his bed he did anyway.

I have always gotten a huge amount of happiness from every dog I have ever shared my life with and I feel very lucky to be living on this little farm of mine. My day-to-day existence is a contented one. I have a great husband who is also my best friend, I wake up in the morning surrounded by lush green hills that I spend a lot of time gazing at, I hear the delightful sounds of livestock out in the open paddocks instead of bumper to bumper traffic car engines and horns, the air I breathe is fresh and pure, I don't live amongst smog. Basically, the pugs and I walk around in a little blissful bubble and I never take for granted how blessed we all are. That is why I make it my mission to help other people as often as I can. If we have any spare money we donate to dog rescue groups and I'm constantly on the lookout for ways to help those who devote their lives to rescuing animals. I have the utmost admiration and respect for the people on the frontline in animal welfare. They see the horrors up close that most of us are protected from, they have had their hearts broken from what they have to witness day after day and yet get up the next day and do it all over again. I feel it is my duty help raise funds so that they can continue helping the many animals in need.

In 2010, I entered Horton in a cutest pug competition. It was to raise money for Pug Rescue. I hadn't been on Facebook long and when I saw they were asking for cute black pugs to enter I thought to myself, "Well, I've got a little black pug here that's so adorably cute I almost faint every time I look at him." So, I went and had a look at their webpage. This group had almost seventy pugs in their care at the time: seventy pugs to restore back to health and find homes for. That just blew my mind. I'd never known of anything like this before. And what about vet bills? Ours were high with eight pugs. What would paying for seventy be like? I knew in my heart I had to do something to help them. I just knew I had to enter Horton in their competition and I reckon if Horton could talk he would have said the same thing. Here he was being loved and adored with all of his needs met every single day while so many pugs on the other side of the world were needy.

Up until that time only fawn pugs had won the competition. I was under no illusions of winning. And I've never been overly competitive. It's just not in my nature. All I wanted to do was help. I just wanted my much-loved little boy to be able to help wherever he could and so I asked if they would allow a pug from Australia to enter. At first I wasn't sure if they'd allow us to be a part of it. I had no idea what the rules were. It may have been a

USA-only competition for all I knew. I'd never entered any of my pugs in anything like this before so it was all new to me. An email came back saying we were very welcome and that all they needed was a photo. They then went on to explain to me how it all worked and told me what the prizes were. There were prizes? Really? That surprised me. I hadn't even thought about prizes. I told them if Horton should win anything they were to keep it or auction it off to make more money for their pugs. We weren't interested in prizes. I didn't even think there should be prizes when it comes to charity organizations. It kind of defeats the purpose. All money, including prize money, should go straight back to the pugs. Well, that's my opinion anyway, but I guess if you don't have prizes some people wouldn't enter. I told them the best prize for me was being able to help them achieve their goal. I just wanted to have a small part in helping all the pugs that were continually streaming through their door.

For a few days I glanced over every single photo I had of Horton and there were hundreds, literally hundreds. David had to keep upgrading my computer because I needed more space to store them. I had days where every time Horton made a move I'd be there capturing it. I thought everything he did was wonderful and didn't want to miss anything. He became a real ham in front of the camera, too; not that he knew what the camera was for. I think he just saw how excited I got, so learnt to become excited too. Whenever he saw the camera in my hand he became happy because he could see how happy I was. I captured his growth spurts, his victories, him with his brothers and sisters and him on his own. I took shots of him trying to chase the sheep and shots of him sitting by the fence watching Gerald. I captured his nappy-on moments and his nappy-free days. Horton in front of the fire woofing is one of my favourite shots; it's not a brilliant photo by any means, the lighting wasn't good, but I love it all the same. I captured Horton in the sunshine and with his face against the window when it was cold outside. I even put the camera in his pram when we went for a walk so I was ready to record his reaction and interest in the many different things happening on the farm and I crept around taking photos of Horton sleeping. I've always been a sucker for sleeping pugs and this little baby was so beautiful when he slept. His little eyes used to vanish into his facial folds. And I took videos of Horton as well: plenty of videos of him discovering the farm. I suppose I could have sent a photo of Horton with his wheels on but I didn't. I guess it may have gotten him a few more votes but they would have been purely for sympathy and I didn't want to do that. I felt that, although it would have helped raise more money for this group, I just couldn't do it to Horton because there was so much more to him than his back legs and crooked spine. When people looked at his photo I wanted them to see his lovely little face and his wonderful expressive eyes. I wanted them to look at him and see him, really see him for what he truly was: a stunning-looking black pug. In time, everybody got to know Horton's story but at the start they saw the part of Horton I wanted to portray. The image they got of him was this sweet little black pug with lovely deep amber eyes and a mischievous face. I've always thought Horton's face reflected his personality. I can always tell when he's up to something because his faces changes. He gives himself away. He thinks he's got you fooled but he never does. I wanted people to see what I consider to be the real Horton before they got to know the real Horton. I knew if I submitted a photo with wheels all they would be concentrating on was the metal frame. He would be forever known as the poor little paraplegic pug and that wasn't him at all because he was beautiful and joyous. Those were the labels I thought should be connected to Horton and anything else would have lessened who he was. They say a photo paints a thousand words and I believe that too. The people in America didn't know the life he was living here or how much he had accomplished with the little body he'd been born into. I knew if they were able to spend an hour with Horton their idea of a paraplegic pug would change. He out-moves almost every other pug in the house. And when he sees his daddy take a seat he goes so fast towards him I'm almost afraid he's going to hurt himself. Horton can be sitting there looking in the opposite direction then he must hear the leather shift as David lowers himself onto the couch and he flips around quickly and scoots across the floor at full speed – head down, front legs going a hundred miles an hour – then he'll look up just before he makes contact with the couch and when he sees his dad's hands being lowered he leaps and jumps up into them. It all happens so fast. I'm not sure if the lower part of his body fully leaves the ground or not, but it sure does look like it. He is leaping up as high as a paraplegic pug can leap that's for sure. Horton adores his daddy time. He sits on David's knee and glances across at the others as if to say, "He's mine. Get your own daddy." He then plasters David's face with kisses. It doesn't matter if David's been home for hours, the welcome he gets when Horton first sits on his knee is the same one he gets when walking in the door after he's been gone all day.

With the cutest pug competition, I wanted Horton to win a few hearts with his face first. After all he's given me, I wanted to give him that and I knew he'd be able to do it. I was hoping he'd make the 2011 calendar. The top twelve pugs would go on to be part of the calendar with the winning pug, the highest money-earning pug, on the cover. I wasn't sure whether it would happen and every Monday morning I'd nervously wait for the page to download wondering if I was going to see my boy's little face in with the eliminated pugs or if he was still in with a chance. I so wanted Horton to be part of their calendar. I wanted him to light up other homes the way he lit ours up every single day. The photo of Horton celebrating his second birthday was the photo I sent in. The photo with his green party hat off to the side has always been special to me. Horton was sitting beside me on an office chair when I found out he'd made it onto their calendar, I looked at the screen, saw his beautiful little face in amongst the eleven other pugs and I thought to myself "Oh you brilliant, brilliant little boy" then I turned and cupped his cheeks in my palms and kissed his forehead repeatedly. Horton had no idea what was going on but welcomed my kisses, he then sat beside me while I rang everyone I knew with the news. A phone call to his Daddy was made first and Horton tilted his head to one side when he heard David cheering down the phone. They asked for another photo for the Calendar and I thought, "Oh hell! I've already sent you what I consider to be the best one." However, Horton's first birthday photos were pretty special too. A close-up shot of his baby face looking straight into the camera all wide-eyed and beautiful caught my eye, so we went with that and added another smaller photo of him sitting on the grass staring across the front paddock.

David spent a lot of time trying to get the perfect shot of Horton for the calendar. He took numerous photos of his son around the farm, but I didn't think any came close to being as cute as his first birthday photos were. Sure, they weren't as colour-coordinated as they could have been but that in a way made them more special.

I was asked to write a little bit about Horton's life to go with the photos so that people could find out more about the pugs representing each month. Honestly, I could have written an essay. I was so proud of him, but I kept it simple, straight to the point and as short as I could make it. Otherwise there'd have been no room for his photos.

Horton became the June pug and his lovely little velvety face sat right in the middle of the calendar. We bought fourteen calendars to give to family and friends and everybody thought it was wonderful to have one of our kids on a calendar.

CHAPTER SEVENTEEN

Sledge Hammer

Tuesday 4th January 2011 started off like any other day. We had just lost our beautiful fifteen-year-old pug, Grace, and were mourning her privately, quietly, together as a family. I was upset and wasn't ready to tell anybody about it yet. I hadn't even told my Mum that we had lost one of the pugs and she was normally the first person I'd ring. We woke up and did our morning routine. David was on holidays so everybody was happy about that. When Dad is home the pugs are ecstatic and so am I. We love being together, just bobbing about the farm. It was a very hot day and as is always the case when the temperature rises the pugs were a bit lethargic. Horton was also lethargic but no more or less than any of the other pugs. Due to the heat we walked early in the morning then settled down inside with the air conditioner on. Nothing was unusual about Horton. I fed him and changed his nappy then as the day got hotter I took the nappy off and laid him on a towel so he would be cooler. I always put him on the largest, thickest towels in the house and layered them. They're king-sized, so there's plenty of room for him and I'd add a pile of toys to keep him occupied. It also gives him room to wander around a bit while still having something absorbent underneath. He was happy lying in the middle of our bed underneath the ceiling fan playing with his toys, he was cool without a nappy on so the rising temperature outside didn't bother him one little bit. He let me know when he wanted a drink and I carried him outside when the others went out for a wee. He sniffed around on the grass like he always did when he was outdoors, then in we'd all come again until another toilet break was needed. I fed the pugs around 4.00 p.m. and Horton ate his normal-sized tea. At around 8.00 p.m., I noticed that Horton wasn't his normal self. He was having trouble settling down for any amount of time, he was restless and seemed uncomfortable in the tummy, so I looked him over to see if I could figure out what the trouble was. His nappy was back on by this time so I checked everything was in place with that and made sure nothing had come loose or was digging into him. I also checked him for cuts and grazes in case he had scooted over the top of a stick when outside during the day. Normally, I would notice something like this as soon as it happened because I was always there keeping an eye on what he was doing, but I did a double check anyway just in case I'd missed something. But everything was okay. Nothing was amiss on the outside of his body. I stroked his little face and asked, "What's wrong, baby?" Grace had gastro the week before she died, so I talked to David about it and we both figured Horton had probably picked up a bit of that. He didn't eat his before-bed mini meal so we gave him some medicine to settle his tummy and went to bed, but I had trouble sleeping. When one of the pugs is ill I never sleep well. I kept getting up and checking on him. Sometimes he'd be lying down; other times, sitting up. Just after midnight I woke David because Horton had diarrhea. We cleaned

him up and sat on the bed with him. I knew that Grace had gone to
the vets after a few days of having gastro. We normally try and
give them a day or so for things to clear up naturally. Sometimes
they'll have just eaten something that doesn't agree with them and
its one or two sloppy stools then everything's back to normal.
With Grace it wasn't the case so she was put on something from
our vet to help clear things up. Being fifteen years old, I didn't
want to prolong things for her and have her becoming dehydrated,
so expert advice was sought. Horton sat on a fresh towel in-
between David and me as we discussed what to do. I was stroking
him and he just sat looking up at me. He was uncomfortable but
not so ill that we needed to panic. We sat talking for a little while
and I said to David, "Look, I know it's the middle of the night and
we're going to have to wake somebody up here, but I'd rather do
that than have Horton wait until morning before being seen." I felt
Horton had enough to deal with in his little body without this.
Maybe his diarrhea would clear up by itself in a day or so but
because he was who he is, I didn't want him being left in
discomfort when we could take him somewhere and have his
tummy pain assessed and hopefully eased quickly. Yes, the vet
was going to charge a fortune for this because of the time of night,
but neither David nor I cared. We just wanted to get Horton's
tummy upset settled as soon as possible. Our country vet is about
twenty minutes away and I figured Horton would be already
feeling better by the time David brought him home again and that
thought made me happy. So David rang the vet and made
arrangements for her to meet him at the surgery then set off into
the night while I began washing his soiled bedding. I got a clean
nappy ready for when he came home; we hadn't put a fresh nappy

back on him because of the discomfort. We didn't want him having to have a nappy put on and taken off multiple times when he wasn't feeling well and besides, he was about to be examined. He needed to be nappy-free so the vet could have a good look at him. David just wrapped Horton in a blanket and headed out the door.

Our country vet looked Horton over and wanted to put him on a drip. She was on-call and knew if he stayed in their surgery he would not be properly monitored. If somebody had a cow calving she would have to go and leave Horton on his own. She didn't want to do that so called ahead to an emergency vet about an hour and a half's drive away and David set off for the 24-hour emergency vets. He rang me on the way to let me know what was going on. I was worried but not panicked. I felt a bit useless being here instead of with Horton, but when they left I thought it was going to be a quick trip up the road and back home again. Half the old pugs were still in their beds asleep. If I'd left the house they would have known and been wandering around looking for me. As it was they had barely opened their eyes. They could sense I was there so carried on sleeping. They were old, they needed to rest and night time disturbances didn't do them any good at their ages.

I decided to get on the computer and begin telling people what had happened to Horton. Within a few seconds, people all over the world began praying for our boy and that gave me comfort. I knew he was going to be okay, but prayer helps a real lot and I instantly felt less alone in this once I knew people were out there praying for my son.

David rang once he arrived to tell me what was going on. It wasn't a nice place but it was the only vets open at that hour so we didn't have a choice. I mean, you drive at high speed with a pug in discomfort, who's in distress, who is having trouble breathing and you walk into this emergency vets at 2.00 a.m. carrying your little boy and they want to see your credit card before they'll even look at him. They knew Horton was coming, they knew all about him before David arrived, but that didn't seem to make the slightest difference to them. All they seemed interest in was getting $800 before even taking one step towards helping our boy. A normal person, a caring person, an animal loving person would have rushed round the desk and taken Horton into their arms and begun helping him. Well, that's what I would have done anyway. If I had a job helping animals that's what would be foremost on my mind, not the money. That could have come later on when the animal in need was settled and comfortable. There was plenty of time to take care of the financial side of things. David wasn't going to do a runner. They had our son. He wasn't going anywhere.

When they finally did look at Horton everything began unravelling fast. They began doing all sorts of tests and asked if we wanted him revived should his system start to fail. David said, "Yes, of course, yes." He told them to do everything in their power to save Horton's life and make him well again. David was there for a few hours before they said he may as well go home. Horton was going to be there a while. We were taken aback by this news but figured he was dehydrated and a few hours on fluids would make the world of difference.

They wanted another thousand dollars to do the tests. David paid them and headed home. When he got home we sat in bed talking. We couldn't sleep. Our minds were in turmoil. David and I didn't understand what was going on in Horton's body, but certainly it was a lot more than gastro. Up until a few hours ago Horton was perfectly healthy. Whatever it was had come on fast and was very nasty. But he was young and had never had a sick day in his life. Whatever this was would be identified and fixed, we were sure of that. How could it not be? Horton had youth and health and prayer on his side.

Was something wrong with his bowel? Due to his condition that could be a possibility. In that case we were glad we had rushed him in instead of waiting till morning. We figured he would probably need an operation.

When it got light David rang for an update. There wasn't much news, so we rushed around getting things ready for when Horton came home. Both of us had a few errands to run and began getting them out of the way so that when we got the call saying Horton could come home neither one of us would have to leave his side. I did a big grocery shop and David went and got his licence renewed. We wanted all the petty things dealt with so that we could both devote all our time and energy to doting on our baby. I figured we'd be squabbling again over who got to change his nappy. Horton had never been sick before and we used to argue over who got to care for him enough when he was well. Now, we would be squabbling even harder over who got to do things for him once he was home recovering. In my mind I was thinking I'd let David do it until he went back to work then once he was gone Horton and I would carry on with our wonderful life together.

As we drove back to the farm we were talking about how Horton would probably be tired after being away from home all this time. There were bright lights on 24/7 where he was so he wouldn't get much rest. Although he was scared of the dark when he first came to us, he was well used to sleeping with the lights out now and the brightness of the room he was in, as well as the extra noise, would have meant very little sleep. We were talking about setting everything up in the bedroom so we could all be together as a family while Horton rested and healed, much like we did after he had been de-sexed.

Many phone calls were made during the day and on Wednesday night we both went to see Horton. They still didn't know what was wrong with him so the tests continued. We paid some more money then sat waiting to see our boy. I knew it would be hard to see Horton so ill and I knew he would be scared and feeling alone and I wouldn't be able to help him in that area just yet. I knew he would be looking up thinking we had come to take him home and I'd have to disappoint him. I missed him so much. Up until yesterday I'd never spent more than a few hours away from him and even then I was constantly ringing home to ask David how he was. Being apart from Horton for this amount of time was agonizing, but I knew he would be coming home soon and we'd both be able to put all of this behind us.

They kept us waiting for the longest time when we got there. All I wanted to do was run through those doors and see my son, but the nurse muttered something about vets changing shifts and walked off leaving us sitting there with worried expressions on our faces. My chair was opposite a wall with framed certificates plastered all over it. I walked across for a closer look; they sure had a lot of vets working here but each one had graduated with honours. This gave me hope. Okay, they were money hungry, but they also had the expertise to find out what was wrong with Horton and make him better. It gave me peace of mind and I really needed that at this moment in time. I read all the vet names and all the titles they had. It looked like my boy was being taken care of by some of the best vets in the country. They may not have had great bedside manners but they were super intelligent people. They were going to save our son. I walked back to David with a new sense that everything was going to be okay.

When they finally let us in I couldn't wait to see Horton and couldn't turn the corner fast enough. I couldn't wait to stoke him and tell him that I loved him. I glanced across the large room to the cages. Horton was on top. A few other dogs were at the other end of the room looking worse for wear and a golden retriever was under him, but one cage over, the retriever looked fine to me, as if it shouldn't have even been in there. I wondered if the presence of such a large dog bothered Horton but looking at him now I doubt he even knew it was there. Seeing my son with all those tubes coming out of him was hard. This once-full-of-life little boy was now unable to lift his little head up. It tore my heart out seeing him that way but at that time I still believed he was going to get better. I mean, how could he not? We had so many people praying for him and we had already lost one pug. Life would be pretty cruel to take another one from us in the same week. And because it had come on so fast I assumed they would be able to find out the cause and have him on the mend in no time. Yes, he was very sick now, but the thought hadn't yet entered my head that Horton may not get better. This was a hard time for our little boy but he was going to come through it and soon be back on the farm enjoying the life he loved. My mind kept going over the twenty-four hours before he'd gotten ill, trying to work out what could have caused this, but nothing had gone on. He hadn't hurt himself or had an accident.

Everything was just like any other day. I went over and over every single detail in my mind a good many times and came up with nothing. Could he have been bitten by a snake they asked us. No. A spider? Maybe, but I very much doubt it. Did we have poisons on the property? Weed sprays and the like? NO. Are you sure? Beyond positive. Okay then, could he have gotten onto a neighbour's property and been poisoned there? NO, our fences are well secured because with so many old blind pugs they have to be. If Horton is on a neighbour's property then I'm there with him. He's rarely out of my sight. They'd asked these same questions on the first day and even though Horton being poisoned or bitten had now been ruled out, they kept on asking because they were unable to find out what was actually wrong with him. The tests weren't bringing the usual answers. We were not just talking to one vet either; there seemed to be a different vet on duty every time we rang and each time we explained to them how Horton lived his life. He was not a little puppy left outside all day long, fending for himself and only seen at mealtimes. He was a big part of what made up our lives. Horton's wellbeing was the most important part of my day. He was the first pug I attended to when I woke up in the mornings and his routine of care was constantly in the back of my mind all day long. Basically, all the other pugs had to fit in with Horton because he was the one who needed the most care. What I did with my days had to fit in around Horton. That's how it was because that's how it had to be. He couldn't do things for himself. It was my job to make sure his life ran smoothly. The horses, the sheep, the farm chores, the housework, all had to fit in around Horton. It got tedious having to go through it every time we spoke to somebody different. At times I felt like screaming at them to stop asking the same set of questions over and over again and get back in there and tend to our son, but we knew it was a way of helping them help Horton so we kept on going over it with them.

The vet showed us some x-rays and talked to us for a while, then I went back to be with Horton. The first time I'd stood by his cage he hadn't known I was there. This time, he opened up his eyes a bit when I spoke to him. I got the nurse to open the cage so I could put my hand in. I cupped his little face in my palm and massaged his ear with my thumb the way I had done when he was a puppy. I kept telling him over and over again how much I loved him, how special he was and how much joy he'd brought into my life. As I stroked him all I wanted to do was unhook those tubes and carry him out of there and bring him home. He wasn't happy in that place, I could tell, and I just wanted to see him happy again. He was opposite the operating table. I didn't think that was a good thing to do on their part. He should have been off in a separate room instead of right up close to where the action was. He would have seen and heard everything going on in that room. He would have heard the dogs just brought in squealing in pain before being sedated. That wasn't fair on Horton at all. I leant in close and kept telling him to hang on, to fight, to be strong. He had always been a little fighter. I knew the strength and determination he possessed. He had the spirit dwelling within him of a true champion. I had witnessed that great strength of character many a time over the years. When he came up against an obstacle he tackled it. He never backed off. He just tackled it head on.

I stayed with Horton for a long time and it constantly bothered me that he was not happy in that place. Every time a vet nurse or vet walked past he lifted his head just slightly as if he was scared of what they were going to do to him next. He'd had so many tests performed, so much interference in such a short time. His little body had been prodded and poked over and over again, blood samples taken, x-rays. He'd been handled so many times by people he wasn't familiar with. This was as far away from Horton's normal existence as he could get.

When it came time for us to go I didn't want to leave him. I just wanted to stay there like that, stroking Horton's little head and talking to him. A vet came over to talk to David but I didn't acknowledge him. I turned away and concentrated on Horton. Again, I started telling him to fight but then I felt strongly that I had to give him an option so I told him if he couldn't fight, if he felt too ill, too sick to carry on it was all right for him to go. I told him I loved him and that his Daddy and I would understand if he couldn't be with us anymore, that we would both be okay. I felt I needed to let him know this. I still thought he was going to live but I also wanted him to know that it was all right if he no longer could. He was my baby, he was so little and I didn't want him being that ill and thinking he had to keep on fighting for me, for us, for his daddy and me. I didn't want him struggling on for my sake. I couldn't ask that of him. He was too precious and I loved him too much to be that selfish. I wanted him to truly know whatever the outcome we understood and that everything was going to be all right. Once again I thanked him for coming into our lives and for all the joy he'd given me and again, I told him how very much I loved him. Turning and walking away from Horton that night was hard but I made sure I was all the way round the corner before I started crying. I didn't want him seeing that. It would have been very unfair if he had to witness me falling apart.

Thursday 6th of January started out frantically. Ruby wasn't doing well. While David was on the phone to the vet about Horton I carried Ruby outside for her morning wee. She was unable to walk and had not much life in her. She didn't want to eat. Ruby and Grace had always been close. They'd lived their entire lives together. That was how they came into our care. The rescue group wanted to find them a home where they could stay together and not too many people wanted one old pug, let alone two. We knew Ruby was coming to the end of her life. She had been slowing down for a while. Grace, on the other hand, could run rings around pugs half her age. I always thought Grace would live to seventeen but she passed away a few days before Horton got sick due to a heart attack. She was fifteen years old. Once Grace died Ruby just seemed to give up on living. I believe she missed her little friend so badly that she just wanted to be with her again.

David got off the phone and said there was no improvement in Horton and that the emergency vets wanted more money. David and I wanted to make sure there was nothing else we could do for Ruby so he set off again to our country vets while I gave the other pugs their breakfast. We were trying to keep the pug routine going at home and keep their life as normal as we possibly could and it was hard because there was so much else going on. We were both worried about Horton and grieving over the loss of little Gracie and also concerned about Ruby. But we knew those five old pugs on the farm deserved to have their breakfast on time and their morning walk on time and so we split tasks at a time when we would have much preferred being together. It's what you do at times like this and in a few seconds it's decided who goes to the vet and who stays behind and keeps things going on the farm. But I really do wish I could have been with Ruby at the end. Oh I know she loved her Daddy best, she chose him over me the first week she arrived, still I would have liked to have been there with the two of them. But I knew my role was to try and keep things at home as normal as possible so that's what I did. And I think it was probably the best thing for me to do as the pugs seemed happy that morning, and their happiness was important to David and to me. They walked, they ate and they settle down to sleep and it warmed my heart seeing them all sleeping side by side in their beds.

The rest of the day wasn't so calm though and it passed quickly with saying goodbye to and burying Ruby, and constantly ringing the vets for progress reports on Horton. The latest news on Horton was that he had gotten slightly worse in the past few hours. Before David left for the emergency vet, while he was still on the phone trying to work out exactly what they were telling us and how much money they wanted, I was pacing round and round in circles. I couldn't help David with what they were saying and was making it worse for him when he was trying to find out, so I left the bedroom and began pacing in the lounge room. The pacing thing is something I always do when my mind is twirling and I can't stand still. I went round and round the lounge a few times with a cloud of elderly pugs scurrying after me. I could hear by the way they were walking that they were getting anxious. It wasn't a normal calm pitter-pattering on floorboards, but a scurrying, scampering at my heel. Normally, I would have stopped and tried to calm them down – they were getting caught up in what was going on and feeding off David's and my emotions – but my mind wasn't on them; it was on Horton. I should have just bent down for a moment and given each one of them a reassuring pat. The poor little things had no idea what was happening. This was not how they normally lived. This was not our normal calm home. They were restless and apprehensive because we were, but I couldn't think about that now. I had already lost two of my children and we were trying desperately to keep the third one alive.

Suddenly, I stopped pacing and began looking at a photo of Horton hanging on the wall near the back door. I put my hand to the frame and rested it there for a few moments, my mind stopped twirling and a real peace came over me. I decided to go back and join David. As I entered the room he was still on the phone. The atmosphere in the bedroom was different to what I had felt in the lounge and I began getting anxious again. This time I thought about my other pugs, about taking the sensitive little souls back into the calmer room so they weren't involved with what David was caught up in. Everything in that moment was confusing. It was hard talking to the vets over the phone. Things weren't being said clearly, or perhaps they were and we just weren't listening correctly. I didn't even know if David was talking to the deaf vet. Whenever she was involved it got confusing because there had to be a third person relaying the messages back and forth and a lot of things got lost in translation. This was not the right time for such a thing to be happening. I didn't have anything against the deaf vet. I thought her lack of hearing would make her an excellent vet actually, because she would be more in tune with the animals; she'd be able to block out the world and concentrate on her furry patients; she would pick up on things hearing vets miss and for that reason I believe she was an asset. But when you're using a voice-to-text mechanism there are pauses and time delays and things are not straightforward and it becomes confusing. Horton was our son; we needed to know fully what was happening with him and I believed another vet should have been there on duty making such calls.

Later in the evening, David left to give the vets the money they were demanding and I stayed at home. I wanted to see Horton but I was an emotional mess. David and I talked about it and again decided I should stay home with the pugs, keep them cool and try and restore the order that had been disturbed in the past few hours. Elderly pugs are like elderly people. They can get upset when their regular routine is disturbed. David would race up there this evening for a quick visit and pay them some more money then we would both go for a longer visit in the morning. Horton had a fight on his hands and I didn't want him to see me all puffy-faced from crying about Ruby and Grace. I needed him to see me strong so he could be strong. In the morning I would be in a better state for him to see me, but I never got the chance to see Horton alive again.

A few hours later, David rang from the vets and told me Horton wasn't going to make it. This was the worst thing I could have heard. This wasn't meant to be happening. More tests were being done. They hadn't even told us what the problem was yet. We were still waiting for answers to what was actually going on in Horton's body. This can't be right. Surely there was more they could do. They were expert vets after all. Besides, we were going to visit Horton tomorrow, the two of us, but now they were telling us that we were going to have to bury our son. In less than a week we had lost three of our babies. I sat in disbelief. No! No! No!

This can't be happening. Horton can't be dying. They wanted more money. That's what tonight's mad dash up there was about. Horton's vet bill was going through the roof and they wanted us to pay some more. They had said he had gotten slightly worse but we just thought it was a setback, just a little setback and he was going to improve and come home. There was a little bit of doubt but deep down we still both thought Horton was going to get better. But in two short days he was gone. He went from being healthy to dead in forty-eight hours and our entire world collapsed.

A lot of Horton's life is clear in my mind as if it merely happened yesterday, but this part, the time around the phone call and all that went with it, is not so clear. I can remember parts of it, but not the sequence that took place and not clearly everything that was said. Perhaps because it was such a difficult thing to go through, perhaps my mind doesn't want to go back there because it was hard enough living through it the first time. Maybe part of me did realize they were saying he was dying because I remember hoping for a miracle as David walked out the door. Looking back now, I fully believe that Horton was dying from the time he went in to see the first vet in the early hours of Wednesday morning and that there was never going to be anything anybody could have done to save him. I think if we were the types to not have our dogs sleeping in our bedroom that Horton would have been found dead in his kennel in the morning. I believe if we hadn't rushed him to our local vet, then onto the emergency vet clinic, that he would have died at home in pain and discomfort during the night. At least we could spare him that. We may not have been able to save him but at least we know he was administered painkillers in his final two days of life. As nice as it would have been for him to die here at the farm, simply slipped into the other world in a place he loved with all his family around him, at least he was not in pain at the end and I was grateful for that.

We could have found out more about what was going on inside Horton's body, but that would have meant an autopsy and we both felt we couldn't do that to him. No way was I going let them cut his little body up, not after all the love and care I had put into looking after that beautiful body of his every day in every single way. It would have broken my heart to make him go through that. Besides, it wasn't going to bring him back to us. But in the back of my mind there was a feeling that one day I would regret this decision. In years to come, I would regret that I would never fully have an answer to why Horton died, but that was only a one percent chance and my heart couldn't bear to have him cut into. I couldn't do that to Horton or to us. We wanted to put our baby in the ground in one piece. I wanted to protect Horton. Even after he died I wanted to protect him. I suppose I was looking after his little body in death just as I had done in life. I wanted to put him into the ground beside his two elderly sisters, whole.

It was a shock when David rang and told me Horton's little body had turned toxic and he was dying. I can clearly remember how that felt. David said Horton didn't even look like our Horton anymore. He no longer had his puppy eyes; he now had the eyes of an elderly dog that was at the end of its life. That was hard to hear. The days of praying – people all over the world were praying for our son – the days of getting everything ready for when our boy came home had come to an end. As hard as we had tried we couldn't make him well again and that just hit me like a sledge hammer. Why couldn't all those prayers have been answered? Why couldn't we have had our miracle? Why take Horton from me now when I had already lost so much this week? Why couldn't he have been given a few more years of life? If anybody deserved to be given more time it was Horton. Horton loved life. Why take it away from him? He hadn't asked to be born into that body and yet he had done brilliantly with it. He didn't deserve to have his life cut short, not when he took so much joy in living. He didn't deserve to be dying now. He wasn't even three years old yet. That was the cruelest blow for me, that he was taken so fast and so young. I had plans for his third birthday. I'd already bought him a hat and we were going to make a big deal out of it.

David put the phone to Horton's ear so I could say goodbye. That was one of the most difficult things I have ever done in my life. I wished I had gone in with David more than ever now. I wished I was there with Horton in his final moments. As hard as I would have found it, I just wished I had been there with him, to talk to him, to comfort him, to tell him how much I loved him and how much happiness he had brought me, tell him how he had changed my life and that I felt like the luckiest person in the world because I was his mother. I wanted to tell him over and over again that he was one of the best things that had ever happened to me in my entire life. Horton would have known all this already, though. Every single day of his life I gushed about how special he was and told him time and time again what he meant to me, but I wished I could have been there and told him over and over again how much I loved him as he slipped from this world.

I also thought about David and how hard this was going to be for him. He had already said goodbye to his special girl, Ruby, only a couple of hours ago. He'd dug a hole and lovingly placed her in the ground only a few hours before he left for the vet. This was going to destroy him. He'd had so much sadness today already. David loved Horton deeply and he too had thought Horton was going to survive, going to turn a corner and start slowly turning towards health again. David hadn't gone in there to say goodbye; I'm sure that wasn't on his mind when he left. He had gone in merely to give the vets some more money. I started thinking about how much I wished we hadn't taken Horton to that particular place. Neither David nor myself felt happy about him being there. We wished we had found a nicer place for Horton to have spent his final days with nicer people looking after him. This is something I would think about for many months afterwards. But in the middle of the night, when David took Horton to our closest vet, we didn't have a backup plan. We just thought he had an upset tummy. If we'd known what was going to happen we would have started searching for a better facility to take Horton to, just to get him out of the place as soon as possible. Up until this happened to Horton we had never had a pug of ours get that sick that quickly. Seven weeks after Horton died one of our other pugs, Arthur, needed complicated back surgery and we found the most wonderful vet surgeon for him. We had time then. We found a lovely place with an entirely different atmosphere. You just felt better walking in to see this other vet and the nurses there were wonderful, kind, caring people. They truly loved animals. You could feel it and see it and that made all the difference in the world. The place we took Arthur to was worlds apart from the place Horton was in and we wished we had known about it back then. It may not have saved his life but it would have been a nicer place with nicer people in it to look after him. David and I have deep regrets over Horton being at that particular emergency vets. If we had to lose him we would have preferred it had been in a pleasanter place with better people. After being so loved throughout his life, why couldn't it have been like that in his final two days? I felt guilty because all Horton's life I had told him that I would never leave him. As I snuggled him I would whisper in his ear that Mummy would never leave him. Horton had felt abandonment early on in his life and I wanted him to know that I was never going to do that to him, but in the end I did, didn't I? I didn't leave him long when he got de-sexed, we worked around that one, but this time everything was different. I had no control over it. I felt horrible because not only did I go back on my word, but I left him in that place. I thought it was for his own good. I thought they were going to make him better and I told him that when I visited. But they didn't make him better. He got worse and he died. Do you know how terribly awful it is to promise your son something then go back on your word? It kills you. Deep inside it kills you. You are dealing with the loss of your boy and the fact that you broke a promise to him as well. I didn't like the vet at the start and it grew from there and every dealing I had with them I lost more faith. I hated walking out and leaving Horton with those people, but consoled myself with the fact that he wouldn't be there for too long. I knew how sick Horton had become and so did David. I remember sitting in the waiting room telling David how much I hated the place and how Horton must hate it too. David said with Horton being so ill he probably wouldn't be fully aware of the place he was in or what was going on around him.

Arthur needed many visits and a great deal of care and every time he went to see his vet in the back of your mind was the thought that Horton should have come here too. That is one thing we had no control over and we would both feel bad about it for a very long time.

Everything happened so fast. Horton was in there for forty-eight hours or so. Everything was a blur of confusion and there was a lot of not knowing fully what was going on. I was an emotional mess, worried sick. I doubt I was an asset to David at this time and I do feel awful about that. My pugs are my life and when one gets this sick this fast and nobody can tell you why or what is happening to his little body and you've already buried two of your children in the past four days, you tend to just lose it, emotionally, physically, everything. The person you normally are leaves and you lose control. You don't eat, you don't sleep, you don't know what you are doing or saying half the time. Nothing is as it should be and you don't know how to cope or make it right again. I do believe that place could only operate as an emergency surgery where people have to walk through those doors because there is no other choice, either because of the time of day or the condition of their dog or, as in our case, both. They would have gone out of business if operating as a normal veterinary practice.

David was particularly hurt and angry too because they didn't want to give him a towel to wrap Horton in. They asked if he had something in the car he could use. Of course we didn't have anything in the car. We didn't think we would be bringing Horton's body home. We had just paid them thousands and thousands and thousands of dollars, and they didn't even want to give us an old towel to put our son in.

When I spoke to David on the phone I told him to be strong, you know, for our boy so that he wouldn't be scared. I told him to be brave. If Horton saw that his Daddy wasn't scared he wouldn't be either, then David put the phone up to Horton's little ear so I could say the last few words I would ever say to him. I told him how much I loved him and how much joy he had given me since he came into my life, I knew he was in pain now because he was off the drip, so I wanted to be fast. I didn't want him suffering any longer. I told him to go into the light and that his sisters would be there waiting so he would be okay. I told him to go find Ruby, Grace and Harper. I said that he would be going to a beautiful place and to wait because one day Daddy and I would be joining him. Then I started crying. I didn't want to cry but I couldn't stop the tears coming. This was another thing I will always feel bad about because I should have been stronger, for Horton, you know. I just wished he hadn't heard me crying in those final moments of his life. That was so unfair to him and I shouldn't have done that.

David must have heard me breaking down because he took the phone away from Horton's ear. We spoke a few words then hung up. When I put the phone down my body started going nuts. I was half-screaming, half-crying. I heard an odd wailing sound and turned around sharply but then realised it was coming from me. My brain was going a hundred miles an hour. My pulse, my heartbeat, my breathing all started going berserk. Nothing was working as it should do. I felt like vomiting. I also felt as though my legs were going from under me. I was in our ensuite and don't know why I was in there. I guess I must have been pacing round the house while talking on the phone and ended up in that room. I held onto the sink, leant against the wall and cried my heart out. My heart was going ballistic. It hurt. It physically hurt. The pressure in that area was enormous. I thought I was going to have a massive coronary. I thought my heart was going to explode, come bursting through my chest. It was beating so fast. My mind was reeling.

I felt sorry for David having to go through this on his own. And worrying about him made everything worse. The pain in my chest became unbearable. I felt like I was dying. I couldn't breathe, couldn't breathe, couldn't get any air into my lungs. It was like I could physically feel my heart changing, like it was literally splitting straight down the middle and I could feel every tear, every fracture as it became two separate pieces. I began to panic, which made trying to breathe worse. It had been a boiling hot day and the house was stifling. I felt lightheaded. David, my rock, the one person who would be able to help me, wasn't here. He was miles away with our baby boy, helping him into the next world as calmly and peacefully as he could. He was over an hour's drive away and was about to go through one of the saddest, most difficult times of his life. I was on the farm on my own. I knew I had to help myself, start breathing normally and settle down my heartbeat otherwise I could be dead by the time David came home and how would that be for him? Walking towards the house with our lifeless little son in his arms and finding me not breathing? I had to talk myself through this. I had to try and calm myself down and start to breathe normally. All this going through my head made my breathing worse. I felt like I was going to faint. One of the pugs knocked against my leg and as I looked down to see who it was, Sarah's old worried face looked up at me and then the room started spinning. Our ensuite is a very small room with only one tiny window in it. I knew I had to get out of that room, get out of the house, get some fresh air into my lungs, calm down and start concentrating on my breathing. But I didn't think I could make it all the way outside. I glanced in the mirror and all the colour had gone from my face. Red-rimmed eyes looked back at me as I began talking to myself. "Inhale, exhale, inhale, exhale," I repeated over and over again until I felt I was able walk without collapsing.

The pugs were all with me in the ensuite, panting. They were hot too. As I made my way to the back door I felt them fall in behind me like they normally do. But I didn't look back to make sure they were all there. I was just concentrating on moving forward, getting outside as quickly as I could. I walked halfway down the back ramp and stopped. I didn't feel good. I remembered reading in a yoga magazine that slow, deep breathing calms the body, spirit and mind, and stills the soul. I desperately needed that right now. I stood holding onto the rail and started to count my breath as it entered and left my body. The counting made me concentrate on what I was doing. It also gave me something else to think about and after a while I started to settle down a bit.

The pugs had all raced down the ramp ahead of me and begun sniffing in the garden. I watched them looking around for somewhere to wee. It seemed like such a small amount of pugs there now; no Grace, no Ruby and no Horton. In a few short days my beautiful pug family had been reduced by almost half. I wondered if they could sense that we were about to lose Horton. They didn't seem to be behaving any differently to how they normally did. They were just circling each other contently. One or two ran off to the row of trees and began sniffing there and in a few minutes a few of the others followed. I watched them walking off happily in a group, like they always do. No, nothing seemed out of place in their little world, whereas a bomb had just exploded in mine.

CHAPTER EIGHTEEN

The Carnival is over and I will Love You till I Die

Waiting for David and Horton to get back to the farm that night was terribly difficult. I was going through a lot of emotions and hadn't stopped crying from the moment I put down the phone after saying goodbye to my little boy. It was everything from slow, single trickles down my cheeks to gushing rivers of tears. I wanted them home but at the same time I didn't want to view Horton's lifeless body because I knew it would hurt to see that which was once so full of life now lying still. And I felt really guilty about that, as if I was rejecting Horton, and that made me feel all the worse.

It was dark by the time David got home. He'd sat in the vet's car park for the longest time unable to drive, just sat there holding Horton in his arms. I wished I had been with him, with both of them. It was one of those moments in life when you just need to be together and here I was miles away on the farm with no mode of transport. I put the back porch light on when the pugs started barking. They always barked when they heard Dad's car pull into the drive. They were happy, dancing in circles, spinning and running from window to window like they always did when they knew who was about to walk in the door. I was leaning with my back against the kitchen bench. I just didn't know what to do with myself. A lot about this moment reminded me of the night David brought Horton home for the very first time. I'd waited in the exact same position then as well because it gave me the best view of the back ramp. The pugs were barking and circling and dancing then too. The only difference between then and now was that last time I felt like joining them in the dance.

I heard David's car door close and watched him carrying Horton towards the house. He was wrapped in a towel with his little head peeping out. David had wrapped him the way he always wrapped him after a bath. He walked in the door and handed Horton to me then went and patted all the other pugs. I kissed Horton's head and told him over and over again how sorry I was, but then I handed him back to David as quickly as I could. It just seemed so very wrong that Horton's heart was no longer beating. This little body once so full of life now lay so still and I couldn't bear it. I walked out onto the veranda and closed the door behind me so the pugs couldn't get out. I didn't want to upset them. I then leant against a post and cried my heart out.

We didn't want to bury Horton right then. We simply couldn't bring ourselves to do it, not tonight anyway. It had been a hell of a day and we had already buried one pug this morning. We were both wrecked, emotionally and physically. David put Horton in his little dog bed on our bed and that's where he spent the night. He always slept on the bed with us and tonight he was going to do so again for one last time. Tomorrow would come soon enough. We would bury him then.

I got on the computer pretty quickly to tell people Horton had died. I can't remember if I did it that night or early the next morning. All I know is that it was a very difficult thing to do. I didn't want to face it. I didn't know where to start but I knew I had to do it because so many people were still praying for Horton. They all thought he was still alive, still fighting. They had been so kind to us and I couldn't leave them out there worrying about our son. I owed it to them to let them know Horton was no longer with us.

Everything was still and quiet the morning we buried Horton. If the birds were chirping I certainly didn't notice them. David and I have always been great talkers; from the time we first met we have been able to talk for hours about anything, but there was not much conversation to be had that morning or for the rest of the day. It wasn't that we didn't want to talk to one another; we just didn't have anything much to say. Our minds were on other things and we were totally exhausted. Not much sleep had been gotten and the strain of the previous few days had taken everything out of us. We didn't know what to do with ourselves either. It was like everything just came to an abrupt stop. For the past few days it was rush, rush, rush, crying, worrying, making and receiving phone calls. A lot of the time we'd be standing there with the home phone in one hand and our mobiles in the other. The phone never stopped ringing with people desperately wanting to know how Horton was doing. Now everything was deadly quiet. We'd give each other a hug as we passed by, but mainly we just sat or stood around the house like two broken people, two empty shells.

Only a few days ago we were an eight-pug family. Now we had five. In less than a week our beautiful little family of pugs had been reduced by almost half. The pugs we had left were worn out too. They slept in their beds for most of the day. We tried to keep their routine as normal as possible, tried to keep things the same for their sake, but I don't think we managed to pull it off. How could we really? The true reality of the situation was that nothing was ever going to be the same again here on the farm. We had lost too much, gone through too much. It was like a hurricane had hit us and we were left swaying, reeling, rocking to and fro. Totally consumed, oblivious to everything else around us, we didn't eat and we didn't sleep. We just ceased to exist really. It was both the feeling of being completely numb and in excruciating pain all at the same time. We had fought hard over the past few days. All our energy had been caught up in doing all we could to save Horton and the loss of Ruby and Grace had been put on the backburner. When you have one little pug so desperately ill but who's still fighting everything you have goes directly into that, into making him better, into keeping him alive, and our elderly pugs had borne witness to all of that. Over the past few days I'd often looked down and wondered what on earth these poor little old babies of mine were thinking. As much as we tried to protect them from it, the truth of the matter is that we are a close-knit family. What touches one touches us all. Whether it be happiness, pain or sorrow we all get caught up in it because that is how we've always lived our lives.

The pugs all had a walk and ate their breakfast. After that they just shuffled off to the nearest bed and settled down to sleep. I suppose it made it easier in a way because it let David and I bury

Horton on our own. Perhaps that was how it was meant to be. Perhaps they realized Mummy and Daddy needed to do this on their own. We didn't close the doors when we walked out of the house so the pugs were free to come with us if they wanted to, but I don't remember a single pug being beside us when we buried Horton, which was unusual because they normally followed me everywhere I go.

I held Horton in my arms while David dug a hole. It was the third hole he had dug this week and that was hard on both of us. David stopped and leant on the shovel many times. It was as if this final hole was the hardest one to dig. I glanced across at the two fresh mounds of dirt sitting side by side. I thought Ruby and Grace would have been happy for their final resting place to be together just as it had always been when they were alive. I didn't want to watch David digging the hole that Horton's body was to be placed in. I just couldn't look at it. It was just too hard to see so I turned my back and began talking to Horton. By this time I was a bit more used to the fact that he was no longer breathing. During the night I'd woken up almost every half hour and each time I leant over, stroked Horton's tiny head and told him that loved him. I always rocked Horton like a baby when he was wrapped in a blanket and I began rocking him now. At first it was difficult to do. It just didn't seem right. Normally, he would be looking up at me, giving kisses and I longed for those kisses now. Then, all of a sudden, a feeling of pure peace came over me. It was the most beautiful feeling, one of the most tranquil moments of my entire life. It didn't feel at all like I was holding a lifeless body in my arms; it felt exactly like it felt when Horton was alive. I heard David say the hole was ready but I couldn't put Horton in it; I just stayed there like that with my back turned, talking to my baby and feeling so very, very peaceful and happy. After a little while it felt as if I was once again holding a lifeless body in my arms. It was then that I handed Horton to his Daddy so that he could say goodbye to his son.

Over the years I've often thought about my friend in rescue, about how she entrusted me with this special gift and how I would always be grateful to her for that, but mainly I've thought about how hard it would have been for her to give Horton up: putting him in that car that day, the thoughts going through her head, how difficult it must have been for her seeing him being driven away. I know if I was in her shoes I wouldn't have been able to do it. I would have begun running after the car, throwing myself across the bonnet. She told me how after she had placed Horton in the car seat he had turned and looked at her. She said that in that one small moment she knew he was going to be okay. I believe he was letting her know this so she could have peace of mind. She loved him a lot and he knew that. I believe our home was chosen because of how well we look after our pugs. A wishy-washy home wouldn't have been right for Horton. This precious little baby needed one hundred percent dedication. He needed an excellent diet and the best care and that is exactly what we give all of our pugs. Over these past few years I have often wondered why Horton's life couldn't have been extended, why this excellent diet that had prolonged the life of so many pugs before him hadn't done the same for Horton. David and I have had a good many conversation about this and we've come to the conclusion that perhaps the diet Horton was on and the clean lifestyle did in fact give him more time than he would have had living somewhere else. Maybe the care we gave him, the fresh air, the quiet life in the country caused him to live a lot longer than he would have done if living a different lifestyle, but of course that's something we will never ever know. If I could have found out for sure would it have made the grieving period different for me? Yes. I'd say it probably would have.

One thing I never did with Horton was take his presence for granted, not because I thought my time with him was limited, because I never did, but because I was simply besotted with him. I spent my days watching everything he did and loving every moment of it. I'd comment on it too, so he'd know I'd seen his accomplishments, seen what he was interested in. I lived in all his moments, I experienced all his experiences, stopped what I was doing, stood back and watched him living his life and got so much enjoyment out of it. Before Horton I used to rush a lot. I'm busy, we all are, there is always something to do, but I adored this little pug and the absolute love I had for him caused me to never want to miss a moment of his life. And I'm glad I lived this way. Horton made me realize how important it is to stop and enjoy what's going on around you, to make time for those you love. Life goes by quickly enough; you don't want to make it go faster because you're always on the go. Slow down because these moments are the ones that make your life worthwhile and at the end of your days I believe these are the things you are going to remember. They're going to be some of the best moments of your life. I'm glad I let the dishes wait and the housework pile up. I'm still doing housework now long after he has gone; that's all still here and it will always be here, whereas Horton no longer is.

In the early days, did I think I may have been able to get Horton to walk? Yes, there were times I did think that, fleeting moments that quickly passed, moments when he was balancing really well on his back legs and I'd look at him and think maybe, just maybe there could be a miracle happening with this little soul. And was I disappointed when he couldn't achieve that? Maybe a tiny bit but it didn't last because I was able to see all that he could do and that which he wasn't ever going to do didn't seem anywhere near as important anymore. I mean, how could I not think what Horton was achieving wasn't wonderful, wasn't marvelous, wasn't a miracle in itself? He got around with such ease and such speed. You just didn't have your mind on what he couldn't do when you were there right up close seeing what he could do: the beautiful way he handled himself regardless of his limitations.

I've talked about it being a shock losing Horton so young; would I have lived differently if I'd known what was coming? The answer is yes. I probably would have because it would have always been in the back of my mind, affecting everything I did, and I believe Horton would have picked up on it and that was no way for him to live. Instead, we talked about the future. All the time we talked to him about our future plans, the pugs he would see coming into and being taken out of our lives. We thought he would be the one seeing loss after loss of his older brothers and sisters and we wanted to prepare him for that. We wanted him to know what was coming so he wouldn't get too upset about it. Looking back, I should have been preparing the older pugs for Horton's loss because most of them outlived him, but I didn't know it at the time. And I'm glad I didn't know how short a time we were going to have with Horton. I'm not good at hiding my emotions and Horton was such an intelligent little boy. I wouldn't have been able to fool him, because everything I feel is always written clearly all over my face and heard in my voice. And that would have been no good for either Horton or me. Instead, I thought Horton was going to make double figures and that's how I talked to him every day. I'd bought party hats years in advance, stocked up on them because I'd found some beautiful ones and I wasn't sure if I'd be able to find such nice ones again when his birthday came around. It just goes to show that you must never take any life for granted. There are no guarantees; no matter how young they are they can be taken from you in a heartbeat. I learnt this the hard way.

One of the hardest things that happened after Horton died was when people started saying that he should never have been allowed to live. To this day I don't understand why they said what they did at the time they did. Unless they were blind or deaf they would have seen what I was going through. Did they say it without thinking? I don't know. Probably not, because if they did, on seeing the effect it had on me, they would have stopped, but they didn't. Their words saddened me but it they didn't crush me. They only saddened me because these same people saw Horton when he was alive and commented on how happy and healthy he was. Why change their minds once he'd gone? That didn't make any sense. Was it to hurt me? I don't know, but they couldn't have hurt me any more than I was already hurting. I'd lost my baby. Anything other than that, no matter how malicious, simply couldn't touch me. I couldn't be hurt any deeper because there were no other levels for me to go. At one time such words would have had a greater effect on me but not anymore. When you've experienced that much loss you look at everything differently. That which is and isn't worth worrying about becomes clearer.

It wasn't just the loss I was reeling from; it was the shock as well. It seriously shocked me. The first week in January wasn't the only time of loss that we would endure that year. In May we lost our thirteen-year-old black pug, Sarah, and on June 30th David's brother, Chris, my brother-in-law and friend, lost his battle with cancer. 2011 was one of the hardest years we have ever lived through.

I think the loss of Horton would have been agonizing at any time but to come on the back of losing Ruby and Grace took me to a new level of suffering. And the first thing you are always asked when you lose three pugs so quickly is what they died of. And it can be difficult to talk about it but they don't think about that; they're not in the same place you are. They're more curious than they are sensitive and so you continue to be asked that very same question over and over again. I found that a really difficult thing to have to deal with.

The grief felt and the period of mourning for Ruby and Grace was different to what I was going through with Horton. They passed due to old age and in time I was able to find closure in their deaths because they got to live long beautiful lives. But Horton wasn't granted such longevity. That's why I struggled so terribly over his loss and besides, he was my baby and needed the care of a human baby. Everything about Horton's loss was different. A human response is to make some form of sense out of it, some way of trying to lessen the pain that is like a sharp-edged blade constantly stabbing and twisting in your heart. We used to say things like, "At least he didn't get lost and was never found. At least it wasn't this and at least he didn't die that way". You go through all sorts of ways that Horton could have been taken from you. It's a tormenting game you play to try and make some of the hurt go away. And it made us realize that as hard as it was at the end, at least Horton went to sleep in his daddy's arms where he felt safe and loved and protected. I told David that when my time comes if I too can leave this world like that then I would consider myself very lucky. I do feel that Horton would have felt peaceful in those final moments of his life. He would have been in those loving arms, those arms that had held him and helped him and looked after him all his life. At least he wasn't alone in a strange scary place. He didn't go out of this world with fear in his heart; his last moments alive weren't spent with a stranger. As hard as it was for David, at least Horton had his Daddy there with him and I will forever feel proud of and grateful to David for all he did for our son that day. I knew the pain it caused him, not only in that moment but for months afterwards. I knew the toil it took because he went grey almost overnight. But he did what any good parent would do; he put the needs of his child before his own and that makes me very proud.

I used to see ads on TV with human babies in them and had to turn the television off. It hurt my heart too much to see those mothers and babies being happy together because I had lost a baby, my baby. Horton was our son, whether we were human and he was a pug made not one ounce of difference; he was our son, our son pure and simple. Horton wore nappies, needed changing and he needed special care. It was constant, the same way human babies' care is constant. It was as if I had a six-month-old human baby to look after for three lovely years and I loved doing it. I wanted to go on changing Horton and caring for him for many, many years, but in the blink of an eye he was gone. When I'd lost other pugs such ads didn't have the slightest effect on me. Horton's loss hit me so hard. People I'd known for years said I wasn't the same person anymore and they were right. I thought about counselling. I'd never sought counselling when losing a pug before but this time I was losing the battle to stay afloat. I knew I needed more help with this loss, but I felt they wouldn't have understood my pain. I felt if I went and sat in a support group to talk my feelings through with other mothers they would have made me leave when they found out my son was a pug. They may have thought I was belittling them and what they were going through, but I wouldn't have been. I merely wanted to gain help in the hope of somehow lessening the enormous heartache I was feeling. I felt I couldn't cope on my own, like I was drowning and needed to reach out for a lifeboat. I thought group therapy would be that lifeboat. But I didn't get the chance. The lady I spoke to on the phone was less than encouraging. I thought about buying a book on bereavement but it would tell me to plant a tree or buy a statue and dedicate a little area in the garden. It wouldn't be able to tell me how to stop the sadness or how long I was going to go on crying because nobody has the answer to that. It's not so easy. Nobody can wave a magic wand and take your pain away.

I talked to my Mum asked how she had coped through the saddest moments of her life and she said, "You just do, Andrea, because what other choice do you have?" Mum was right. What other alternative is there but to walk through it. You can't change what happened and you can't make it right. It is what it is and you have to live with it, but I did a lot of pretending to be okay, to be healing. Not to David – he was well aware of all that I was going through – but to the people who stopped by the farm to see how I was. They were the ones I felt I had to put a front on for because if I didn't things became awkward. They'd been nice enough to think of me and drop by but everything about those visits was a sham. I put on a front, not a big happy, smiling ball of fakeness – Lord knows I couldn't have managed that – but more that I was just sitting there pretending, acting as if I was interested in their conversations, saying the right things, giving the right responses, doing everything I could to appear normal, be like the old me, you know, the person they were used to spending time with. But I wasn't the old me anymore. They didn't know it, but I did, and I used to sit there watching their mouths move, wondering how long I was going to have to keep up with the exhausting act when all I wanted to do was be left alone. I just didn't know how long I could keep it up. I used to avoid eye contact with people because I was afraid of giving the game away. I thought that if they looked in my eyes they'd be able to see the hell going on inside of me.

David used to say he couldn't allow himself to go back to that first week in January because it hurt too much, but I couldn't get myself out of it. I relived that week over and over and over again. Your mind can be your best friend or your worst enemy and mine was playing havoc with me. You blame everyone for his death: the first vet, the second vet, the third and fourth vet, the vet surgeons, yourself, even your husband. You start believing you caused it. Was there something you missed, something you should have seen but didn't? What if you'd managed to housetrain him? Would that have made a difference? My mind kept ticking over and over. It became like poison. It kept me asking question after question that had already been answered or question after question that I knew I would never have the answers to. You sit up all night wondering if by allowing Horton to live a full life, experience everything, did you actually cause his life to be shortened? By the early hours of the morning you've reasoned it all out. You know deep in your heart that a half life wouldn't have been right for Horton. You kept him safe from harm – that was your role – but you also allowed him to truly live and you know it was the right thing to do. You spend hours going over everything and you are glad you worked through it on your own this time. This time you didn't have to wake your exhausted husband up and torment him as well, like you have done so many times in the past couple of months. You feel proud of yourself for letting him rest. But the next night you're sitting up again wondering what else you could have done wrong. It's virtually impossible to heal when you're putting your head on the pillow every night with the thought in the back of your mind that you may have been responsible for the death of somebody you loved. The torment you put yourself through doesn't help in the slightest; it makes it worse if anything, but you go on doing it because you don't know how to stop. Your mind has to make somebody pay, you have to make somebody responsible for what happened, because then you have somebody to focus your anger on. To just say it was one of those things in life or it was just nature's way doesn't sit right in your heart. They are crap responses and you know it. I think the worst thing people said to me was, "You did your best." I'd erupt. I loathed that saying, because if I did my best then why wasn't Horton still alive today? It's patronizing in a way too, like you did your best but it still wasn't good enough, whereas somebody else's best may have been. It's like some pathetic person patting you on the shoulder. They don't physically do it of course but they may as well because those words sound like they should come with a pitiful shoulder pat. Because I was blaming myself for Horton's death I thought they were too. They weren't, but I gave them hell all the same. Looking back I realized I should have kept my mouth shut. Nobody knows what to say in these situations. They were trying to be nice, comforting even. Everybody was merely trying to help in some small way. They didn't mean any harm; these are just things people say to make you feel better about a situation that nobody feels good about. I'd rather they just said nothing at all. Sometimes silence is the only response needed. An honest look in the eye that tells you in that one quick instant that the other person understands fully all that you are going through is a lot better than tired, meaningless sayings repeated in every single instance in life when somebody doesn't know what else to say.

I did think of giving up rescuing after Horton died. I thought about it a real lot actually. I was at a crossroads, my heart going in all directions. But then I thought how could I let the little boy I loved so much be the reason I stopped, I couldn't dump that on him, how could I let that be his legacy. That was no way of honouring Horton so I carried on doing what I really love doing. And besides I was only in my mid-forties when he died. I figured I had at least another twenty or thirty rescuing years left in me. And really what else was I going to do with my life? Muddle around the farm by myself with no little shadows scurrying after me or sit on the veranda alone while elderly and special needs pugs piled up in rescue groups and pounds all across the country? Or, worse, let these beauties be put to sleep simply because people didn't want them?

Writing this book has been quite a rollercoaster of emotions. Some chapters flowed easily and had me laughing real loud, others were extremely difficult to write, but I believe Horton's beautiful life story needed to be shared and so I pressed on. Besides, I couldn't just tell you the good parts. That wouldn't have been his whole story and I wanted to tell you everything about him. I mean, how could I have Horton come into this world and then go out of it without any record of how wonderful he was? Some days had me in tears, getting up from the computer and going outside onto the veranda to try and catch my breath. On those days I wrote very little because that's all I could manage. The days I wrote a lot were when I was sitting there typing away happily with a pile of old pugs at my feet and a big smile on my face. Those days I didn't want to shut the computer down; I just wanted to sit there allowing all those precious memories to come flooding back. If I look across at the veranda I can still picture him out there in the sunshine, nappy-free and happy. If I close my eyes real tight and concentrate hard I can almost hear Horton's puppy barks, those precious little woofs that brought me so much joy.

The first time I entered my friend's antique shop without Horton was hard. It was so painful to be in there without him. The backroom with its high step remained empty and the fridge door remained shut. It was the same when I ventured out to the supermarket. Horton had never come into the supermarket with me. He always stayed in the car with David and bounced up and down as soon as I came into view. I used to love watching him do that. I'd come out of the store carrying my bags and keep my eye on the little black bundle sitting in his daddy's arms. I'd see him sitting there looking all around. You could just see the top of his little head above the steering wheel and although I couldn't see his eyes, I always knew the exact moment he had seen me. He'd be looking around, watching everyone coming and going. He used to love watching people going about their business. He was always interested in what was going on around him. He'd sit in the safety of David's arms and watch the world from his advantaged view. When the bouncing started I knew he'd recognized me from the other shoppers. I once followed a woman out of the store whom I thought looked very similar to me. Okay, she was probably a good dress size smaller than me (two if I'm being honest), but the hair was the same length and colour and she was wearing a similar outfit to mine. I stayed a few steps behind her and was able to get close enough to the car without Horton seeing me. I saw his face change and he began bouncing then he stopped, looked closer at the woman and his face changed again as if to say, "You're not her. You're not the one I love, the one I'm waiting for." She passed by our car and I watched Horton watching her go, then he turned and saw me. His face lit up with excitement as soon as he recognized his real mummy.

Coming back to the car was a joyous time, both for Horton and for me. He knew I always had a treat in one of the bags for him. I loved watching him watch me going through the bags looking for his treat and he was never disappointed with what I bought for him. He would sit bouncing on David's knee as I broke the food into small pieces and feed him then we'd drive back to the farm with Horton asleep in my arms. The ride home was never anywhere near as exciting for him as the trip up was. The ride up, the waiting and the anticipation of when I was actually going to emerge from the shop tired him out so he was usually fast asleep before the car turned onto the main road.

In my saddest moments of missing Horton I used to say to David that if he had been born normal he would still be alive today, but David would say, "Yes, but then we would never have known him." And he was right because if Horton didn't have hemivertebra he would have never come into our care. Yes, he would still be alive today but not on this farm and not here with us. He would simply have never crossed our paths. He would have been sold on just like his brothers and sisters and countless other pug puppies born into breeding circles. If fate had allowed it, he may have come to us when he was old and frail and his family no longer wanted him, but the chances of that were very slim. What would have happened is that we simply would have gone on with our lives never knowing anything about him and I think never having Horton share our lives. To never have been able to love him and have him love us and touch us the way he did, well, that to me would have been a great misfortune.

I think Horton did live the best life he could. I do think he lived for all those who had gone before him and been put to sleep. Horton may not have been granted a long life but he packed a heck of a lot into those three years he was given. Perhaps that's why he was so joyous all the time, so curious, so involved in everything that was going on. Rain, hail or shine, Horton was happy. He didn't care what was going down, he wanted to be part of it. Perhaps he actually did know his time on earth would be short, or maybe he just listened intently when I explained to him about all those other pugs born with hemivertebra, and decided right there and then that he was going to make every day count. I believe we can all learn from that.

People have often asked me if I would do it all over again with Horton, or if, given the opportunity, I would take in another one just like him. And my answer to that will always be one hundred and fifty percent yes. I wouldn't even have to think about it, both of my hands would be up in the air waving around madly and I'd be shouting at the top of my lungs "ME ME ME" because although the loss was devastating I do not for one minute regret having him, because the gifts Horton brought, what he gave us, well, things like this don't come around very often and their worth is beyond measure. Grief is hard, it is always going to be the saddest part of all. It's not meant to be easy is it. The loving part, that's the easy part. But where there is love there will eventually be sorrow and that is just how it is with life. You cannot escape it. The loss is short, only one day really, but the missing them, well that is what lasts a lifetime.

Grief, to me, is like floating alone in a sea of pain, an ocean even, a huge overwhelming ocean of emotions with your heart, mind and soul in a broken state. You can see those you love on dry land reaching out for you, but you don't react because you can't react. At that point in time your world is different to their world. They call your name, beg you to respond, beg you to come over, but sound is too painful and touch is too painful and interaction is too painful. At that point all you can do is go on floating, bobbing about on the surface with no control over where it's going to take you. You've no idea how far out you are going to drift or the time and place you'll float back in again. Sometimes you almost see the shore then it's gone again before you have time to acknowledge it was there. Sometimes you hear their voices but they quickly fade. Your pain stifles them before you hear what was said. Your sorrow is so vast, so powerful and so consuming that there is nobody else in the world but you. You drift back and forth, back and forth, barely keeping your head above water. But one day you open your eyes and the sun is shining and your friends are standing on the shore gesturing and you turn, and you smile, and you start to swim.

The End

I hope you have enjoyed reading about Horton's life as much as he enjoyed living it. Horton and I would like to thank you for buying his book. 100% of all profits from the sale of The Joy of Horton will go directly into making the lives of the animals of this world better and brighter and happier, because I know that is how Horton would have wanted it to be. Please tell your animal loving friends about The Joy of Horton.

God bless you and take care.

ABOUT THE AUTHOR

Andrea Comer was born in the United Kingdom and migrated to Australia with her family when she was six years old. From a very young age Andrea became aware of the way animals were treated in this world and vowed that one day she would create a place where elderly animals could live out their natural lifespan without knowing fear, feeling pain or enduring suffering. Grace Farm Senior Pug Sanctuary was a dream she carried in her heart for a very long time before it became a reality. Andrea lives with her husband and a cloud of elderly pugs, sheep and horses. Her days are spent taking care of her large four legged family, but sometimes in the late afternoon when the pugs are sleeping she has time to write. The Joy of Horton is Andrea's first book. Andrea says she has at least seven more books in her, she just needs to find the time to write them.

Made in the USA
Lexington, KY
25 October 2016